# Praise for *Video Generation with AI*

With practical, industry-relevant examples throughout, this book makes modern video AI approachable and actionable. Readers will gain the confidence to build, fine-tune, and deploy cutting-edge video generation systems while mastering diffusion transformers, multimodal learning, and production-ready workflows.

*—Maxime Dehaut, head of product and application development, Luxembourg Stock Exchange*

A definitive technical standard. This text masterfully bridges theoretical foundations and cutting-edge multimodal research with the rigorous, distributed system design necessary for production-scale generative deployments, offering practitioners a masterful, hands-on roadmap to modern video generation.

*—Debanshu Das, senior technical lead for AI video generation and recommendation*

Open-sourcing LTX was about empowering builders. Seeing it taught in a book is exactly the kind of impact we hoped for.

*—Dr. Zeev Farbman, cofounder and CEO, LTX*

# Video Generation with AI

*Working with Diffusion Transformers and Multimodal Learning*

*Joseph Enochs*

O'REILLY®

**Video Generation with AI**
by Joseph Enochs



Published by O'Reilly Media, Inc., 141 Stony Circle, Suite 195, Santa Rosa, CA 95401.

O'Reilly books may be purchased for educational, business, or sales promotional use. Online editions are also available for most titles (*https://oreilly.com*). For more information, contact our corporate/institutional sales department: 800-998-9938 or *corporate@oreilly.com*.

**Acquisitions Editor:** Nicole Butterfield
**Development Editor:** Corbin Collins
**Production Editor:** Ashley Stussy
**Copyeditor:** nSight, Inc.
**Proofreader:** Dwight Ramsey
**Indexer:** nSight, Inc.
**Cover Designer:** Karen Montgomery
**Cover Illustrator:** José Marzan Jr.
**Interior Designer:** David Futato
**Interior Illustrator:** Kate Dullea

August 2026: First Edition

**Revision History for the First Edition**
2026-07-21: First Release

See *https://oreilly.com/catalog/errata.csp?isbn=9798341653344* for release details.



979-8-341-65334-4

[LSI]

# Table of Contents

# Preface

Video generation is advancing at a remarkable pace. New models and techniques appear almost monthly, each improving realism, consistency, and multimodal reasoning. Yet often the difficult part is not using these models. It is understanding why they work.

I wrote this book because I believe that real understanding comes from connecting theory with implementation. Reading a paper is valuable. Building a model is valuable. The greatest insight comes from understanding how the architecture, training process, and engineering decisions fit together to produce the final result.

This is not a catalog of every video generation model or a survey of every research paper. The field is moving too quickly for that. Instead, this book focuses on the core ideas that appear across modern systems and explains them through practical examples and working implementations.

My hope is that this book helps the next generation of builders move beyond treating these models as black boxes and gives them the foundation to build what comes next.

## Who Should Use This Book

This book is intended for software developers, machine learning engineers, AI researchers, data scientists, and technical architects who want to understand how modern video generation systems are designed, trained, and deployed.

It assumes a basic familiarity with Python and machine learning concepts but does not require prior experience with video generation. By connecting theory with implementation, the book aims to help you understand not only how these systems work, but why they work.

## Conventions Used in This Book

The following typographical conventions are used in this book:

*Italic*
: Indicates new terms, URLs, email addresses, filenames, and file extensions.

`Constant width`
: Used for program listings, as well as within paragraphs to refer to program elements such as variable or function names, databases, data types, environment variables, statements, and keywords.

**`Constant width bold`**
: Shows commands or other text that should be typed literally by the user.

*`Constant width italic`*
: Shows text that should be replaced with user-supplied values or by values determined by context.

This element signifies a tip or suggestion.

This element signifies a general note.

This element indicates a warning or caution.

## Using Code Examples

Supplemental material (code examples, exercises, etc.) is available for download at *https://github.com/jenochs/video-ai-book-companion*.

If you have a technical question or a problem using the code examples, please send email to *support@oreilly.com*.

This book is here to help you get your job done. In general, if example code is offered with this book, you may use it in your programs and documentation. You do not need to contact us for permission unless you're reproducing a significant portion of the code. For example, writing a program that uses several chunks of code from this book does not require permission. Selling or distributing examples from O'Reilly books does require permission. Answering a question by citing this book and quoting example code does not require permission. Incorporating a significant amount of example code from this book into your product's documentation does require permission.

We appreciate, but generally do not require, attribution. An attribution usually includes the title, author, publisher, and ISBN. For example: "*Video Generation with AI* by Joseph Enochs (O'Reilly). Copyright 2026 Joseph Enochs, 979-8-341-65334-4."

If you feel your use of code examples falls outside fair use or the permission given above, feel free to contact us at *permissions@oreilly.com*.

## O'Reilly Online Learning

For more than 40 years, O'Reilly Media has provided technology and business training, knowledge, and insight to help companies succeed.

Our unique network of experts and innovators share their knowledge and expertise through books, articles, and our online learning platform. O'Reilly's online learning platform gives you on-demand access to live training courses, in-depth learning paths, interactive coding environments, and a vast collection of text and video from O'Reilly and 200+ other publishers. For more information, visit *https://oreilly.com*.

## How to Contact Us

Please address comments and questions concerning this book to the publisher:


O'Reilly Media, Inc.
141 Stony Circle, Suite 195
Santa Rosa, CA 95401
800-889-8969 (in the United States or Canada)
707-827-7019 (international or local)
707-829-0104 (fax)
*support@oreilly.com*
*https://oreilly.com/about/contact.html*


We have a web page for this book, where we list errata and any additional information. You can access this page at *https://oreil.ly/video-generation-with-ai-1e*.

For news and information about our books and courses, visit *https://oreilly.com*.

Find us on LinkedIn: *https://linkedin.com/company/oreilly-media*.

Watch us on YouTube: *https://youtube.com/oreillymedia*.

## Acknowledgments

No book is written alone, and this one is no exception.

I would like to thank the team at O'Reilly Media for their guidance and support throughout this project. My sincere thanks go to Nicole Butterfield, Corbin Collins, Ashley Stussy, Adam Lawrence, and Kristen Brown for helping shape and bring this manuscript to publication.

I am especially grateful to Michael Demers, Seb de Greef, Jordan Harvey, Maxime Dehaut, and Debanshu Das for their collaboration, technical insight, thoughtful feedback, and encouragement throughout the writing process.

I also want to recognize the researchers, engineers, and open source communities whose work forms the foundation of modern AI video generation. Their willingness to publish research, share ideas, and contribute code has accelerated innovation across the industry and made books like this one possible.

Finally, I want to thank my family, especially my children. Your patience, encouragement, and unwavering support gave me the time and space to complete this book. My greatest hope is that the world you inherit is one where curiosity, creativity, and technology are used to make life better for everyone.

CHAPTER 1

# Foundations of Video Generation

*Learning objective:* In this chapter, you'll learn the foundational principles and emerging methods used to generate video with AI.

Video generation represents one of the most challenging frontiers in AI. While generating a single image requires understanding spatial relationships within a frame, video generation introduces challenges that exponentially multiply this complexity. Models must account not only for the content of each frame but also for how those elements change logically and coherently over time.

This chapter guides you from understanding these challenges to creating high-resolution videos with advanced generative models. By the end, you'll realize why diffusion transformers (DiTs) have transformed the field and you'll gain practical skills for working with cutting-edge video AI systems.

We begin with immediate, hands-on success—generating a sample video in minutes—then build a deeper understanding of the technology that makes it possible.

## Hands-On: Your First AI Video

Let's start by generating a video. You'll use CogVideoX (*https://oreil.ly/wLCDN*), one of the most advanced open source models, selected for its accessibility and compatibility with a wide range of consumer-grade hardware and cloud platforms, such as Google Colab (*https://oreil.ly/TBgFF*).

While not a replacement for full production pipelines, CogVideoX can produce high-resolution, temporally coherent video outputs suitable for prototyping, experimentation, and creative development. This initial success sets the stage for a more in-depth exploration of the architecture and techniques behind modern generative video models.

## Environment Setup

First, you'll need to prepare your environment with modern AI tooling. Please open the Chapter 1 Notebook (*https://oreil.ly/lNK0I*) and create a copy for your experimentation. The tooling selected here is based on the foundational requirements for video generation. You'll mainly need the torch library (*https://oreil.ly/Gip_K*) at this point:

```
import torch
import numpy as np
import time
import matplotlib.pyplot as plt
from IPython.display import Video, display, HTML
```

Next, verify your computational environment, since video generation requires significant resources. I have chosen a model with moderate resource requirements for you to use for the demonstration exercises in this chapter:

```
print("Video Generation AI Environment (2025 Edition)")
print(f"PyTorch: {torch.__version__}")
print(f"GPU Available: {torch.cuda.is_available()}")
if torch.cuda.is_available():
    print(f"GPU: {torch.cuda.get_device_name(0)}")
    print(
        f"VRAM: "
        f"{torch.cuda.get_device_properties(0).total_memory / 1024**3:.1f}GB"
    )
else:
    print("No GPU detected - video generation will be slower")
print("\n Environment ready for state-of-the-art video AI!")
```

Next, install the necessary libraries for video generation. If you're running this process for the first time locally, you may need to install the Diffusers (*https://oreil.ly/4zayM*) library and other required dependencies. If you're using Google Colab, the notebooks provided by Google are likely preconfigured with compatible versions:

```
# Install the video AI stack
# Reference environment (known-good configuration used in this book)
!pip install diffusers==0.33.1 transformers==4.52.4 accelerate safetensors \
    --quiet
!pip install imageio-ffmpeg opencv-python scikit-image --quiet

# Import tools required for video generation
from diffusers import CogVideoXPipeline
from diffusers.utils import export_to_video
import diffusers
```

## Loading the Model

You'll now load the CogVideoX model:

```
# Start the timer
start_time = time.time()
# Load the CogVideoX Pipeline
pipe = CogVideoXPipeline.from_pretrained(
    "THUDM/CogVideoX-2b",          # Accessible model
    # "THUDM/CogVideoX-5b",        # Larger model optional
    torch_dtype=torch.float16,     # float 16 precision
)
```

Now you can apply model optimizations, which can have a significant impact on whether your model runs successfully on your selected platform. The main components to be concerned about are VRAM on the GPU and system memory. These resources can become overloaded during the video generation process, so applying available optimizations is crucial to a successful generation:

```
# Apply optimizations
pipe.enable_model_cpu_offload()        # Move unused comps to CPU.
pipe.vae.enable_tiling()               # Process in tiles
pipe.vae.enable_slicing()              # VAE optimizations

# Track our load time and display results
load_time = time.time() - start_time
print(f"\n✅ CogVideoX loaded and optimized in {load_time:.1f}s!")
```

## Generate Your First Video

With the model loaded and optimizations set, you're ready to begin generating your first AI-generated video.

The foundation of successful AI video is the prompt. A well-structured natural-language prompt can guide models toward generating outputs with strong visual impact. At the same time, prompts often need a "negative" counterpart to reduce common generation artifacts. These artifacts refer to visual flaws that arise during synthesis, such as distorted body parts, unnatural movements, or inconsistent backgrounds. By pairing positive and negative prompts, we can guide the model to produce imagery that is both compelling and technically clean:

```
# Craft a prompt and negative prompt
prompt = (
    "A majestic golden retriever running through a sunlit "
    "meadow, cinematic quality, slow motion"
)
negative_prompt = "blurry, low quality, distorted, text"
```

Now run the generation process:

```
# Track the generation process
start_time = time.time()
# Generate with settings optimized for quality and success
video_frames = pipe(
    prompt=prompt,
    negative_prompt=negative_prompt,
    num_frames=49,                    # ~2 seconds at 24fps
    height=480,                       # Balanced quality/memory
    width=720,                        # Standard aspect ratio
    num_inference_steps=50,           # 50 refinement steps
    guidance_scale=6.0,               # Text conditioning
    generator=torch.Generator().manual_seed(42)
).frames[0]
generation_time = time.time() - start_time
print(f"\n Generation completed successfully!")
print(f"Time: {generation_time:.1f} seconds")
print(
    f"Generated: {len(video_frames)} frames "
    f"({len(video_frames)/24:.1f}s of video)"
)
```

## Save and Display Your Achievement

Once your video is generated, you can save and preview it so you can review your progress, share your work, and use it as a reference in future experiments and evaluations:

```
# Save and display your achievement
output_filename = "my_first_ai_video.mp4"
export_to_video(video_frames, output_filename, fps=24)
print(f"\n Video saved as: {output_filename}")
print("\n Your First AI-Generated Video:")
display(Video(output_filename, width=720, height=480, embed=True))
print("\n🎉 Congratulations! You've just created your first video using AI.")
```

Congratulations! You've just created your first video using AI. Figure 1-1 shows the output I got.

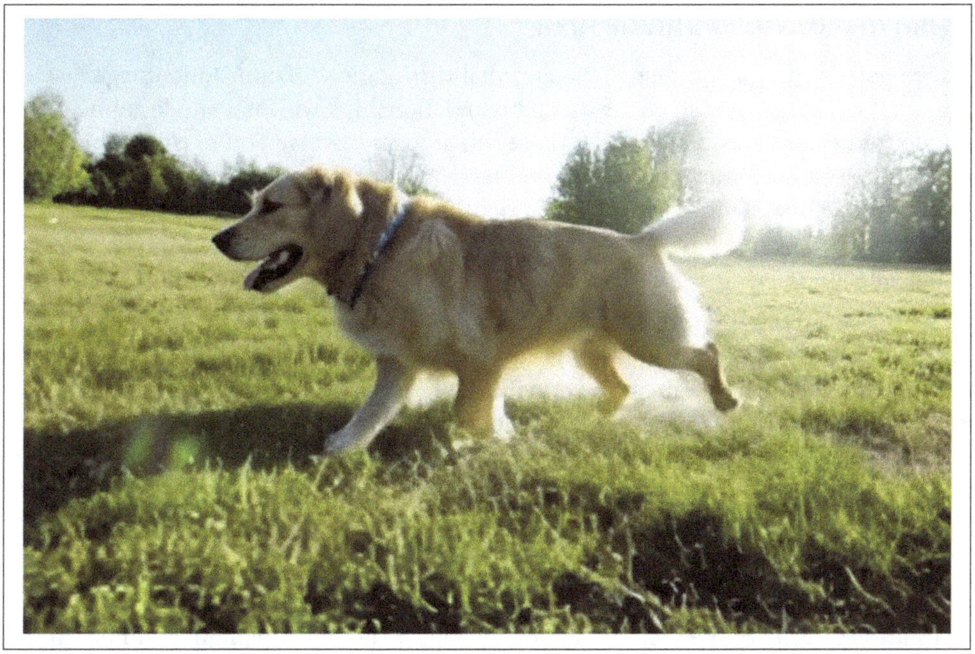

*Figure 1-1. A majestic golden retriever running through a sunlit park, generated by CogVideoX, July 2025*

## Introduction to Generative Video Models

The video you just created represents the culmination of years of research in AI. To understand why this achievement is so significant, we must examine what makes video generation fundamentally distinct from other AI tasks.

Video generative models represent a groundbreaking collaboration between artist and algorithm. Imagine a paintbrush that not only understands your creative vision but evolves with you, suggesting possibilities while remaining firmly guided by your direction. These emerging AI systems represent a growing component of creative collaboration, engaging in dynamic dialogue with professionals to push the boundaries of what's possible in video creation while preserving the essence of artistic vision.

These models are emerging as intelligent, creative partners that learn from and build upon vast repositories of visual knowledge. They use advanced machine learning (ML) techniques to predict how images should flow from one frame sequence to another.

## What Makes Video Unique in AI

Video generation has unique challenges that distinguish it from static image generation. While image models focus on spatial relationships within a single frame, video models must also account for how those relationships evolve across time. This introduces a temporal dimension to the problem, which requires consistency in motion, character identity, lighting dynamics, and visual perspective across multiple frames.

### Temporal consistency

The first and perhaps most critical challenge is *temporal consistency*. Unlike static images, videos require maintaining coherent motion and scene continuity across multiple frames. Objects must move naturally, lighting conditions must remain consistent, and camera movements must follow realistic physics. Consider a simple scene of a person walking: each frame must show the walker in a slightly different position, with clothing that moves naturally, shadows that shift appropriately, and background elements that maintain their relative positions.

### Higher computational demands

This leads directly to the second major challenge: exponentially higher computational demands. Generating multiple frames in sequence requires significantly more computational resources than producing single images. A 2-second video at 24 frames per second contains 48 individual photos, each of which must maintain coherent relationships with all others—a 48x multiplication in raw data complexity. To put this in perspective, a single frame at 720 × 480 resolution with three color channels contains 1,036,800 values to model. The same content, as a 2-second video, balloons to 49,766,400 values, creating an exponential increase in complexity as we extend the video generation sequence. (See Figure 1-2 for an illustration of this increase.)

### Sequence of events

The third dimension of complexity involves how videos tell stories through sequences of events. Videos convey the narrative of the story and require the AI models to understand the relationships between action sequences, along with the natural flow of events. This temporal storytelling dimension adds layers of complexity beyond spatial composition. A video of a glass falling and breaking must show not just the individual frames but the physics of acceleration, the moment of impact, and the fragments scattering realistically.

These massive data requirements explain why video generation requires revolutionary architectural breakthroughs, particularly the development of models with billions of parameters. Models have to keep track of how objects and scenes should look within each frame, ensure temporal coherence across frames, and maintain physical realism in motion patterns and semantic understanding of text prompts, all while ensuring smooth motion and narrative flow throughout the sequence.

Figure 1-2 illustrates the exponential complexity of video generation, along with the time steps required for your video pipeline.

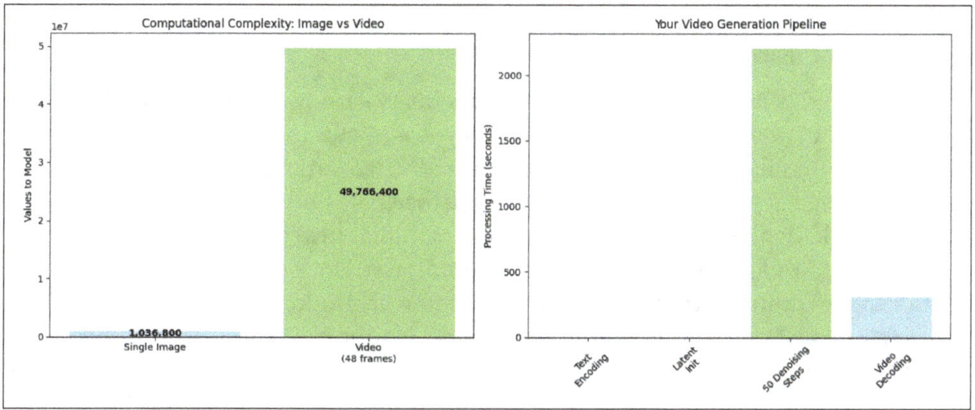


*Figure 1-2. Video generation comparison and processing pipeline*

## Key Use Cases for Generative Video

Video generative models are becoming more than theoretical concepts. In recent times, they have become transformative in industries, driving innovation across entertainment, advertising, healthcare, and beyond.

### Entertainment and media

Google's Veo (*https://oreil.ly/dgr10*) series of models represents a significant leap forward among the first video generation models to support native audio, enabling creators to produce synchronized sound effects, ambient noise, and dialogue along with visuals in a single pass. This advancement could significantly reduce the manual effort required for separate audio production.

Meta's Movie Gen (*https://oreil.ly/CrRO2*), introduced in late 2024, brings generative video capabilities into the social media ecosystem. Although, as of mid-2025, its full integration with platforms like Instagram has not been publicly confirmed, Movie Gen is positioned for short-form content creation. It offers 1080p resolution and synchronized audio output, supporting experimental workflows for creators and marketing teams. Early collaborations (*https://oreil.ly/OMzsB*) with filmmakers and studios, including Blumhouse Productions and Casey Affleck, are exploring its potential.

Runway (*https://oreil.ly/CtS9i*) has also introduced many notable improvements in character and object consistency across scenes, a longstanding challenge with video generation. Runway leverages reference objects and tags to condition the output and maintain character consistency, to maintain coherent identities throughout multishot sequences, which is paramount for narrative storytelling.

#### Advertising and marketing

In advertising, generative video is driving a shift toward hyperpersonalized, scalable content production. Kling AI (*https://oreil.ly/gy6Y-*), with over 22 million users globally, enables brands to experiment with localized video variations, using features such as multi-image reference, a localization tool that helps advertisers maintain brand identity while dynamically adapting visuals for different regions and demographics. For example, a global sportswear brand could generate localized ads featuring the same athlete running through different cities worldwide, adapting their clothing styles to regional preferences and inserting local landmarks. The cost efficiency could be remarkable.

Meanwhile, Open-Sora (*https://oreil.ly/OzuJ-*) introduces a new level of cost efficiency in video AI. Trained for just $200,000—10% to 20% of the cost of comparable models—it enables small and midsized businesses to access high-quality video generation tools that were once limited to large organizations.

#### Healthcare and medical training

Video AI is also transforming medical education (*https://oreil.ly/Le3M2*) by creating comprehensive, repeatable training libraries that offer cost-effective training for critical medical resources, making high-quality simulations more attainable. Modern simulation models can generate medically accurate content with sufficient visual fidelity for training purposes. Integrated audio features strive to replicate the surgical environment—including heart monitors and realistic machine sounds—and virtual patient interactions, enhancing the training experience.

#### Cultural preservation and accessibility

AI video tools are also helping cultural institutions (*https://oreil.ly/KuK6u*) reimagine preservation and accessibility. With native audio generation, historians can now recreate period-appropriate soundscapes for silent films or historical footage, including ambient sounds, music, and dialogue inspired by archival records.

Modern models also allow museums to create immersive, accessible virtual experiences, generating multiple viewing angles of historical events from a single archival photograph.

With the support of these emerging technologies, archives can generate audio descriptions for visually impaired visitors, create multiple language versions with culturally appropriate narration, and even produce educational content that offers "behind-the-scenes" perspectives on historical events.

# The Architectures Behind the Models

The journey to today's breakthrough video generation capabilities represents a fascinating evolution of architectural innovations. Understanding these foundational approaches is essential for grasping why DiTs now dominate the field and how they're addressing challenges that seemed insurmountable just years ago.

## GANs, Diffusion Models, and Variational Autoencoders

The evolution of video generative models has brought together multiple architectural innovations, each adding its strengths to the field. Understanding these foundational architectures is essential for making informed decisions about which approaches best suit your creative or business goals. This section reviews three key architectures.

Figures 1-3 and 1-4 trace the architectural evolution that led to your CogVideoX model. Figure 1-3 specifically focuses on the evolution of video generation quality.

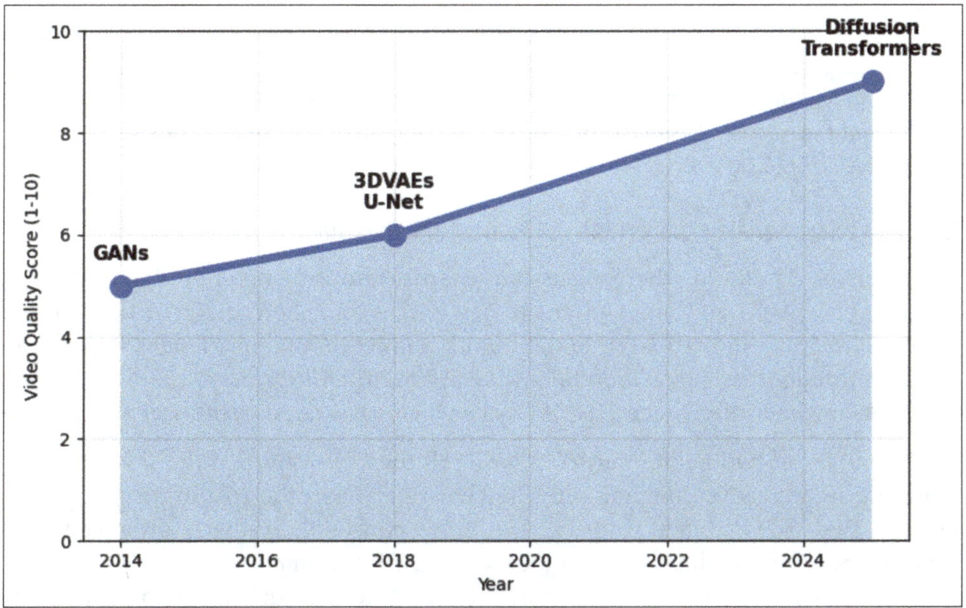


*Figure 1-3. Evolution of video generation model frameworks*

Figure 1-4 shows the evolution of model quality.

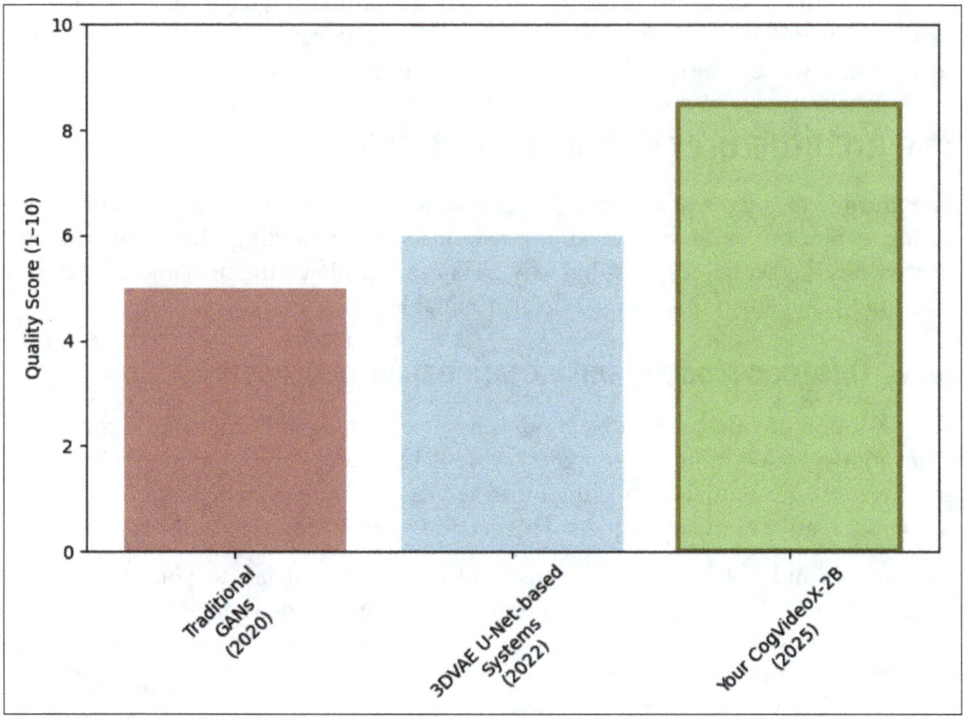


*Figure 1-4. Comparison of model quality scores over time, showing improvements from traditional GANs to U-Net-based systems and finally to Diffusion Transformers CogVideoX2B (2025)*

#### Generative adversarial networks (GANs): The artist and the critic

Consider an art studio where a passionate artist and a demanding art critic work together. The artist continues to create new pieces and the critic provides detailed feedback, helping the artist refine their work with each attempt. This is how GANs work. Introduced by Ian J. Goodfellow et al. in 2014 (*https://oreil.ly/w67JD*), these networks revolutionized generative AI by using an adversarial training approach.

GANs consist of two neural networks we'll call the *Generator* and the *Discriminator*, engaging in a creative competition. The Generator takes the role of an artist who's creating new video content from random noise, constantly trying to produce videos that are indistinguishable from real footage. The Discriminator acts as critic, evaluating each video to determine whether it's real or AI-generated. This ongoing feedback process improves the generator process over millions of iterations.

This adversarial process drives both networks to improve continuously. Early video GANs such as MoCoGAN (2018) (*https://oreil.ly/TXEb3*) further developed this concept by decoupling motion and content generation, learning separate latent spaces for each component, which enabled more controlled video synthesis.

GANs can produce detailed videos with stunning detail. However, they have some problems that make them tricky to leverage in the video generation process. The training can go off the rails and create instability in the adversarial process. This can lead to what's known as *mode collapse*, where the model generates repetitive outputs one after another. GANs can also struggle with *temporal flickering*, making it difficult to maintain consistency across frames. These limitations become especially pronounced with more extended video sequences, motivating researchers to explore alternative architectures.

#### Variational autoencoders (VAEs): The magical middle ground

Imagine teaching someone to draw a cat by providing a set of simple instructions rather than describing every detail. VAEs (*https://oreil.ly/IZEiT*) date back to 2013 and work similarly, compressing videos into a *latent space*, a condensed representation that captures essential features while enabling smooth transformations and interpolations.

VAEs operate through a two-stage process. First, they encode video into a lower-dimensional latent representation, which is a compact version of the data that captures the essential patterns such as shapes, motion, or textures while leaving out unnecessary detail. You can think of this as distilling a high-definition video into a kind of blueprint, which still contains the critical information needed to rebuild it. Second, they decode this latent space representation, reconstructing the footage using learned probability distributions. This compression/decompression process enables several powerful capabilities: smooth transitions that allow natural morphing between different scenes or styles, intuitive style manipulation through control over visual characteristics, and more stable training compared to GANs.

While VAEs provide excellent control and stability, with additional guidance elements, they typically produce softer, less detailed outputs than GANs. This trade-off makes VAEs especially useful for tasks that benefit from smooth, gradual changes in appearance, such as interpolations (blending one scene or image into another) or style transfer (re-creating the content of one video while applying the visual look of another, such as turning live-action footage into the style of an oil painting). Because of this ability to compress and reconstruct data, VAEs are often used inside larger systems, including diffusion-based video generation models, where they provide an efficient way to handle the latent representation of video data (see the article by Diederik P. Kingma and Max Welling) (*https://oreil.ly/OY4D1*).

### Diffusion models: The digital restoration artists

Picture a restoration artist working on an ancient, weathered painting. Instead of creating art from scratch, they carefully remove layers of dust and damage, gradually revealing the masterpiece underneath. This analogy captures the essence of how *diffusion models* approach video generation.

Pioneered by Jonathan Ho et al. in 2020 (*https://oreil.ly/MRu8q*), diffusion models work through a fascinating reverse journey. They begin with a forward process that gradually adds Gaussian noise to training videos until they become pure static. Then they learn the reverse process—how to remove noise step by step, recovering the original video. During the generation process, diffusion models start with random noise and then apply the learned denoising process to generate the resulting video.

The CogVideoX model you used follows a similar approach. Figure 1-5 visualizes how your golden retriever video emerged from noise over 50 denoising steps.

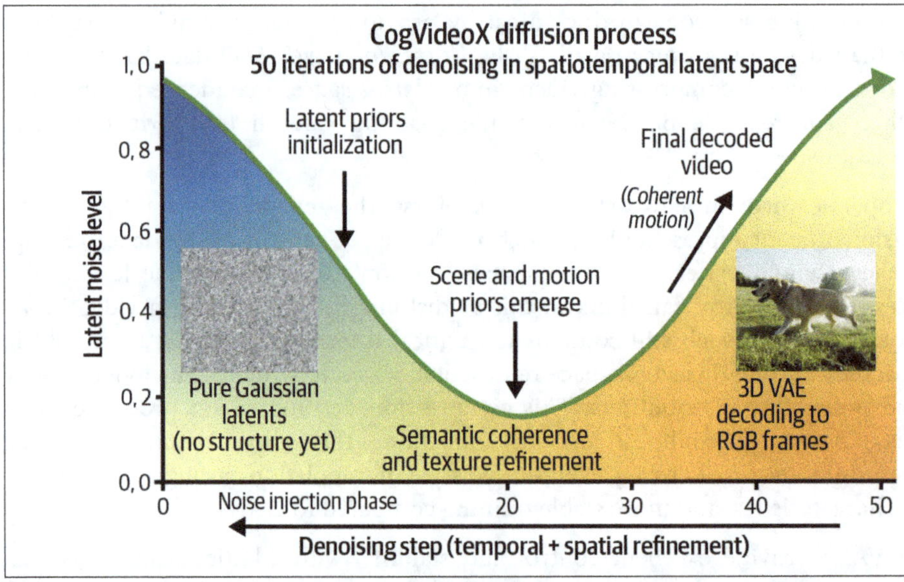


*Figure 1-5. Diffusion models generate video by starting with pure noise and gradually removing it step by step until a clear video emerges*

In the first phase, the model operates entirely in latent space, beginning with near-total noise. At this point, there are no visible objects—only high-dimensional latent representations without semantic meaning. As denoising begins, broad structural patterns start to emerge: the model organizes spatial and temporal relationships that define the rough layout of the scene and large-scale objects.

As the noise recedes, coherent forms take shape, the golden retriever begins to materialize, and environmental elements such as grass and sky become distinct within the latent representation. Further iterations refine the latent sequence, adding texture, resolving motion, and ensuring smooth transitions across frames. In the final steps, the model decodes the denoised latent space into pixel space, enhancing realism, lighting, and coherence to produce a polished, high-quality video.

Figure 1-6 breaks down the model's internal attention allocation. CogVideoX-2B uses its 2 billion parameters to coordinate three primary tasks: ensuring spatial consistency within each frame, maintaining temporal consistency across frames, and aligning the output with the text prompt. These components work in tandem at every step to transform random noise into videos that maintain the attributes of realistic video creations.

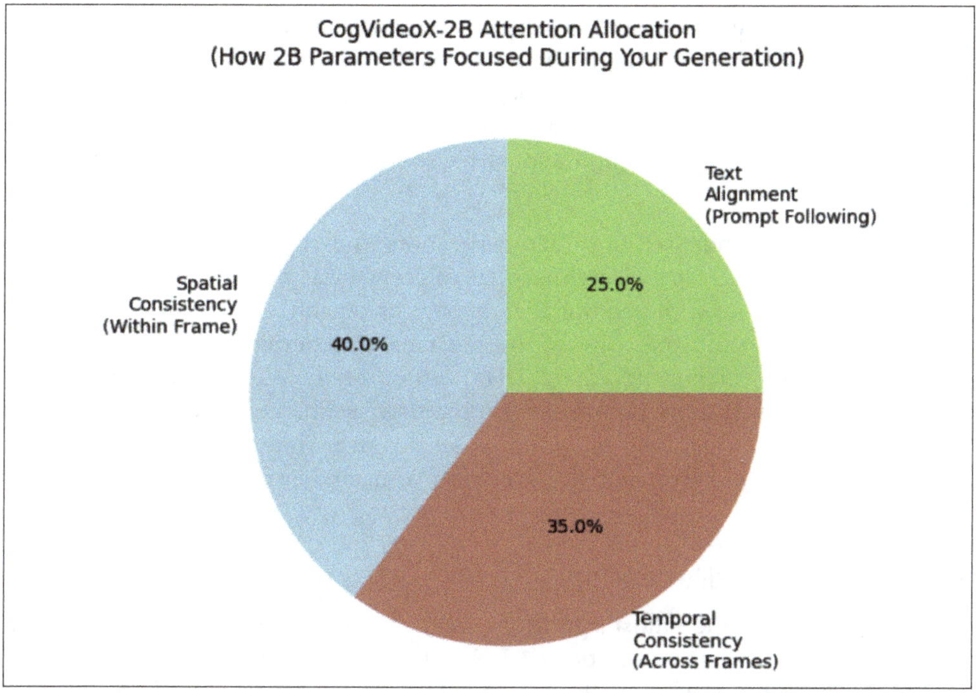


*Figure 1-6. Attention allocation in CogVideoX-2B, showing how parameters are distributed across spatial consistency, temporal consistency, and text alignment during generation*

The key advancement comes in separating the generation process into a sequence of small, manageable steps rather than attempting to generate the entire sequence at once. Each denoising step is guided by neural networks that have been trained to learn the statistical properties of real videos and to predict whether the input is video content or random noise. We will break these steps down in detail in Chapter 3. For now we will begin to build your intuition on how these models function.

## Modern Generative Techniques for Video

Diffusion models are rapidly becoming the architecture of choice for video generation. They offer improved quality and additional refinements while producing more detail. By building up videos slowly, they provide added consistency frame by frame, which helps maintain coherence over time. Diffusion models also avoid the instability often seen in GANs and are easy to integrate with text conditioning and other guidance signals. Text conditioning means guiding the model with natural-language prompts, such as "a dog running through tall grass." Most importantly, diffusion models scale effectively with model size and compute resources.

The breakthrough came with the realization that diffusion could be performed in compressed latent spaces rather than directly in pixel space. Pixel space refers to the raw grid of values for every pixel in an image or frame. Latent space, by contrast, is a compact representation learned by models like VAEs previously mentioned, where only the most important patterns are captured. Working in this smaller, abstract space dramatically reduces computational requirements while still preserving visual quality.

Building on that foundation, the video generation landscape has progressed toward more structured and capable architectures. Recent systems combine step-by-step refinement techniques with additional architectures capable of learning relationships across both space and time. One of the most notable developments has been the introduction of *diffusion transformers* (DiTs) (*https://oreil.ly/Co4X6*). This framework combines two powerful mechanisms: the progressive refinement process of diffusion and the ability to model long-range dependencies over time. The architecture that powers the model you leveraged in generating your golden retriever is built on this approach.

### The revolutionary DiT architecture

DiTs represent one of the most significant architectural innovations in video generation to date. Replacing the traditional U-Net (*https://oreil.ly/w3D2x*) backbone used in earlier diffusion models with transformer-based architectures (*https://oreil.ly/GnQzr*) can better capture the spatial details and temporal relationships in your video. Andrej Karpathy describes the transformer as a type of cortical tissue similar to how our brains function: it can learn and compress various types of information including text, video, audio, and images, along with robotic embodiments and motion.

Figure 1-7 illustrates a sample inference pipeline, from initial text prompt to rendered video. This diagram shows how key components, including a text encoder, a DiT, and a 3D variational autoencoder (3D VAE), operate in a consistent workflow to generate a high-resolution, temporally consistent output.

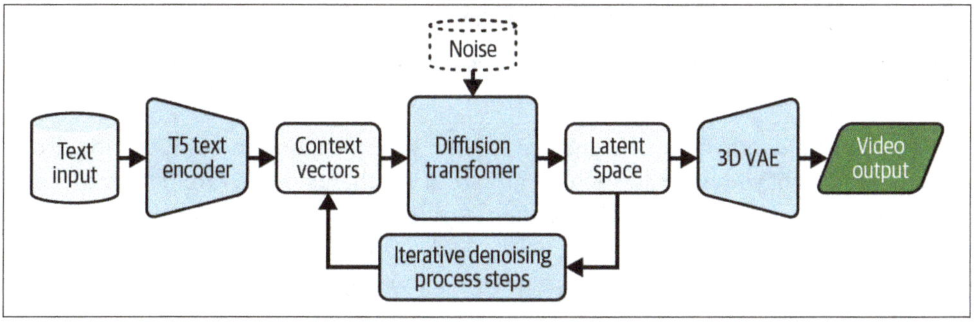


*Figure 1-7. Illustrative text-to-video inference process*

Chapter 3 takes a detailed look at each of the architectural elements. For now, let's take a high-level, step-by-step walkthrough.

First, the *prompt* (text input, step 1 in Figure 1-7) is processed by the T5 text encoder (*https://oreil.ly/f3Qx6*) (step 2), converting natural-language prompts into dense, high-dimensional context vector embeddings. These embeddings guide the *DiT in* (step 3), which models video using 3D full attention across space and time. The iterative denoising process unfolds over dozens of steps, with each step refining the latent space representation toward a coherent video. Once complete, the output is decoded by a 3D variational autoencoder (*https://oreil.ly/rV7Je*) (3D VAE, step 4), which reconstructs the full resolution of the frames, preserving both motion elements and visual details. This architecture enables video generation models like CogVideoX to generate high-quality *results* using hardware with modest amounts of GPU memory in our case, and increasing amount based on the model's size.

Leading models are refining this core architecture. Many integrate 3D VAE structures and hierarchical attention mechanisms (*https://oreil.ly/-Sibn*) to model long-range dependencies while preserving fine-grained motion. Hierarchical attention processes information at multiple scales, recognizing small details like the movement of a hand alongside the broader context of a scene. Rather than processing frames independently, these systems divide video into 3D spatiotemporal patches (*https://oreil.ly/21Ted*)—such as 2 × 2 × 2 or 4 × 4 × 4 blocks—that encode motion and spatial continuity. These architectures are increasingly evaluated on public benchmarks, such as the "Artificial Analysis Text to Video Arena Leaderboard" hosted on Hugging Face (*https://oreil.ly/pih-J*), which enables head-to-head comparisons across quality, coherence, prompt fidelity, and multimodal alignment. They also point toward the emergence of open-world video generation models (*https://oreil.ly/sxEk1*), systems capable of producing interactive audiovisual environments with minimal input.

While these innovations signal the future of generative video, the remainder of this chapter will focus on foundational architecture principles, the building blocks that enable such capabilities, and the methods you'll apply in your own experiments.

### Architectural components of modern video models

Today's state-of-the-art video generation systems share their approach to consistency with many architectural elements.

To balance the depth of consistency over time and to maintain computational efficiency, models have begun to include attention mechanisms hierarchically, focusing on different time scales. *Local attention layers* focus on short-term elements to address frame transitions and movement. *Global attention layers* track broader arcs, enabling models to maintain visual narratives and logical consistency across dozens of frames.

*Text conditioning* plays an equally critical role. Models such as T5-XXL and custom language encoders enrich and enhance the user's prompts to better construct and embed more comprehensive information into high-dimensional vectors. Chapter 5 will deep dive into prompt construction and how the models have been trained to follow user guidance for cinematic prompting.

## Open Models and Baseline Tools

Starting in late 2024 and 2025, video generation has rapidly become more accessible to anyone with basic knowledge of Python and access to Google Colab. The open source ecosystem continues to mature, and community models have shown the ability to rival or exceed many proprietary alternatives. Understanding this landscape enables readers to select appropriate tools and infrastructure for their specific use case.

### Leading open source models

The landscape of open source video generation models offers many options for creators at every level. For example, the Wan series of models, released by Alibaba, at the time of writing offers a 14B and 1.3B parameter model. The 14B variant supports up to 8K resolution and 720p standard generation, while the lightweight 1.3B model runs on consumer GPUs, such as the RTX 4070, requiring only ~8 GB of VRAM. Wan was also among the first video models to support both Chinese and English text effects within videos.

CogVideoX Family from Tsinghua University offers an excellent balance of quality and accessibility. The 2B variant available in late 2025 runs on consumer GPUs with 8 GB or more VRAM, while the 5B version provides enhanced quality for those with more powerful hardware. Integration with the Hugging Face Diffusers library makes deployment straightforward for developers at all levels.

Open-Sora 2.0, released in March 2025, represented a breakthrough in cost-efficient training. This 11B parameter model was developed for only $200,000, 5 to 10 times less than competitors. It supports resolutions of 256px and 768px, generates videos ranging from 2 to 15 seconds in length, and accommodates various aspect ratios. The model combines text-to-video and image-to-video capabilities in a single architecture, using MM-DiT (multimodal diffusion transformer) with flow matching.

HunyuanVideo introduced a comprehensive 13B parameter model that outperformed many commercial alternatives upon its release. While requiring 24 GB or more of VRAM for full capabilities, it includes video-to-audio synthesis and supports the generation of multiminute content. The model is available on GitHub and Hugging Face, accompanied by comprehensive documentation.

Stable Video Diffusion (SVD) rounds out the options with enhanced capabilities for novel-view synthesis. At the time of writing, SVD runs efficiently on consumer hardware with 8 GB VRAM and excels at camera motion and scene consistency.

### Essential development stack

The modern video AI toolkit has converged around several key frameworks that form the foundation of most video generation projects. The Diffusers (*https://oreil.ly/VMrHc*) library serves as the cornerstone library, featuring native quantization support for running large models on consumer hardware; integrated pipelines for CogVideoX, HunyuanVideo, and SVD; VAE tiling; and CPU offloading for memory optimization. It also provides a simple, consistent API across different model architectures.

PyTorch (*https://pytorch.org*) provides the foundation for all modern video AI, with optimized video processing operations, mixed-precision training and inference, and distributed generation for production deployments.

When considering hardware, consumer setups with 8–16 GB VRAM can handle Wan2.1-1.3B (requiring 8.19 GB), CogVideoX-2B, SVD, and quantized models. Professional workstations with 24–48 GB VRAM can run Wan2.1-14B, HunyuanVideo, CogVideoX-5B, and Open-Sora 2.0, and generate more extended sequences. For those preferring cloud solutions, options include Google Veo 3 through Ultra subscription and access to commercial models, such as Kling AI.

## Evaluation and Early Experiments

Rating AI video quality mixes science with personal judgment. We can measure certain technical aspects, but ultimately, video evaluation comes down to individual taste and specific needs. A "good" video depends on how you plan to use it.

Consider this paradox: a video with perfect frame-to-frame consistency (high SSIM score (*https://oreil.ly/GgbXt*)) might be a static image repeated 50 times. While that's technically *consistent*, it's not what anyone wants. Similarly, a dynamic action scene might have lower consistency scores, but it may be precisely what was intended.

When you're trying to figure out if your AI video is good, you'll want to look at the numbers and trust your judgment. Following are four common ways people measure video quality, along with what each one tells you and where they might lead you astray:

*Temporal consistency*
: The Structural Similarity Index (SSIM) measures how similar consecutive frames are. A high score means gradual transitions and smooth motion. However, a video that is simply one frame repeated may score perfectly yet be visually unengaging. This metric is ideal for evaluating calm, slow-changing scenes, such as sunsets or drifting clouds.

*Motion magnitude*
: Captures the level of motion across frames. High scores reflect frequent movement, which might be suitable for sports or action content. However, random noise or flickering can also inflate the score, even if the output is chaotic or incoherent. For our baseline metric, we will calculate the SSIM between the first and last frames.

*Visual sharpness (Laplacian)*
: Assesses clarity and edge definition in the image. High sharpness often translates to better detail and visual quality. Still, creative blur (such as depth-of-field effects) may reduce scores even when artistically justified. This metric is beneficial for evaluating scenes where detail and legibility are crucial.

*Prompt adherence*
: This assesses how closely your video aligns with the requirements outlined in your text prompt. It's probably the trickiest one to measure since it's so subjective: you can't just run some automated test to figure it out. You need a human to watch the video and decide whether it captures what you had in mind. We will tackle this one later in the book. For now, you will be the judge of prompt adherence.

No single metric can provide a complete picture. The most effective evaluations strike a delicate balance between numeric observation and human interpretation. Always keep the intended use case top of mind.

# Getting Started with AI Video Generation

This section guides you through the practical aspects of generating your first AI videos while building your understanding of the underlying technology.

## Exercise 1: Implementing Basic Evaluation Functions

To evaluate your AI-generated video, we'll build a Python function that performs three core tasks: measuring temporal consistency, analyzing visual sharpness, and estimating motion. In this section, I take you step by step through implementing it, explaining as we go.

You'll begin by importing the necessary libraries to help with video frame extraction, metric calculations, and visual display:

```
import cv2
from skimage.metrics import structural_similarity as ssim
import numpy as np
import matplotlib.pyplot as plt
```

Next, you'll create a function that opens a video file and extracts its frames. This function converts each frame to RGB format for consistent analysis and comparison. It also checks that the video contains enough frames for evaluation:

```
def evaluate_video_basics(video_path):
    print(f"\nBasic Video Evaluation: {video_path}")
    print("=" * 40)

    cap = cv2.VideoCapture(video_path)
    frames = []
    while True:
        ret, frame = cap.read()
        if not ret:
            break
        frames.append(cv2.cvtColor(frame, cv2.COLOR_BGR2RGB))
    cap.release()

    if len(frames) < 2:
        print("Not enough frames to evaluate")
        return None
```

Once the video loads, you can print out some basic metadata, including the number of frames, approximate duration (assuming a frame rate of 24 frames per second, or FPS), and resolution:

```
    print(f"📹 Video Properties:")
    print(f"   • Total frames: {len(frames)}")
    print(f"   • Duration: {len(frames)/24:.1f} seconds (at 24 FPS)")
    print(f"   • Resolution: {frames[0].shape[1]}×{frames[0].shape[0]}")
```

Now, using the SSIM, measure the similarity between consecutive frames. A high average SSIM implies smooth transitions, but excessively high scores could indicate that the video is too static:

```
    print(f"\n🔄 Temporal Consistency:")
    consistency_scores = []
    for i in range(1, min(len(frames), 10)):
```

```
        gray1 = cv2.cvtColor(frames[i-1], cv2.COLOR_RGB2GRAY)
        gray2 = cv2.cvtColor(frames[i], cv2.COLOR_RGB2GRAY)
        score = ssim(gray1, gray2)
        consistency_scores.append(score)
    avg_consistency = np.mean(consistency_scores)
    print(f"   • Average consistency: {avg_consistency:.3f}")
```

You can interpret the result using the following thresholds:

```
    if avg_consistency > 0.95:
        print("   • 🟢 Very smooth transitions (might be too static?)")
    elif avg_consistency > 0.85:
        print("   • 🟢 Good temporal consistency")
    elif avg_consistency > 0.75:
        print("   • 🟡 Moderate consistency (dynamic content)")
    else:
        print("   • 🔴 Low consistency (very dynamic or flickering)")
```

For this exercise, you'll assess sharpness by calculating the variance of the Laplacian of the middle frame. The Laplacian is an image-processing filter that highlights *edges*, meaning areas where brightness changes sharply, like the boundary between an object and the background. Taking the variance measures how spread out those edge responses are. A higher variance indicates more edges and therefore a sharper, more detailed image:

```
    print(f"\n🔍 Visual Quality:")
    middle_frame = frames[len(frames)//2]
    gray_middle = cv2.cvtColor(middle_frame, cv2.COLOR_RGB2GRAY)
    sharpness = cv2.Laplacian(gray_middle, cv2.CV_64F).var()
    print(f"   • Sharpness score: {sharpness:.0f}")
```

Now you can add some components for interpreting the sharpness score:

```
    if sharpness > 500:
        print("   • 🟢 Very sharp and detailed")
    elif sharpness > 200:
        print("   • 🟢 Good visual clarity")
    elif sharpness > 100:
        print("   • 🟡 Moderate sharpness")
    else:
        print("   • 🔴 Soft or blurry appearance")
```

For this initial exercise, you'll estimate motion by comparing the first and last frames of the sequence. Subtract the SSIM of these two frames from 1 to create a simple motion score:

```
    print(f"\n🏃 Motion Characteristics:")
    motion_score = 1 - ssim(cv2.cvtColor(frames[0], cv2.COLOR_RGB2GRAY),
                            cv2.cvtColor(frames[-1], cv2.COLOR_RGB2GRAY))
    print(f"   • Overall motion: {motion_score:.3f}")
```

This score is followed by interpretations:

```
    if motion_score < 0.1:
        print("    • 🟡 Very little motion (static scene?)")
    elif motion_score < 0.3:
        print("    • 🟢 Subtle, controlled motion")
    elif motion_score < 0.5:
        print("    • 🟢 Moderate motion")
    else:
        print("    • 🟢 Dynamic scene with significant motion")
```

To complement the numeric evaluation, plot the first, middle, and last frames, as shown in Figure 1-8, to inspect the video's progression visually:

```
    fig, axes = plt.subplots(1, 3, figsize=(15, 5))
    axes[0].imshow(frames[0]); axes[0].set_title('First Frame');
    axes[0].axis('off')
    axes[1].imshow(frames[len(frames)//2])
    axes[1].set_title('Middle Frame')
    axes[1].axis('off')
    axes[2].imshow(frames[-1]); axes[2].set_title('Last Frame');
    axes[2].axis('off')
    plt.suptitle('Video Frame Samples', fontsize=16)
    plt.tight_layout()
    plt.show()
```

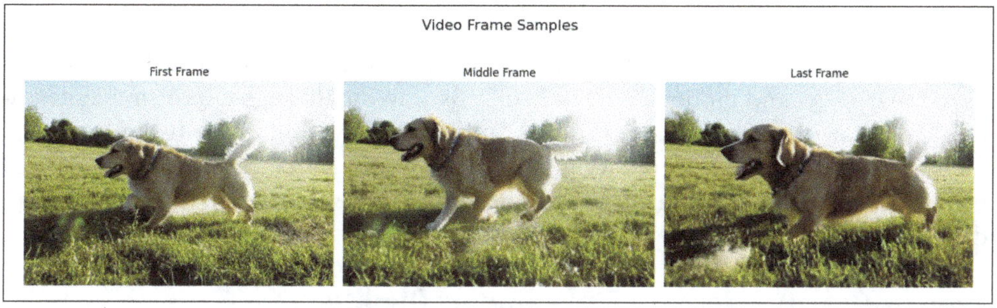


*Figure 1-8. Plotting first, middle, and last frames*

Finally, the function returns a dictionary of the computed metrics for downstream use:

```
    return {
        'consistency': avg_consistency,
        'sharpness': sharpness,
        'motion': motion_score,
        'frames': len(frames)
    }
```

Once you've completed these steps in the companion notebook, you can review the results for your first video. Here are the results I received:

```
📊 Basic Video Evaluation: my_first_ai_video.mp4
========================================
📹 Video Properties:
```

```
    • Total frames: 48
    • Duration: 2.0 seconds (at 24 FPS)
    • Resolution: 720×480

🔄 Temporal Consistency:
    • Average consistency: 0.556
    • 🔴 Low consistency (very dynamic or flickering)

🔍 Visual Quality:
    • Sharpness score: 154
    • 🟡 Moderate sharpness

🏃 Motion Characteristics:
    • Overall motion: 0.648
    • 🟢 Dynamic scene with significant motion
```

As you can see, evaluating AI-generated video requires a balance between quantitative analysis and qualitative insight. You can see that when I generated my golden retriever video, these measurements gave me mixed results, including the introductory SSIM-based temporal consistency score and Laplacian estimate of sharpness. However, applying some thresholds and incorporating the Motion Characteristics score helped clarify the interpretation, since the golden retriever in the video is indeed running.

This section demonstrated how to compute three basic metrics: temporal consistency, visual sharpness, and motion characteristics. By walking through a basic implementation, you learned how to extract frames, apply standard evaluation techniques, and interpret results within the creative goals of your video. As we develop more complex projects, these foundational tools will help you model behavior, improve prompt design, and guide iterative refinement.

## Exercise 2: How Inference Steps Impact Quality

One of the most effective ways to track your progress is through structured experimentation. This section and "Exercise 3: How Prompt Styles Influence Output" will guide your initial explorations by providing two hands-on experiments you can try. As you do, you'll build your intuition about how these models work.

This experiment investigates the impact of the number of inference steps on video quality, generation time, and key evaluation metrics. More inference steps often lead to higher fidelity outputs but at the cost of increased compute time. Let's test two settings and compare the results.

You'll begin by defining a function to manage your experiment and display metadata for each test. You'll use a consistent prompt across both tests to isolate the effect of the change. One setting uses 25 refinement steps for speed, while the other uses 50 steps for a more balanced output:

```
def experiment_inference_steps():
    test_prompt = "A red rose blooming in timelapse, nature documentary style"
    experiments = [
        {
            "steps": 25,
            "name": "Fast (25 steps)",
            "expectation": "Quick but potentially less refined",
        },
        {
            "steps": 50, "name": "Balanced (50 steps)",
            "expectation": "Good quality/speed tradeoff"
        }
    ]
    results = []
```

For each configuration, you'll generate the video, time the process, save the result, and evaluate it using the evaluation function:

```
    for exp in experiments:
        print(f"\n🔬 Testing: {exp['name']}")
        print(f"   Expectation: {exp['expectation']}")

        start_time = time.time()

        video = pipe(
            prompt=test_prompt,
            num_frames=25,  # Shorter clip for faster experimentation
            height=480,
            width=720,
            num_inference_steps=exp['steps'],
            guidance_scale=6.0,
            generator=torch.Generator().manual_seed(123)
        ).frames[0]

        gen_time = time.time() - start_time
```

The function stores these metrics for later comparisons:

```
        filename = f"experiment_steps_{exp['steps']}.mp4"
        export_to_video(video, filename, fps=24)

        print(f"   ⏱️  Generation time: {gen_time:.1f}s")
        print(f"   💾 Saved as: {filename}")

        eval_result = evaluate_video_basics(filename)

        results.append({
            'name': exp['name'],
            'steps': exp['steps'],
            'time': gen_time,
            'evaluation': eval_result
        })
```

After all tests are complete, compare the results side by side to see how increasing the number of inference steps affects quality and performance:

```
print("\n📊 Results Comparison:")
print("Setting         | Time     | Consistency | Sharpness | Motion")
print("-" * 60)

for r in results:
    e = r['evaluation']
    print(
        f"{r['name']:<15} | {r['time']:>6.1f}s | "
        f"{e['consistency']:>10.3f} | {e['sharpness']:>9.0f} | "
        f"{e['motion']:>6.3f}"
    )
```

Now call the function to perform the test and store the output:

```
step_experiment_results = experiment_inference_steps()
```

Once you've completed the exercise in the companion notebook, return to this section to analyze your results. For comparison, here are the results I got:

```
📊 Basic Video Evaluation: experiment_steps_25.mp4
========================================
📹 Video Properties:
   • Total frames: 25
   • Duration: 1.0 seconds (at 24 FPS)
   • Resolution: 720×480

🔄 Temporal Consistency:
   • Average consistency: 0.999
   • 🟢 Very smooth transitions (might be too static?)

🔍 Visual Quality:
   • Sharpness score: 18
   • 🔴 Soft or blurry appearance

🏃 Motion Characteristics:
   • Overall motion: 0.012
   • 🟡 Very little motion (static scene?)
```

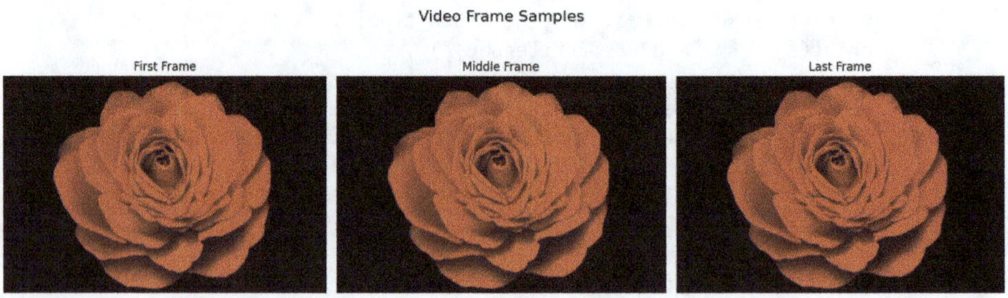

```
📊 Basic Video Evaluation: experiment_steps_50.mp4
========================================
📹 Video Properties:
   • Total frames: 25
   • Duration: 1.0 seconds (at 24 FPS)
   • Resolution: 720×480

🔄 Temporal Consistency:
   • Average consistency: 0.979
   • 🟢 Very smooth transitions (might be too static?)

🔍 Visual Quality:
   • Sharpness score: 31
   • 🔴 Soft or blurry appearance

🏃 Motion Characteristics:
   • Overall motion: 0.359
   • 🟢 Moderate motion
```

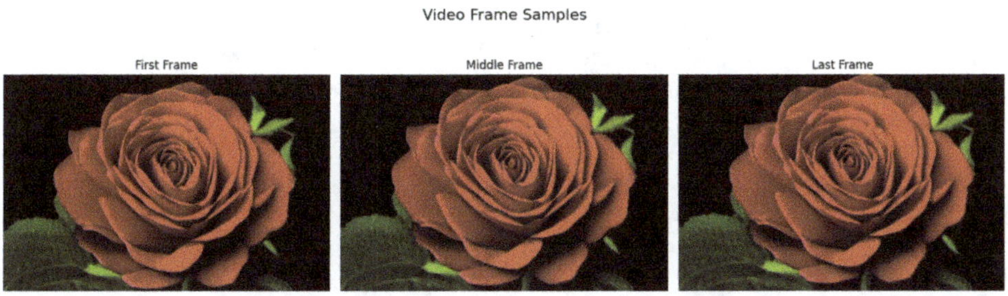


Great job. You've completed your first experiment comparing inferencing steps for refinement. The results revealed both videos exhibited high temporal consistency, with the 50-step version achieving a slightly lower score. This indicates the transitions between frames were smooth in both cases, though the 25-step version was even more stable, perhaps to the point of being nearly static. This illustrates the subjective nature of evaluation. Temporal consistency alone does not guarantee a compelling video, especially when there is insufficient motion to convey growth or change.

Visual sharpness was another area where additional steps helped. The 25-step version scored just 18 for sharpness, resulting in a soft, somewhat fuzzy appearance. The 50-step video scored 31: not perfect but noticeably sharper, with more precise edges and better detail in the petals.

The primary difference between the inference steps in this scenario lies in the amount of movement each video exhibited. The 25-step version barely moved with a motion score of 0.012, looking almost like a photograph. The 50-step video had much more motion, with a motion score of 0.359. This iteration showed fundamental changes over time and created a more compelling effect. The higher-step video captured the rose opening in a much more significant way.

Overall, this experiment confirms that increasing the number of inference steps can significantly enhance the perceptual quality of AI-generated video. While gains in temporal consistency may plateau, improvements in motion and sharpness make the additional computational cost worthwhile in many scenarios. Still, the 25-step video offers a viable alternative when speed is more critical than fidelity.

## Exercise 3: How Prompt Styles Influence Output

Let's examine how various prompt styles change the quality, appearance, and consistency of AI-generated videos. You'll keep the subject the same—a butterfly—while changing how you describe it to see how prompt structure influences the results. You'll test several prompt approaches that offer different levels of creative control, ranging from basic descriptions to highly detailed, artistic language. This will help you see how language guides the model's visual interpretation.

Define your experiment:

```
def experiment_prompt_styles():
    """Explore how prompt engineering affects video generation."""
    print("\n🧪 Experiment 2: Prompt Engineering Impact")
    print("=" * 45)
    print("How do different prompt styles affect the generated video?\n")
```

Now provide the prompts in different styles:

```
    base_subject = "a butterfly"

    prompt_styles = [
        {
            "prompt": "a butterfly",
            "style": "Minimal",
            "expectation": "AI has maximum creative freedom"
        },
        {
            "prompt": "a colorful butterfly landing on a flower, high quality",
            "style": "Detailed",
            "expectation": "More control over the output"
        },
        {
            "prompt": (
                "ethereal glowing butterfly in magical forest, "
                "cinematic lighting, fantasy style"
            ),
            "style": "Artistic",
            "expectation": "Creative and stylized result"
        }
    ]
```

For each style, generate a short video using the same model settings, so that the only change is the prompt:

```
print("Testing different prompt styles with the same subject...\n")

for i, style in enumerate(prompt_styles):
    print(f"🎨 Style {i+1}: {style['style']}")
    print(f"   Prompt: \"{style['prompt']}\"")
    print(f"   Expectation: {style['expectation']}")

    video = pipe(
        prompt=style['prompt'],
        num_frames=25,
        height=480,
        width=720,
        num_inference_steps=30,
        guidance_scale=6.0,
        generator=torch.Generator().manual_seed(456)
    ).frames[0]

    filename = f"experiment_prompt_{i+1}_{style['style'].lower()}.mp4"
    export_to_video(video, filename, fps=24)

    print(f"   💾 Generated: {filename}")
    print()
```

Finally, run the whole experiment to observe the results:

```
experiment_prompt_styles()
```

Once you've completed the exercise in the companion notebook, return to this section to analyze your results. Well done—you've completed your second experiment with video generation. Here are my results:

```
🧪 Experiment 2: Prompt Engineering Impact
=============================================
How do different prompt styles affect the generated video?

Testing different prompt styles with the same subject...

🎨 Style 1: Minimal
   Prompt: "a butterfly"
   Expectation: AI has maximum creative freedom

🎨 Style 2: Detailed
   Prompt: "a colorful butterfly landing on a flower, high quality"
   Expectation: More control over the output

🎨 Style 3: Artistic
   Prompt: (
       "ethereal glowing butterfly in magical forest, "
       "cinematic lighting, fantasy style"
   )
   Expectation: Creative and stylized result
```

You can see the difference in Figure 1-9.

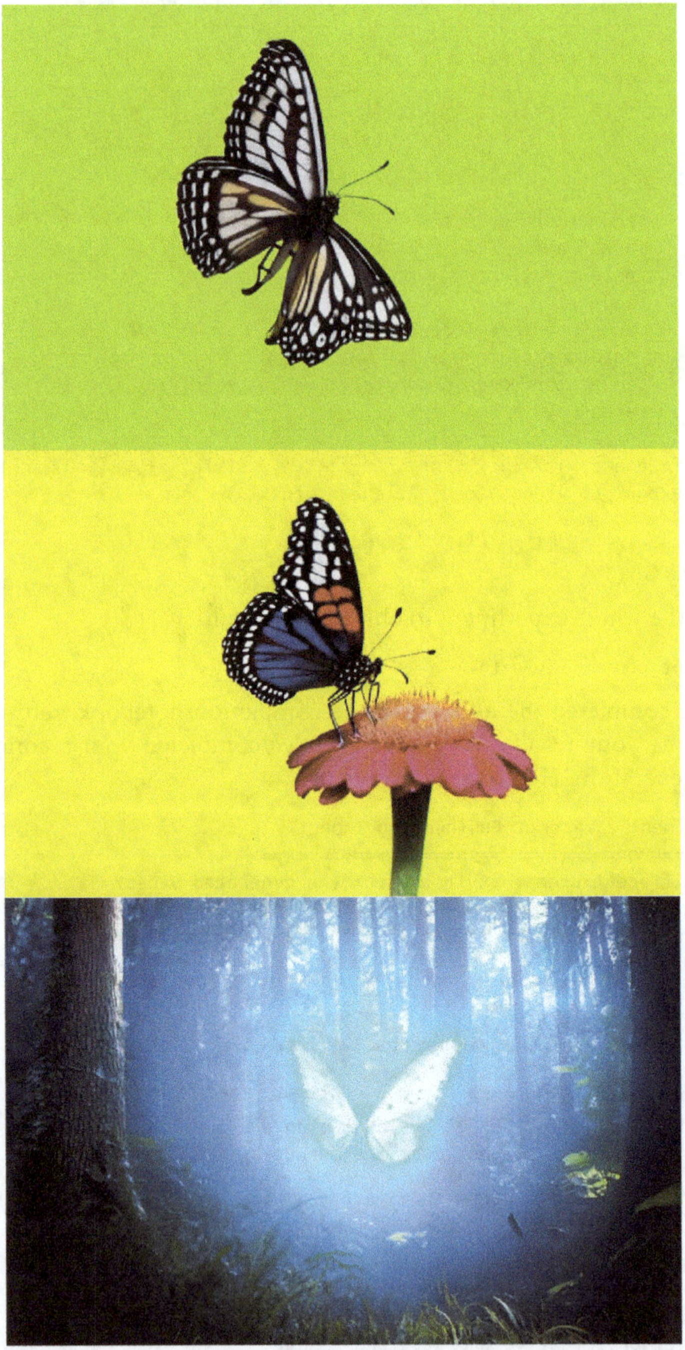

*Figure 1-9. Stills from the videos generated by prompt styles 1, 2, and 3 (top to bottom)*

The minimal prompt, simply *a butterfly*, allowed the model maximum interpretive freedom. The result was a clean but generic visual with a flat background and a single butterfly in flight. While this approach is fast and flexible, it provides limited control over composition, lighting, or context.

The detailed prompt, *a colorful butterfly landing on a flower, high quality*, added specificity to guide the model's generation. This produced a much more controlled and realistic scene, with the butterfly interacting with a vibrant flower against a transparent, high-quality background. This indicates that additional descriptive words enable the model to ground its generation more closely to the user's intent.

For the last test, I tried a more creative prompt: *ethereal glowing butterfly in magical forest, cinematic lighting, fantasy style*. This one used much more artistic language to describe the scene, background, and main subject. The AI created a video featuring both the forest and a luminous butterfly set against a backdrop that resembled a dreamscape. It demonstrates how selecting the right descriptive words can guide the AI toward the exact mood and visual style you're after.

Overall, the exercises show that proficiency in writing prompts is a valuable skill in modern video generation. Minimal prompts initiate the process, and more detailed prompts as you iterate will provide greater creative direction. Detailed prompts deliver greater control and creative direction.

> Start simple, then add details as needed to achieve your desired outcome.

## Learning from Your Experiments

As you've worked through your first video generation tasks, several essential principles have likely become clear.

One of the most fundamental lessons is the trade-off between quality and speed. Increasing the number of inference steps typically improves video quality, but the gains taper off—especially beyond a certain threshold—resulting in longer generation times with minimal visual benefit.

Another key insight is the importance of prompt engineering. The way you describe your desired scene directly influences the output. Specific, vivid prompts tend to yield more accurate and compelling results than vague descriptions.

Quantitative metrics can help guide experimentation, but they only tell part of the story. Visual inspection remains essential—ultimately, your eyes are the final judge of what "works."

Perhaps most important of all is the realization that context shapes everything. What qualifies as "good" output depends entirely on your use case. A marketing team may value visual clarity and branding alignment, while a filmmaker may prioritize emotional tone or narrative consistency.

There isn't one perfect setting that works for everything. The best results are those that match what you're trying to create.

Let's look at what you've learned through some visual summaries. These charts consolidate the key takeaways from your experiments, illustrating both the numerical patterns and the broader concepts to help everything fall into place.

## Trade-Off Between Inference Steps and Quality

Let's begin by defining the learning summary:

```
def visualize_learning_summary():
    """Create a visual summary of evaluation concepts."""

    fig, ((ax1, ax2), (ax3, ax4)) = plt.subplots(2, 2, figsize=(14, 10))
```

This first chart (Figure 1-10) illustrates the relationship between the number of inference steps and the resulting video quality and generation time. As shown in the plot, quality improves with more steps, but so does generation time, demonstrating a classic trade-off:

```
steps = [25, 35, 50, 75]
quality = [7, 8.5, 9.2, 9.5]
time = [2, 3, 4.5, 7]

ax1_twin = ax1.twinx()
ax1.plot(steps, quality, 'b-o', linewidth=2, markersize=8, label='Quality')
ax1_twin.plot(steps, time, 'r-s', linewidth=2, markersize=8, label='Time')

ax1.set_xlabel('Inference Steps')
ax1.set_ylabel('Quality Score', color='b')
ax1_twin.set_ylabel('Generation Time (min)', color='r')
ax1.set_title('Quality vs Speed Tradeoff')
```

This helps clarify why 30 to 50 steps is often a sweet spot for practical generation: good quality at a manageable cost.

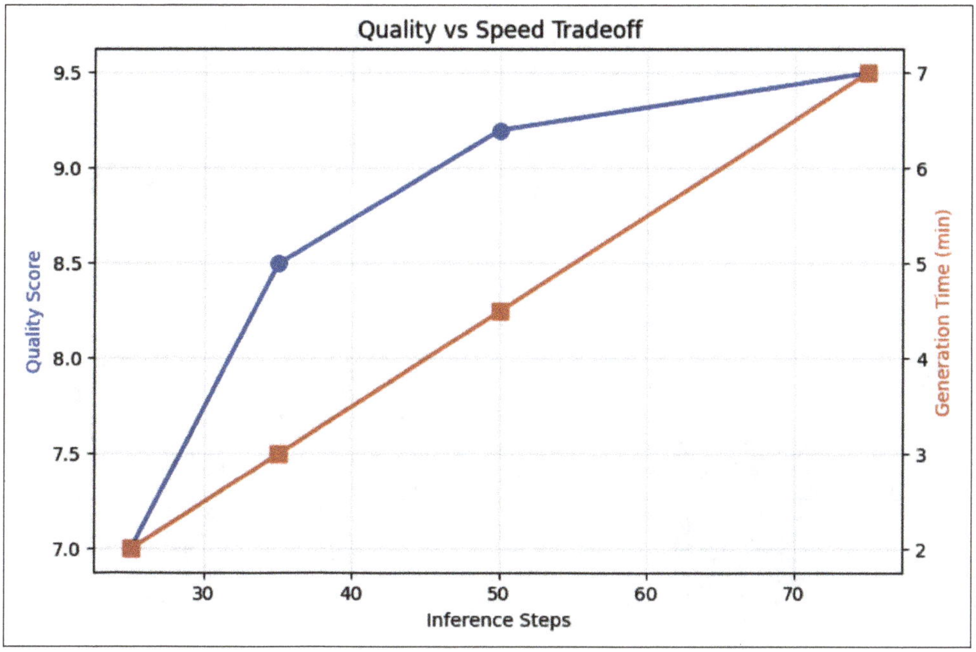


*Figure 1-10. Plotting number of inference steps and resulting video quality and generation time*

## Subjectivity of Evaluation Metrics

The second chart ranks evaluation metrics by their subjectivity. For example, prompt adherence is highly subjective, as it depends on human interpretation, whereas SSIM is more objective:

```
metrics = ['Consistency\n(SSIM)', 'Sharpness', 'Motion', 'Prompt\nAdherence']
subjectivity = [0.3, 0.4, 0.5, 0.9]

bars = ax2.bar(metrics, subjectivity, color=['green', 'yellow', 'orange', 'red'])
ax2.set_ylabel('Subjectivity Level')
ax2.set_title('How Subjective Are Video Metrics?')
```

Figure 1-11 shows the resulting chart.

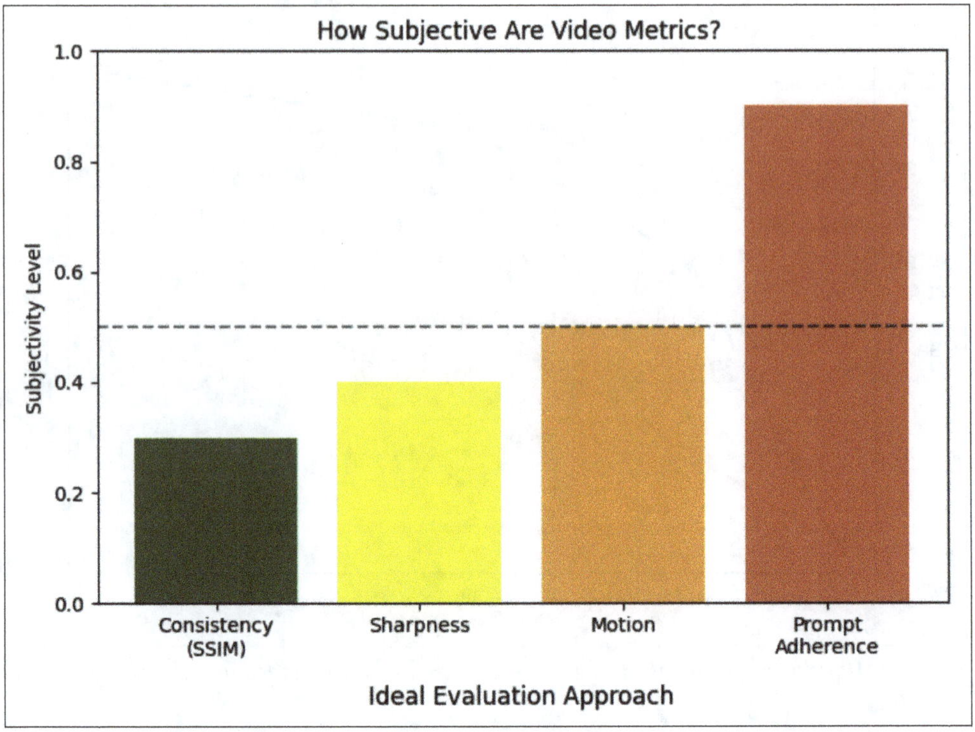


*Figure 1-11. Evaluation metrics ranked by subjectivity*

## Recommended Settings by Use Case

Not all projects require the same level of detail. The bar chart in Figure 1-12 matches different use cases to suggest inference step settings, reinforcing that there is no one-size-fits-all approach. Please note that these settings may vary depending on the model you use. We're aiming for practical metrics you can track along the way:

```
use_cases = [
    'Social\nMedia',
    'Professional\nDemo',
    'Artistic\nProject',
    'Quick\nPrototype',
]
recommended_steps = [30, 50, 60, 25]

ax3.bar(use_cases, recommended_steps, color='skyblue', alpha=0.7)
ax3.set_ylabel('Recommended Inference Steps')
ax3.set_title('Settings by Use Case')
```

Figure 1-12 illustrates how the number of inference steps can be adjusted based on the intended use case. Increasing the number of inference steps typically allows the diffusion model to perform more refinement during the denoising process, often improving visual quality, motion coherence, and prompt adherence. However, additional steps also increase generation time and computational cost. In practice, users must balance quality against speed, selecting settings that align with their specific requirements.

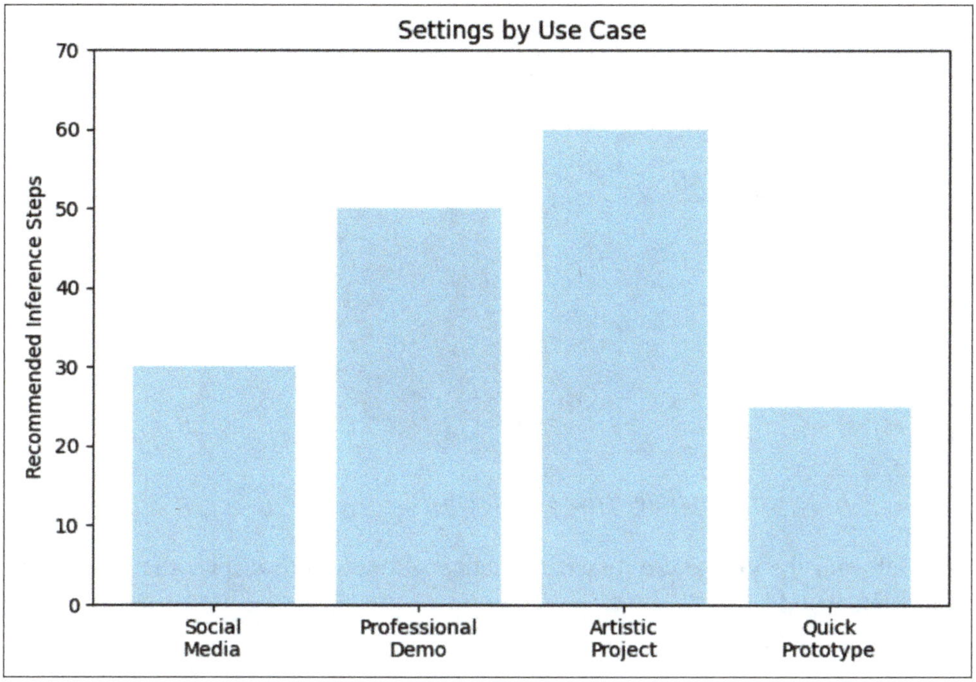


*Figure 1-12. Suggested inference step settings for different use cases*

The final pie chart (Figure 1-13) illustrates a core observation of this chapter: video evaluations combine analysis and intuition. Metrics alone are insufficient to judge the impact of a generated video:

```
labels = ['Objective\nMetrics', 'Subjective\nJudgment']
sizes = [40, 60]
colors = ['lightblue', 'lightcoral']

ax4.pie(sizes, labels=labels, colors=colors, autopct='%1.0f%%',
        startangle=90, textprops={'fontsize': 12})
ax4.set_title('Ideal Evaluation Approach')

plt.suptitle(
    'Video Generation: Key Concepts Summary',
    fontsize=16,
    fontweight='bold',
)
    plt.tight_layout()
    plt.show()
```

Figure 1-13 illustrates a balanced approach to evaluating generated video. While objective metrics provide valuable quantitative measurements of video quality, temporal consistency, and prompt alignment, they cannot fully capture the human perception of realism, creativity, and storytelling effectiveness.

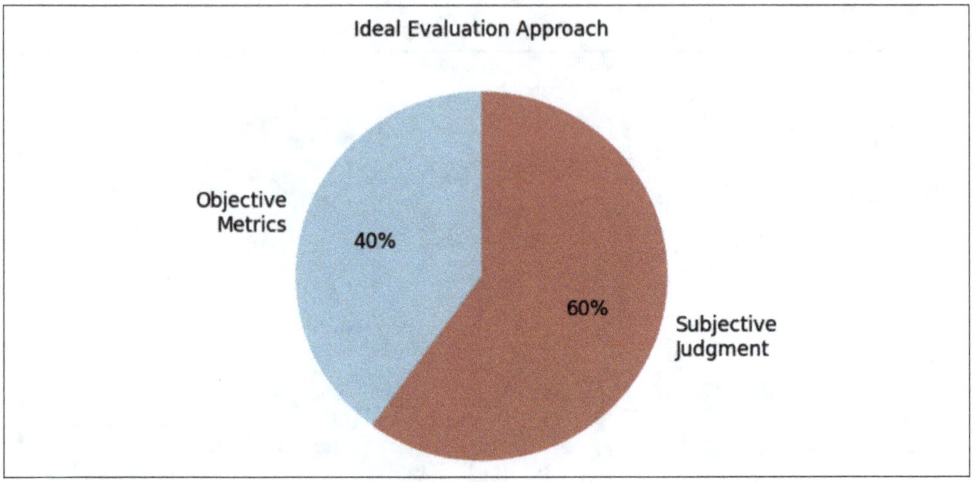


*Figure 1-13. Objective and subjective evaluation*

Now let's run the `visualize_learning_summary` function to display the visual summary (Figure 1-14):

```
visualize_learning_summary()
```

Figure 1-14 summarizes several of the key concepts introduced throughout this chapter. The upper-left chart illustrates the trade-off between inference steps, output quality, and generation time. The upper-right chart highlights the varying degrees of subjectivity present in common video evaluation metrics, demonstrating that some aspects of video quality are easier to measure objectively than others. The lower-left chart presents example inference-step configurations for different use cases, while the lower-right chart emphasizes the importance of balancing objective measurements with human evaluation. Together, these concepts form a practical framework for understanding how modern video generation systems are configured, evaluated, and optimized.

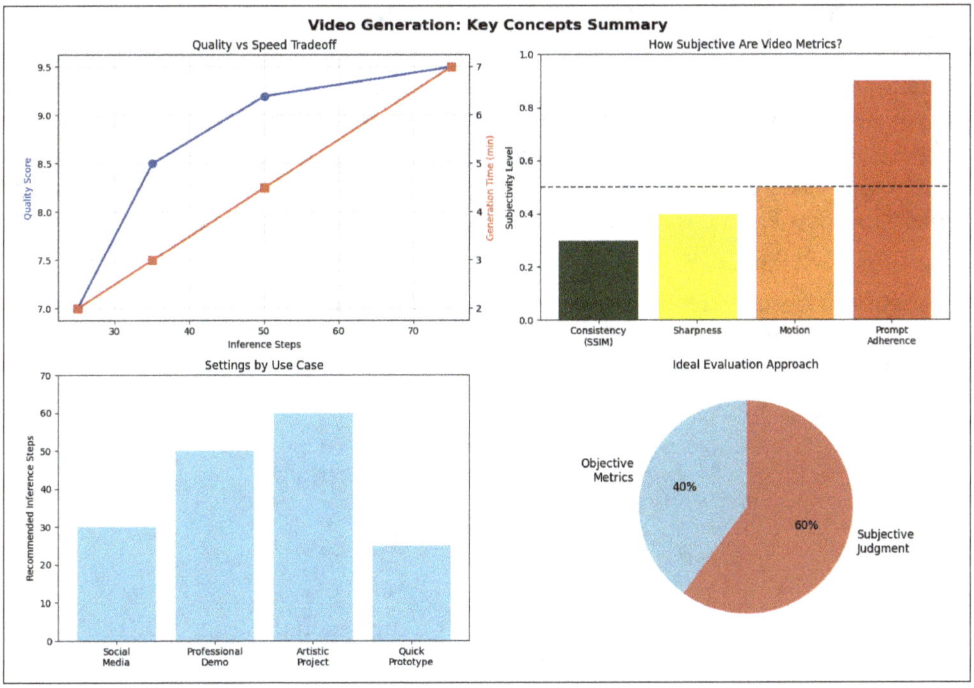


*Figure 1-14. The summary combines all of the charts you've just generated*

## Evaluation Guide

When evaluating the quality of your videos, consider various factors to gain a comprehensive understanding of the content:

- Technical quality encompasses sharpness, consistency, and absence of artifacts.
- Motion realism assesses whether movement appears natural and adheres to physical laws.
- Prompt alignment checks how well the video matches your description.
- Artistic merit considers the overall visual appeal and creative value.
- Practical utility determines suitability for your intended use case.

Remember that the *best* video is the one that achieves your creative vision—it's not necessarily the one with the highest technical scores. A slightly softer video with perfect motion might be far superior to a sharp but jerky one, depending on your needs.

## Hands-On Exercise: Create and Evaluate Your Own Video

Time to put everything into practice! For this last hands-on part, you're going to create your own AI video from scratch. You'll come up with a creative concept, select the proper settings to achieve your desired outcome, and then determine how well it turned out, using both the data we've presented and your judgment on what output looks appropriate. This is often when real learning takes place, as you try things out on your own and learn as you go.

I'll begin by offering a few prompts to get your imagination going. These suggestions span different styles, camera effects, and scene types to help you explore visual diversity:

```
prompt_ideas = [
    "A lighthouse beam sweeping across foggy ocean at night",
    "Time-lapse of clouds rolling over mountain peaks",
    "Hummingbird hovering near tropical flowers, macro lens",
    "Northern lights dancing across starry sky",
    "Coffee being poured in slow motion, steam rising"
]
```

Now it's time to fill in your own prompt and run the generation pipeline. The following template gives you a starting point:

```
# Your creative prompt
my_prompt = "Your creative idea here"
my_negative_prompt = "blurry, low quality, distorted"

# Generate your video
print(f"\n🎬 Generating: {my_prompt}")

my_video = pipe(
    prompt=my_prompt,
    negative_prompt=my_negative_prompt,
    num_frames=49,
    height=480,
    width=720,
    num_inference_steps=40,  # Adjust based on your needs
    guidance_scale=6.0,
    generator=torch.Generator().manual_seed(789)
).frames[0]
```

Once the video is generated, save it to disk, evaluate it using your existing tools, and then watch the output. Reflect on the results and identify areas you want to improve in your next iteration:

```
# Save and evaluate
my_filename = "my_creative_video.mp4"
export_to_video(my_video, my_filename, fps=24)
print(f"\n✅ Video saved as: {my_filename}")

# Evaluate your creation
my_evaluation = evaluate_video_basics(my_filename)

# Display your video
display(Video(my_filename, width=720, height=480, embed=True))
```

You now know how to leverage these foundational tools to go from concept to output. You can iterate creatively, evaluate the results, and use this framework as a launchpad for future explorations in generative video.

## Summary

In this chapter, you've come to understand the fundamental challenges of video generation and gained hands-on experience creating AI videos. You've learned why video generation is exponentially more complex than image generation, requiring models to maintain coherence across spatial, temporal, and semantic dimensions. And you've seen how the field evolved from GANs through VAEs to today's dominant DiTs, with each architecture contributing crucial innovations.

You now understand the practical landscape of the video AI ecosystem, from open source models like Wan and Open-Sora, which are accessible on consumer hardware, to commercial platforms that push the boundaries of what's possible. You've also learned that evaluation is both objective and subjective, requiring a balanced approach that considers technical metrics alongside creative intent. Most importantly, you know how to generate your own videos using state-of-the-art models and evaluate their quality.

As you continue your journey, remember that the best models and settings are those that help you achieve your creative vision. The technology is a tool; your imagination provides the direction.

Chapter 2 dives deeper into understanding and preparing video data, exploring how to curate datasets, preprocess video for optimal results, and understand the data requirements for different video generation tasks.

## CHAPTER 2

# Understanding and Preparing Video Data for Model Training

*Learning objective:* In this chapter, you'll learn how to identify different types of video data, understand their unique challenges, and use practical tools leveraged in scalable data pipelines for AI.

This chapter introduces the methods and tools required to prepare video data for generative pipelines. Why is this important? Video is high-dimensional, storage-intensive, and often inconsistent across sources. Without systematic preprocessing, datasets become redundant or biased, which reduces model quality and makes training harder to scale. Clean, well-prepared video data enables models to learn more efficiently, improves generalization, and reduces wasted computation.

Traditional workflows such as manual editing, one-off filters, or ad hoc cleaning can work for small projects, but they fail at the scale required for generative models. Modern pipelines rely on reproducible processes that can ingest video, detect scenes, extract representative frames, apply augmentations, and generate annotations. This structured approach ensures that downstream models are trained on consistent, balanced data.

Recent open projects demonstrate the effectiveness of these methods. Open-Sora (*https://oreil.ly/MImG1*) and HunyuanVideo (*https://oreil.ly/Vx-ns*), for example, filtered tens of millions of raw clips into just a few million high-quality samples while still achieving state-of-the-art results. In this chapter, we introduce the concepts and foundational tools for working with video datasets, and in Chapter 3 we will work through a scaled-down but realistic version of those pipelines using a curated video dataset.

We will begin by setting up the workspace and running a notebook that demonstrates the initial stages of the pipeline: ingesting clips, extracting frames, and managing annotations with metadata. By the end of the chapter, you will also have a toolkit for preparing video datasets that can be adapted to larger projects and real-world training tasks.

## Hands-On: Working with Video Datasets

Remember the videos you generated in Chapter 1?

They weren't just fun examples—they are real data structures. In this chapter, you'll use them and other sourced videos to explore how to prepare and process video for AI workflows.

### Setting Up the Workspace

The first step in our preprocessing pipeline is to create an organized workspace for raw files, processed outputs, and metadata. Every stage of a production pipeline will write results into the supporting folders, so having a consistent structure is important. In production systems, this may scale to millions of files; here, we'll build a simplified structure for demonstration.

Open the Chapter 2 notebook (*https://oreil.ly/github-ch02-notebook*) and run the following cell. This will create the directories needed for the pipeline:

```
from pathlib import Path

workspace = Path("/content/video_pipeline_demo")

subdirs = [
        "raw", "compressed", "frames", "scenes",
        "annotations", "metadata", "analysis",
        "checkpoints", "pet_videos"
]

print("🎬 Setting up your video pipeline workspace...")

workspace.mkdir(exist_ok=True)
for folder in subdirs:
        (workspace / folder).mkdir(exist_ok=True)
        print(f"    📁 {folder}/")

print("\n✅ Workspace ready!")
print(f"   Working directory: {workspace}")
```

Running this cell creates a `video_pipeline_demo` directory with subfolders for each stage of the workflow. We won't reproduce the printed output here, since you will see it directly in the notebook, but note that you should now have folders such as *raw/*, *frames/*, *scenes/*, *annotations/*, and *metadata/* in place. These and other examples will be used throughout the chapter as the pipeline produces new data.

## Loading the Dataset

With the workspace folders in place, the next step is to load a sample dataset that we can use throughout the pipeline. In production, this stage can be among the most resource-intensive. For example, Open-Sora (*https://oreil.ly/O9G1B*) filtered millions of raw clips before training. To keep things manageable here, we will use a curated gallery of videos.

This dataset is not intended for training a production model. Instead, it serves as a lightweight example to illustrate how preprocessing works at each stage of the pipeline. By working with a small, consistent set of videos, we can demonstrate how to organize, inspect, and transform data without requiring large-scale compute resources.

Open the Chapter 2 notebook (*https://oreil.ly/github-ch02-notebook*) and run the following cell to load the dataset:

```
#Import gallery class from notebook
import gallery

# Download all pet videos
videos = gallery.download_all_videos()

# Display video statistics
print("\n📊 Video Statistics")
print("="*60)
stats_df = gallery.get_video_stats()
display(stats_df)
```

A quick way to build intuition is to look at the videos directly. Using the `gallery` utilities, we can display thumbnails from our dataset:

```
print("\n🖼 Pet Video Thumbnail Gallery")
print("="*60)
print("Here's your collection of amazing AI-generated pet videos!\n")

gallery.display_gallery()
```

Output:

```
🖼 Pet Video Thumbnail Gallery
============================================================
Here's your collection of amazing AI-generated pet videos!
```

Figure 2-1 shows a sample collection of AI-generated pet videos, which we'll use as a toy dataset to demonstrate preprocessing steps.

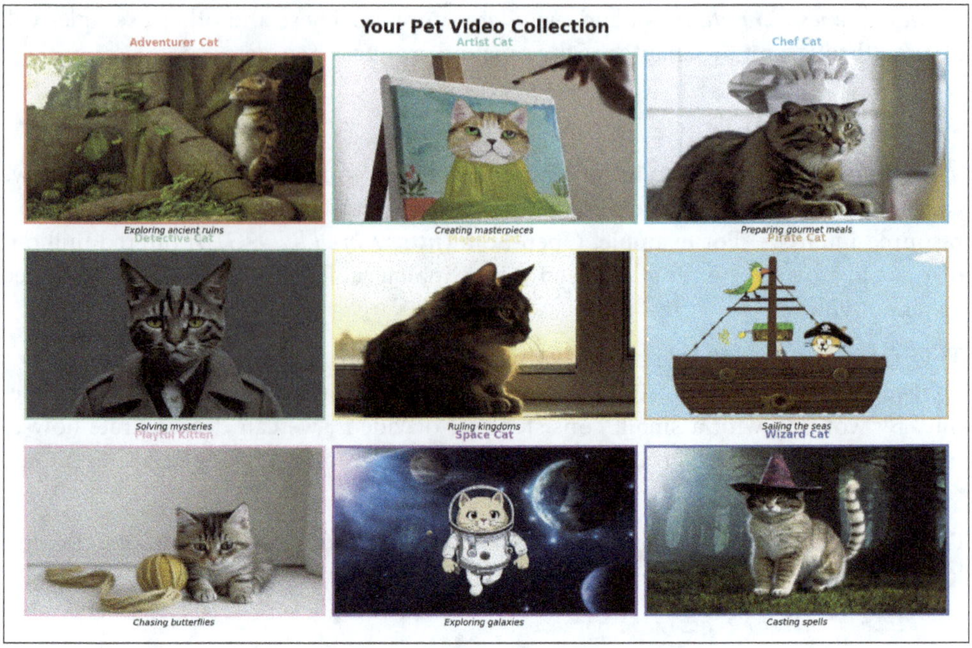


*Figure 2-1. Pet video gallery including images generated in Chapter 1*

Now we have our workspace organized and sample videos loaded. With these in place, we can step back to see the bigger picture.

## Common Challenges in Handling Video Data

Working with video data at scale introduces challenges that cut across infrastructure and platform, as well as provenance, privacy, and governance. Understanding these limitations and challenges is core to building end-to-end pipelines that scale beyond lab experiments into production workflows to support enterprise use cases.

### Scalability

One of the most pressing challenges is scalability. The sheer volume, velocity, and variety of video streams are expanding at an unprecedented pace, driven by applications in streaming, sports analytics, gaming, and telemedicine. Meeting these demands requires a clear understanding of system constraints to set accurate requirements for compute acceleration, distributed networks, and storage architectures. Modern systems must be able to scale metadata independently while still managing the movement of massive video files across locations in a consistent and reliable way. Enterprises are actively exploring distributed, hybrid, and on-premises designs to meet these needs. In addition, enterprise teams need to balance per-unit economics and latency requirements with strict control over sensitive, high-value content.

#### Privacy and ethics

Privacy and ethics add an additional layer of complexity. Video data almost always contains *personally identifiable information* (PII)—such as faces, behaviors, or locations—that must be protected under regulations like the EU's General Data Protection Regulation (GDPR) (*https://oreil.ly/bxpgY*) and the California Consumer Privacy Protection Agency (CPPA) (*https://cppa.ca.gov*). Beyond compliance, bias in training data remains a critical concern. When datasets are unbalanced or unrepresentative, they risk reinforcing harmful patterns in areas such as surveillance, personal privacy, and even hiring practices.

To mitigate these risks, techniques like face blurring and identity swapping are increasingly employed. Still, broader debates continue around the use of copyrighted video for AI training, raising unresolved questions about intellectual property and fair use.

#### Compliance and trust

Building trustworthy AI systems requires governance that goes well beyond technical fixes. Emerging standards such as the EU AI Act (*https://oreil.ly/qHVhn*) and ISO/IEC 42001 (*https://oreil.ly/Uy5K3*) highlight the importance of transparency, fairness, and accountability. As compliance becomes mandatory, these principles must be woven directly into the video sourcing, transformation, and training pipelines. Provenance at every step is equally critical, ensuring that data can be traced and validated throughout its lifecycle. To meet these expectations, organizations need to establish defensible policies and practices for data acquisition, curation, and ongoing maintenance. Together, these elements form the foundation of AI systems that are not only compliant and reliable but also built with social responsibility as a core mandate.

## Working with Video Datasets

Preparing video for generative pipelines is not a single step but a sequence of stages. It begins with collecting raw video, moves through filtering and preprocessing, continues with scene-level analysis and annotation, and ends with structuring the data for training.

Two recent projects illustrate how large-scale systems manage these steps.

The Open-Sora (*https://oreil.ly/YjMD_*) project demonstrates how large volumes of raw video are progressively filtered to create a balanced dataset of high-quality clips, as shown in Figure 2-2. Successive filters such as resolution checks, motion filtering, and deduplication reduce tens of millions of inputs to just a few million carefully curated samples.

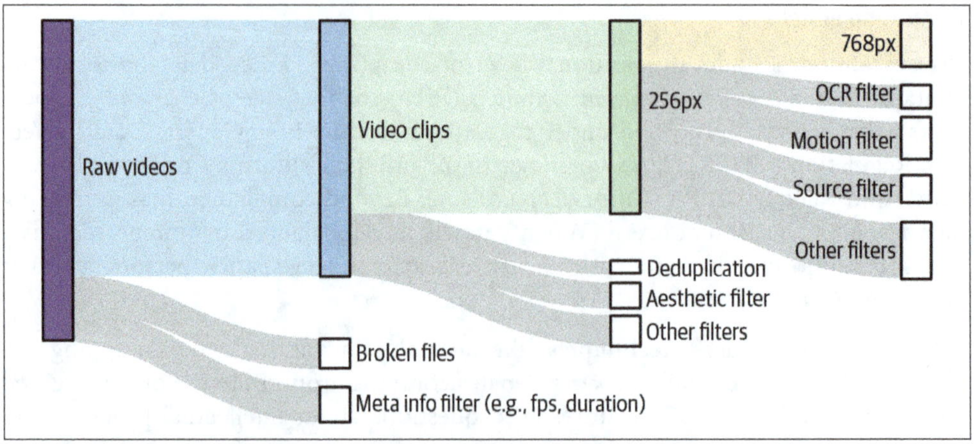


*Figure 2-2. Data preparation workflow from Open-Sora, showing how raw video is reduced step by step into a high-quality dataset suitable for training*

The HunyuanVideo (*https://oreil.ly/0JbhW*) project takes a hierarchical approach. Each stage builds on the results of the previous one, from ingestion through augmentation. This design, shown in Figure 2-3, highlights how structure and reproducibility make large-scale video preprocessing possible.

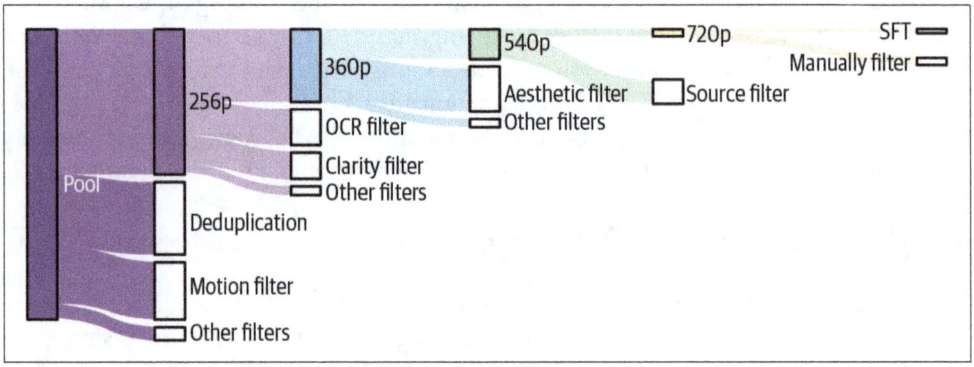


*Figure 2-3. Hierarchical pipeline from HunyuanVideo, where each stage refines the dataset to prepare it for large-scale training*

Together, these examples show why preprocessing pipelines need to be systematic and modular. Each stage contributes to cleaning, organizing, or enriching the data so that the final dataset is both scalable and effective for model development.

Figure 2-4 provides a visual comparison between the example workflow we will build in Chapter 3 and the workflows described by Open-Sora and HunyuanVideo. Open-Sora and HunyuanVideo both describe their dataset creation processes in their respective white papers, but the examples we provide are simplified, designed to make these concepts more accessible.

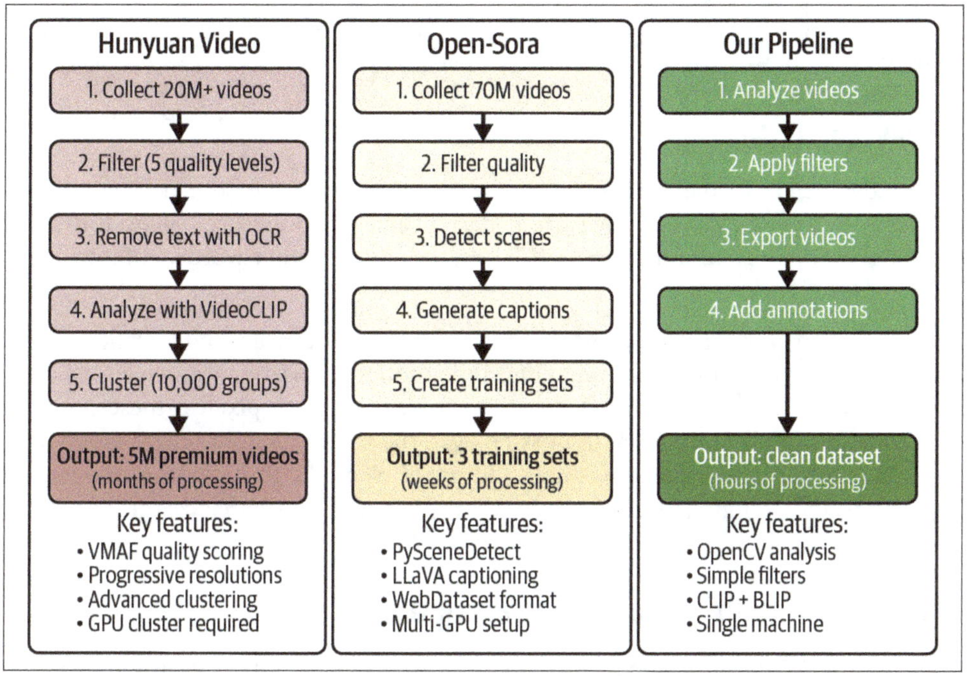


*Figure 2-4. HunyuanVideo versus Open-Sora versus Our Pipeline*

# Types of Video Data

Before we examine the detailed pipelines, it's important to understand primitives associated with video data. Video data isn't uniform. It takes different forms depending on how we capture the data, process it, and plan for deployment. These distinct elements are important as they can impact how rapidly our videos are stored, organized, analyzed, and integrated into our overall workflow. Table 2-1 highlights the main categories we'll examine in this chapter.

*Table 2-1. Common video data types used in video workflows*

| Type | Description | Applications | Key challenges |
|---|---|---|---|
| Raw video | Unprocessed footage at original resolution and frame rate, with maximum fidelity | Professional filmmaking, medical imaging, autonomous driving | Large storage requirements, processing intensive |
| Compressed video | Reduced file size using formats such as MPEG or H.264; optimized for efficient storage and transmission | Streaming platforms, cloud storage, healthcare records | Quality loss, compression artifacts |

| Type | Description | Applications | Key challenges |
|---|---|---|---|
| Annotated video | Video enriched with metadata and labels, prepared for machine learning (ML) tasks | Object detection, activity recognition, supervised ML | Labor-intensive to create, error-prone |
| Streaming video | Real-time video transmitted over a network with low-latency requirements | Videoconferencing, live sports, surveillance | Bandwidth constraints, latency sensitivity |

## Raw Video Data

Raw video refers to the untouched footage captured directly from devices such as cameras, drones, or sensors. Because it hasn't been compressed or altered, it holds onto its original resolution, frame rate, and encoding. In other words, nothing is lost in translation.

Raw footage maintains its greatest value in fields that require absolute quality preservation including healthcare, filmmaking, and autonomous driving systems. The analysis of raw video in autonomous vehicles shows how every pixel in these domains holds critical importance because missing even the tiniest detail would create potential risks. In fact, many methods add additional elements to video including Light Detection and Ranging (LiDAR) (*https://oreil.ly/wzknL*) to enhance the raw video inputs.

## Hands-On: Analyzing Raw Video Properties

Before we can build pipelines or models, it helps to understand the basic properties of raw video files. This function inspects a video and extracts key information such as frame width, height, frame rate (FPS), and total frame count. From those, it derives useful metrics like the video's duration in seconds and an estimated uncompressed file size.

This quick analysis gives us an intuition for the scale of our data: how long a video runs, how many frames it contains, and how much storage it might require. Knowing these properties early helps us design preprocessing steps that are both efficient and scalable:

```
def analyze_raw_video(video_path):
    """Analyze basic properties of raw video data"""
    cap = cv2.VideoCapture(str(video_path))
    if not cap.isOpened():
        raise FileNotFoundError(f"Could not open: {video_path}")

    # Core properties
    width = int(cap.get(cv2.CAP_PROP_FRAME_WIDTH))
    height = int(cap.get(cv2.CAP_PROP_FRAME_HEIGHT))
    fps = cap.get(cv2.CAP_PROP_FPS)
    frame_count = int(cap.get(cv2.CAP_PROP_FRAME_COUNT))
    cap.release()
```

```
    # Derived metrics
    duration_seconds = frame_count / fps if fps > 0 else 0
    bytes_per_frame = width * height * 3  # RGB
    estimated_size_gb = (bytes_per_frame * frame_count) / (1024 ** 3)

    return {
        "width": width, "height": height, "fps": fps,
        "frame_count": frame_count, "duration_seconds": duration_seconds,
        "estimated_size_gb": estimated_size_gb,
    }

# Example: Analyzing a sample raw video
props = analyze_raw_video("wizard_cat_raw.mp4")
print(f"Resolution: {props['width']}x{props['height']} @ {props['fps']} fps")
print(
    f"Frames: {props['frame_count']} | Duration: "
    f"{props['duration_seconds']:.2f} sec"
)
print(f"Estimated raw size: {props['estimated_size_gb']:.2f} GB")
```

```
Resolution: 720x480 @ 8.0 fps
Duration: 6.125 sec  |  Estimated raw size: 0.266 GB
```

Even a short clip of raw footage can consume hundreds of megabytes of space, illustrating why raw video is challenging and often impractical at scale.

## Compressed Video Data

Most real-world video workflows rely on compression to make large datasets manageable. A codec (*https://oreil.ly/GLAgU*)—short for coder-decoder—is the software or hardware that encodes video into a smaller form and decodes it back for playback. Early standards such as MPEG-4 (*https://oreil.ly/fsah9*) were what first made digital video widely accessible. The arrival of H.264 (*https://oreil.ly/1UvvK*) (also known as Advanced Video Coding, AVC) marked another turning point. H.264 delivered excellent visual quality at much smaller file sizes and became a foundational utility for streaming platforms like YouTube, Netflix, and Zoom. More recently, H.265 (*https://oreil.ly/Dz8YB*) (High Efficiency Video Coding, HEVC) has pushed efficiency further, offering the same visual fidelity as H.264 at roughly half the bit rate. This increased efficiency brings with it a heavier computational cost for both encoding and decoding. These codecs leverage a traditional compression process dividing video frames into smaller fixed-sized units called macroblocks (*https://oreil.ly/A8pF9*). The macroblocks are processed using algorithms like Discrete Cosine Transform (DCT) (*https://oreil.ly/XhcRA*) to achieve video compression. A reverse process of macroblocking and inverse DCT restores the compressed data into the output video.

Today, emerging learned codecs like Deep Render's AI codec (*https://oreil.ly/LFwRb*) operate exclusively on neural networks. This process improves upon preexisting codecs and more closely aligns to technologies leveraged in video generation. As we progress into video generation, we see the emergence of technologies similar in nature to the AI codecs known as autoencoders. Autoencoders are neural networks tuned specifically for AI pipelines. We will dive deeper into autoencoders in Chapter 4. For now it's important to understand that these new classes of compression systems are trained with ML and neural networks rather than by hand-engineered rules.

Table 2-2 highlights several of the most widely used codecs, showing when they were adopted, their typical use cases, and the kinds of artifacts that arise as compression ratios increase.

*Table 2-2. Video encoders and decoders (codecs) along with modern learned autoencoders*

| Codec | Era | Typical use cases | Compression | Notes on artifacts |
|---|---|---|---|---|
| MPEG-4 | Early 2000s | DVDs, early web video, mobile playback | Moderate | Noticeable blocking and blurring at higher compression ratios |
| H.264 (AVC) | 2000s to present | Streaming (YouTube, Zoom), cloud storage | High (baseline efficiency) | Mild artifacts at standard quality ratios |
| H.265 (HEVC) | 2013 to present | 4K/8K streams, Netflix, UHD/Blu-ray | ~50% better than H.264 | More efficient, compute-constrained, banding, and ghosting at high ratios |
| AV1(AOM) | 2018 to present | Google-designed for enhanced streaming | > H.265 | Artifact reduction with advanced open techniques |
| AI Codec (Deep Render (*https://www.deeprender.ai*)) | 2024 to present | Emerging NN Codec | Modern AI aligned NN | Optimized using deep neural networks to reduce artifacts |

The codecs listed in Table 2-2 enable commercial streaming platforms like Netflix to maintain viability at scale.

## Hands-On: Comparing Raw and Compressed Video

To see compression in action, let's take a look at one of our sample videos. In this example, we'll use FFmpeg, an open source multimedia framework widely used for video and audio processing. FFmpeg provides command-line tools and libraries that make it possible to convert, compress, and stream media in nearly any format.

Here, we'll use FFmpeg to compress a raw video with the H.264 codec and compare the file sizes before and after:

```
def compress_video(input_path, output_path, codec="libx264", crf=23):
    """Compress video using FFmpeg and compare sizes."""
    import subprocess, os
    cmd = [
        "ffmpeg",
        "-y",
        "-i",
```

```
            input_path,
            "-c:v",
            codec,
            "-crf",
            str(crf),
            output_path,
        ]
        subprocess.run(cmd, check=True, stdout=subprocess.PIPE,
        stderr=subprocess.PIPE)

        # Compare file sizes
        original_size = os.path.getsize(input_path) / (1024 ** 2)
        compressed_size = os.path.getsize(output_path) / (1024 ** 2)
        return {
            "original_size_mb": original_size,
            "compressed_size_mb": compressed_size,
            "compression_ratio": original_size / compressed_size,
        }

    stats = compress_video("wizard_cat_raw.mp4", "wizard_cat_compressed.mp4")
    print(f"Original size   : {stats['original_size_mb']:.2f} MB")
    print(f"Compressed size : {stats['compressed_size_mb']:.2f} MB")
    print(f"Ratio           : {stats['compression_ratio']:.2f}x smaller")
```

The results illustrate why compression algorithms are key in video-related fields:

```
Original size   : 271.87 MB
Compressed size : 45.62 MB
Ratio           : 5.96x smaller
```

Even with a single clip, the file size is reduced by nearly sixfold. At the scale of millions of training videos, these savings become the difference between a dataset that can be stored and streamed efficiently and one that overwhelms available infrastructure.

## Annotated Video Data

For supervised learning, video must often be enriched with annotations that add structure and meaning to the raw footage. A common example is a bounding box, which marks a rectangular region around an object of interest, such as a car or a pedestrian, so that models can learn to detect and localize them. Segmentation masks go a step further, providing pixel-level labels that distinguish the exact shape of an object from its background. In other cases, clips are assigned action labels, short descriptions such as "walking," "jumping," or "opening a door" that enable models to recognize dynamic behaviors.

Datasets such as KITTI (*https://oreil.ly/budBM*) and ActivityNet (*https://oreil.ly/xFsST*) demonstrate how annotations transform raw clips into training resources for object detection, activity recognition, and captioning. Modern large scale systems like Open-Sora extend this concept further. Instead of assigning a single label or bounding box, each clip is annotated with a natural-language caption that describes the scene, action, or event.

Have a look at the following simple example:

```
def extract_annotated_clips(annotations, action_type):
    """Extract video segments containing a specific action"""
    clips = []
    for ann in annotations:
        if ann.get("action") == action_type:
            clips.append({
                "start_frame": ann.get("start_frame", ann["frame_id"]),
                "end_frame": ann.get("end_frame", ann["frame_id"]),
                "confidence": ann.get("confidence", 1.0)
            })
    return clips

# Example: loading JSON annotations
annotations = [
    {"frame_id": 40, "action": "jump", "confidence": 0.95},
    {"frame_id": 42, "action": "jump", "confidence": 0.92},
]
jump_clips = extract_annotated_clips(annotations, "jump")
print(jump_clips)
```

The output shows that this short clip has action annotations embedded at frames 40 and 42:

```
[{'start_frame': 40, 'end_frame': 40, 'confidence': 0.95},
 {'start_frame': 42, 'end_frame': 42, 'confidence': 0.92}]
```

As you'll see later in Chapter 3, annotation remains essential to the training process, but it can be time-consuming and error-prone. Today, AI-assisted methods such as vision-language models (VLMs) (*https://oreil.ly/uG9ZS*), Grounding DINO (*https://oreil.ly/Ua3uU*), SAM (Segment Anything Model) (*https://oreil.ly/Zxv3Z*), and BLIP (Bootstrapping Language-Image Pre-training) (*https://oreil.ly/IPDyA*) are widely used to accelerate and refine labeling and annotation. Grounding DINO, for example, provides fast, open-vocabulary object detection, while SAM produces high-quality segmentation masks for any image region with minimal prompts. BLIP unifies captioning and question-answering over images, enabling richer semantic annotation across large visual datasets and video pipelines. And VLMs provide more modern and comprehensive capabilities for question and answering along with labeling and annotation.

## Hands-On: Simulating Video Streaming

Streaming video data is central to latency-sensitive applications like surveillance, live sports, and telemedicine. Streaming video is becoming a growing focus for real-time systems and modern generative AI approaches, including open-world models like World Labs (*https://www.worldlabs.ai*).

To better understand how streaming works in practice, we'll simulate a simple video stream by reading frames one at a time. This exercise doesn't create a real network stream, but it demonstrates the principle of sequential frame access, which underlies most streaming systems. By examining each frame as it is read, we can see how video is processed incrementally rather than as a single large file:

```
def stream_video(source, max_frames=3):
    """Simulate streaming video by reading frames one by one."""
    import cv2
    cap = cv2.VideoCapture(source)
    frame_count = 0
    buffer = []
    while cap.isOpened() and frame_count < max_frames:
        ret, frame = cap.read()
        if not ret:
            break
        buffer.append(frame)
        print(
            f"Frame {frame_count}: "
            f"{{'frame_shape': {frame.shape}, 'buffer_len': {len(buffer)}}}"
        )
        frame_count += 1

# Example: stream compressed wizard cat video
stream_video("wizard_cat_compressed.mp4")
```

Here is the output:

```
Frame 0: {'frame_shape': (480, 720, 3), 'buffer_len': 1}
Frame 1: {'frame_shape': (480, 720, 3), 'buffer_len': 2}
Frame 2: {'frame_shape': (480, 720, 3), 'buffer_len': 3}
```

Video streaming requires the use of low-latency networks and powerful edge computing to manage jitter, packet loss, and buffering, all requirements for real-time inference in video processing.

## Choosing Data Based on Use Case

Not every project requires the same set of video data. The right choice of data types depends on both the technical requirements of the model and practical constraints on cost, storage, and latency. Recent production deployments, including Open-Sora (*https://oreil.ly/lz8mZ*), have shown that matching your data type to the specific use case can reduce infrastructure costs dramatically while maintaining the trained model's performance characteristics. Table 2-3 summarizes where each type of video fits best.

*Table 2-3. Best fit use cases for video data types*

| Video type | Applications | Best for | Challenges |
|---|---|---|---|
| Raw video | Film, medical imaging, and autonomous driving | Maximum fidelity requirements | Large storage, processing-intensive |
| Compressed | Streaming, cloud archives, health records | Efficient storage and transmission | Quality loss, artifacts/defects |
| Annotated | Object detection, activity recognition, captioning | Training supervised models | Labor-intensive and error-prone |
| Streaming | Sports, conferencing, gaming, and surveillance | Real-time applications | Bandwidth, latency |

## Sourcing and Collecting Video Data

Sourcing video data is the foundation of any dataset preparation pipeline. The value of a model depends not only on the volume of clips collected but also on how representative and ethically sound those clips are. Researchers now collect data from multiple avenues: long-standing public benchmarks, domain-specific capture efforts, automated refinement pipelines, and collaborative sharing agreements. Each of these approaches has its own strengths and limitations, shaping the downstream quality of video AI systems.

### Publicly available datasets

For many researchers, public datasets are the natural starting point when building video AI systems. One of the classics, UCF101 (*https://oreil.ly/WiKdD*), offers over 13,000 clips spread across 101 human action categories and still serves as a go-to reference for activity recognition tasks. Moving up in scale, Kinetics-700 (*https://oreil.ly/hFmMS*) expands the playing field with more than 650,000 clips covering 700 classes—an ideal resource for training models to capture complex motion at scale. At the other end of the spectrum lies AVA, a dataset built around shorter clips but enriched with dense spatiotemporal annotations, making it particularly valuable for studying fine-grained human actions.

Newer datasets expand both scope and modality. WebVid-10M (*https://oreil.ly/qUZHN*) offers large-scale video-text pairs under an AGPL-3.0 (*https://oreil.ly/Ne77e*) license, which requires that any derived work also be shared openly, while OpenVid-1M (*https://oreil.ly/ofhuc*) provides a CC BY 4.0 (*https://oreil.ly/8ruux*) option that's more flexible for commercial use. Panda-70M (*https://oreil.ly/Bf36w*) and InternVid (*https://oreil.ly/j7VXQ*) add diversity and multimodal depth but restrict commercial deployment.

Together, these and other video datasets set shared baselines for progressing the foundations for training video generation models. Still, more isn't always better. Studies in the past few years point out that recognition accuracy improves when the training data reflects a diverse set of distributed activities and settings, including both cultural and demographic variety.

### Custom video capture

While public datasets are essential for benchmarking, many real-world applications demand something more specific: video that reflects the exact environment and tasks of the system being built. This is where *custom capture* comes into play. By tailoring collection strategies to the problem domain, we can create datasets that match real-world conditions much more closely than generic benchmarks ever could.

Take autonomous driving. Autonomous vehicle fleets are often equipped with both LiDAR and high-definition cameras, recording thousands of hours of driving across diverse weather, lighting, and traffic scenarios. These recordings form the foundation of perception systems that must be equally reliable on a quiet rural road at dawn and in the middle of a crowded city intersection at night.

Urban monitoring provides an alternative method of observation. The use of drones now enables the recording of extensive video footage, which shows traffic flow and congestion levels and safety hazards throughout entire urban areas. The aerial vantage point provides insights that would be impossible to achieve through manual observation, creating datasets that are both expansive and context-rich.

What unites these examples is the way custom capture produces task-specific, context-aware datasets. While the investment can be significant—covering everything from equipment to logistics to data management—the payoff is equally substantial. Models trained on this kind of data are more resilient when deployed outside the lab. For this reason, many of today's leading AI efforts combine broad public benchmarks with targeted custom capture, ensuring both scale and situational relevance in their training material.

### Collaborative data sharing

Not all video data can be collected in-house. In many domains, the most valuable footage comes through collaboration and partnership. By working across industries, organizations can access video that would otherwise remain siloed or unavailable.

Healthcare is one clear example. Hospitals and research institutions increasingly share surgical video recordings with academic partners to support clinical AI development. These datasets are critical for training models that can assist surgeons, identify anomalies, or provide decision support in real time.

Collaborative sharing highlights an important reality of video AI: no single team can capture every scenario on its own. By pooling resources and expertise, partners create richer, more representative datasets and, in doing so, lay the groundwork for systems that perform more reliably in the environments where they matter most.

## Automated Filtering Pipelines

Collecting video data is only the first step. Raw footage almost always contains noise, shaky clips, blurry frames, or files that are too short to be useful. Manually checking millions of videos isn't realistic. That's why large-scale projects rely on automated filtering pipelines to clean datasets before they ever reach the training stage.

The idea is simple: run each video through a set of quality checks. Resolution and duration are obvious first filters, removing clips that are too small or too short. The analysis of video quality includes multiple tests, including the Laplacian variance test, used to measure sharpness and optical flow analysis in order to detect motion levels. Scene detection operates as an additional feature that divides extended recordings into smaller sections to maintain consistent quality.

This approach has been validated in practice. For example, the Open-Sora (*https://oreil.ly/EER_w*) framework processed more than 20 million videos, ultimately filtering them down to a high-quality dataset of 7.7 million clips. Without automation, this kind of scale would be unmanageable.

Automated filtering doesn't just save time—it improves downstream model performance by ensuring that only the cleanest and most consistent data makes it into training. Whether you're working with a few thousand videos or millions of them, a pipeline of automated checks is the most reliable way to reduce noise and maximize quality from the start.

Figure 2-5 provides an example of Open-Sora's end-to-end pipeline. It begins with a collection of 20 million raw videos and progressively reduces this set through several preprocessing stages: quality filtering (down to 12 million), motion and scene analysis (10 million), deduplication using perceptual hashing and embedding similarity (8.5 million), and finally concept balancing via clustering and uniform sampling.

The result is a curated dataset of 7.7 million videos sufficiently lean to manage, yet broad and balanced enough to support robust model training. This demonstrates how structured preprocessing can scale without overwhelming researchers while still producing high-quality training data. In our notebook for Chapter 3, we will apply the same principles at a smaller scale, showing how filtering, deduplication, and balancing each contribute to building datasets that are both manageable and effective for downstream modeling.

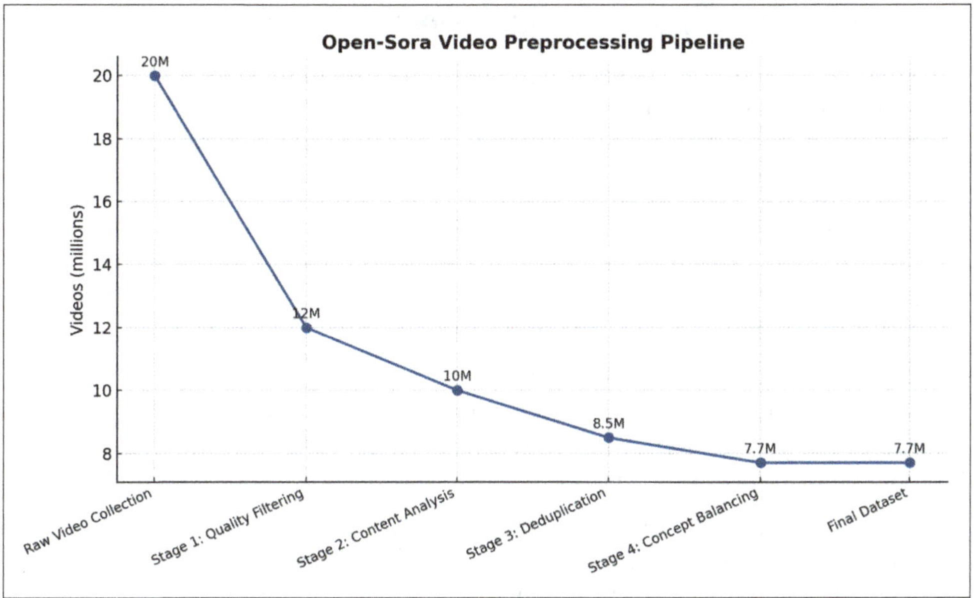


*Figure 2-5. Video preprocessing pipeline for AI-ready datasets*

# Tools for Video Handling

Advancing your work with video will require a reliable set of specialized tools. For tasks like preprocessing, compression, scene segmentation, and augmentation, these tools will act as the core building blocks of your modern AI workflow. They will help to streamline the preparation of raw footage, making it possible to scale from just a handful of clips to millions of files while preserving consistent data quality.

This section focuses on three foundational libraries: OpenCV (*https://opencv.org*), FFmpeg (*https://ffmpeg.org*), and PySceneDetect (*https://scenedetect.com*). Together, they form the support structure for the video generation pipeline you'll be building throughout this book. Each serves a distinct role:

- OpenCV, with its long history and robust community support, excels at frame-level processing.
- FFmpeg is the workhorse for encoding and compression, widely used across industries.
- PySceneDetect adds higher-level structure, breaking long videos into scenes and segments that can then be augmented and used for training.

## Hands-On: Screening Quality with OpenCV

OpenCV is among the most widely used open source libraries in computer vision and has grown into a staple of modern video processing. First released by Intel in 2000, it was built to speed up computer vision research and soon became the go-to toolkit for image and video analysis.

Today, OpenCV supports both Python and C++ and comes with optimized functions for real-time frame handling, geometric transformations, quality filtering, and edge detection. It's the core for many computer vision workflows, powering everything from early research prototypes to large-scale production video systems.

Large-scale generative pipelines such as HunyuanVideo have used OpenCV for data preprocessing before clips are passed to model training. This balance of simplicity, speed, and breadth of functions make OpenCV the go-to library when building low-level components of video pipelines.

Before we do anything fancy, we need to answer a basic question: is this clip worth keeping? In this hands-on, we'll use OpenCV to probe video metadata, sample a few frames, and score sharpness and motion. Let's run it on a wizard-cat clip to quickly flag files that are too small, short, blurry, or static:

```
class OpenCVQualityAssessor:
    """Frame-level quality checks using OpenCV."""
    # ---- metadata ----
    def probe(self, video_path):
        """Return (width, height, fps, frames, duration_s)."""
        cap = cv2.VideoCapture(video_path)
        if not cap.isOpened():
            raise ValueError(f"Cannot open {video_path}")
        fps = cap.get(cv2.CAP_PROP_FPS) or 30.0
        w = int(cap.get(cv2.CAP_PROP_FRAME_WIDTH))
        h = int(cap.get(cv2.CAP_PROP_FRAME_HEIGHT))
        n = int(cap.get(cv2.CAP_PROP_FRAME_COUNT))
        dur = n / fps if fps > 0 else 0
        cap.release()
        return w, h, fps, n, dur
    # ---- sampling ----
    def sample_indices(self, n_frames, n_samples):
        n_samples = min(n_samples, max(1, n_frames))
        return np.linspace(0, n_frames - 1, n_samples, dtype=int).tolist()
    # ---- quality metrics ----
    def _lap_var(self, frame_bgr):
        gray = cv2.cvtColor(frame_bgr, cv2.COLOR_BGR2GRAY)
        return float(cv2.Laplacian(gray, cv2.CV_64F).var())

    def sharpness(self, video_path, indices):
        cap = cv2.VideoCapture(video_path)
        vals = []
        for i in indices:
```

```
            cap.set(cv2.CAP_PROP_POS_FRAMES, i)
            ok, f = cap.read()
            if ok:
                vals.append(self._lap_var(f))
        cap.release()
        return float(np.mean(vals)) if vals else 0.0

    def motion(self, video_path, indices):
        cap = cv2.VideoCapture(video_path)
        prev, vals = None, []
        for i in indices:
            cap.set(cv2.CAP_PROP_POS_FRAMES, i)
            ok, f = cap.read()
            if not ok:
                continue
            g = cv2.cvtColor(f, cv2.COLOR_BGR2GRAY)
            if prev is not None:
                flow = cv2.calcOpticalFlowFarneback(
                    prev,
                    g,
                    None,
                    0.5,
                    3,
                    15,
                    3,
                    5,
                    1.2,
                    0,
                )
                vals.append(float(np.linalg.norm(flow, axis=2).mean()))
            prev = g
        cap.release()
        return float(np.mean(vals)) if vals else 0.0
```

This class shows how to extract simple quality checks from video data. It reports basic metadata (resolution, FPS, duration), samples representative frames, measures sharpness, and estimates motion using optical flow. These quick checks help ensure your dataset is consistent and usable before moving on to heavier preprocessing steps.

## Hands-On: Normalizing and Exporting with FFmpeg

OpenCV works best at the frame-by-frame level; FFmpeg dominates at the stream level. It provides us with a high-performance framework designed for encoding, decoding, transcoding, and streaming media. Its command line provides flexibility and makes it valuable for batch operations, including compressing thousands of videos or converting entire datasets into a consistent format.

FFmpeg is frequently the go-to tool to manage our video dataset at scale. When we apply H.265 compression or extract audio tracks for analysis, FFmpeg keeps our datasets manageable and structured to scale our multimodal workflows.

Once a clip passes quality checks, we want it in a consistent, training-friendly format. Here, we'll use FFmpeg to resize with aspect-ratio preserved, copy audio, and (optionally) export scene-level subclips. This is the *dataset hygiene* step that keeps large collections compact and consistent:

```
class FFmpegExporter:
    """Stream-level operations via FFmpeg CLI."""

    def trim(
        self,
        video_path,
        start_s,
        end_s,
        out_path,
        crf=23,
        preset="veryfast",
    ):
        """Write [start_s, end_s) to out_path (keeps audio, re-encodes video)."""
        dur = max(0.01, end_s - start_s)
        cmd = [
            "ffmpeg", "-y",
            "-ss", f"{start_s:.3f}",
            "-i", video_path,
            "-t", f"{dur:.3f}",
            "-c:v", "libx264", "-crf", str(crf), "-preset", preset,
            "-c:a", "copy",
            out_path,
        ]
    def transcode_resize(
        self,
        video_path,
        out_path,
        size=(512,512),
        crf=23,
        preset="veryfast",
    ):
        """Aspect-ratio-preserving resize; copies audio."""
        w, h = size
        vf = f"scale={w}:{h}:force_original_aspect_ratio=decrease"
        cmd = [
            "ffmpeg", "-y",
            "-i", video_path,
            "-vf", vf,
            "-c:v", "libx264", "-crf", str(crf), "-preset", preset,
            "-c:a", "copy",
            out_path,
        ]
```

This class demonstrates how to carry out stream-level video operations with FFmpeg, a powerful command-line tool for encoding and transcoding. The trim method extracts a segment of a video while preserving audio and re-encoding video with H.264 compression, useful for creating smaller clips from longer footage. The `transcode_resize` method resizes video frames to a target resolution while maintaining aspect ratio, again keeping audio intact. Together, these examples highlight how FFmpeg enables batch processing of video at scale, making it a key tool in preparing data for AI pipelines.

## Hands-On: Detecting Scenes with PySceneDetect

OpenCV and FFmpeg give us the ability to manipulate frames and streams, but they do not directly answer one of the most practical questions in video preparation: where does one scene end and the next begin? PySceneDetect was created to solve this exact problem. It identifies scene boundaries by analyzing changes between frames and marking transitions such as hard cuts or gradual fades.

While PySceneDetect reliably captures hard cuts and gradual transitions, modern GenAI training pipelines often require semantic scene detection, where scene boundaries are defined by changes in meaning rather than purely visual discontinuities. We will return to semantic approaches later in the book when we introduce VLMs in Chapter 7.

In the context of AI workflows, this capability is far from cosmetic. Segmenting a long video into coherent scenes makes it possible to train on meaningful clips rather than overwhelming the model with redundant or contextually mixed footage. A single hour-long video may contain dozens of distinct actions or environments, and PySceneDetect provides the mechanism to isolate them in a consistent and reproducible way.

Recent production pipelines underscore its importance. In Open-Sora 2.0, for example, PySceneDetect is used as part of the preprocessing stage to filter out unstable segments before clips are passed along for training. Other comparative studies have pointed to it as a dependable first stage in large-scale preprocessing, where reproducibility across millions of video samples matters more than fully semantic scene segmentation.

Let's put PySceneDetect to work on a wizard-cat video. We'll use the `ContentDetector` to mark transitions, then grab a keyframe from the middle of each scene. A keyframe is a representative frame that captures the most important visual information from a segment of video. By extracting keyframes, we can summarize scenes, simplify annotation, and make downstream modeling faster and more reproducible. Segmenting long videos into coherent chunks in this way is a standard preprocessing step for scalable pipelines:

```python
class SceneDetector:
    """Educational scene detection using PySceneDetect"""

    def __init__(self, threshold=30.0, min_scene_len=15):
        self.threshold = threshold
        self.min_scene_len = min_scene_len

    def detect_scenes(self, video_path):
        video_manager = VideoManager([video_path])
        scene_manager = SceneManager()
        scene_manager.add_detector(
            ContentDetector(
                threshold=self.threshold,
                min_scene_len=self.min_scene_len,
            )
        )
        video_manager.start()
        scene_manager.detect_scenes(frame_source=video_manager)
        scene_list = scene_manager.get_scene_list()
        video_manager.release()
        return scene_list

    def extract_scene_keyframes(self, video_path, scene_list):
        cap = cv2.VideoCapture(video_path)
        keyframes = []
        for i, (start, end) in enumerate(scene_list):
            mid = (start.get_frames() + end.get_frames()) // 2
            cap.set(cv2.CAP_PROP_POS_FRAMES, mid)
            ret, frame = cap.read()
            if ret:
                keyframes.append({
                    "scene_id": i,
                    "frame_number": mid,
                    "frame": frame,
                })
        cap.release()
        return keyframes

detector = SceneDetector()
scenes = detector.detect_scenes("wizard_cat_compressed.mp4")
print(f"Found {len(scenes)} scenes.")
```

When we run the scene detection against a sample video, PySceneDetect reports that it found a number of distinct scenes in the wizard-cat video.

Each detected scene boundary can be exported as its own clip, providing the complete frame sequence for that segment. From there, additional processing can pull out audio and text, aligning them with transcript elements to add summaries or categories for each scene. Table 2-4 illustrates how these libraries align with one another.

*Table 2-4. Best fit use case for libraries*

| Library | Primary focus | Strengths | Best for | Performance |
|---|---|---|---|---|
| OpenCV | Real-time processing | Versatility/widespread usage | General-purpose CV | 1,000+ FPS for basic ops |
| FFmpeg | Encoding, compression, streaming | Command-line flexibility, high performance | Format conversion and optimization | 10x faster than alternatives |
| PySceneDetect | Scene boundary detection | Automated segmentation/integration | Dataset prep and scene-based analysis | 1,000 videos/hour |

Each of these libraries is powerful on its own, but together they create a repeatable, automated pipeline that turns raw footage into clean, structured, AI-ready datasets. The pipelines that follow demonstrate how these building blocks work in practice, forming a production-ready process that can scale from small experiments to full enterprise deployments.

# Video Processing Pipelines for AI

So far, we have explored individual tools that each handle a distinct part of the video stack. But in practice, what researchers and engineers need is a unified process that links them together end to end.

Think of the pipeline as a production line. The first stage is inspection, where OpenCV runs checks to ensure that each video is sharp, long enough, and meets resolution requirements. From there, FFmpeg compresses oversized files so that storage and bandwidth are no longer bottlenecks. PySceneDetect then steps in to split long footage into meaningful segments, which can be further distilled into representative keyframes. Along the way, the code logs metadata for every clip, capturing codec, resolution, and frame rate, ensuring full traceability and reproducibility.

Manually running those steps one at a time would quickly become unmanageable. Instead, most teams build a pipeline that does it all automatically. On a laptop, that might mean running a handful of videos through a script. At enterprise scale, it could mean deploying the same process on a distributed cluster or in the cloud, where elastic compute and tiered storage help keep costs under control.

# Summary

In this chapter, you learned how to approach video data not just as raw footage but as the essential foundation for generative AI. You have seen how different types of video—raw, compressed, annotated, and streaming—each bring unique strengths and challenges, and you have gained insight into how to choose the correct format for your goals. You now understand why video is so demanding, with its high dimensionality, multimodal signals, and storage requirements, and how modern compression and preprocessing strategies make it manageable at scale.

You also explored practical techniques for sourcing, filtering, annotating, and augmenting datasets, as well as the role of tools such as OpenCV, FFmpeg, and PySceneDetect in transforming disorganized footage into AI-ready training material. As you continue your journey, remember that data preparation is as much about discipline as it is about technology. The most powerful models depend on the quality of their training material, and your ability to curate, preprocess, and structure that data will directly shape the results you achieve.

In Chapter 3, you will build on these learnings and take a deeper dive into the underlying model components and techniques leveraged to generate videos and analyze video generation pipelines.

CHAPTER 3

# Implementing Video Generation Pipelines

*Learning objective:* In this chapter, you'll build intuition for working with video data and learn how to implement staged, modular training pipelines for video generation with AI.

In Chapter 2, you learned about the various types of video data and the challenges related to preparing video data for training. In this chapter, we'll build the architecture foundation that transforms prepared data into a functioning generative model. Using the Latte (*https://oreil.ly/UlSex*) (Latent Diffusion Transformer) architecture as a concrete reference, we'll implement the core components commonly found in modern video generation systems. These components generalize beyond any single generation model.

## Building the Foundation: Data Pipeline and Encoding

Every video generation model begins with a critical challenge of how to transform the continuous, high-dimensional nature of video into something a neural network can process. Raw video data, potentially millions of pixels changing 30 times per second, is simply too massive and redundant to model directly. We need a more robust pipeline that compresses, encodes, and structures this data while preserving the essential information needed for generation.

Think of this process like preparing ingredients for a complex recipe. You wouldn't throw whole vegetables into a pot; you'd wash, peel, chop, and organize them first. Similarly, we need to prepare our video data through a series of transformations before our model can work with it.

## Latent Space Compression with VAE

The first and perhaps most crucial step is establishing a compressed latent space where all subsequent generation occurs. In Latte and many related architectures, this role is played by the variational autoencoder (VAE) (*https://oreil.ly/AqiXn*), mentioned in Chapter 1. The VAE acts as a learned compression engine. By operating in latent space rather than pixel space, the model reduces the computational requirements by one to two orders of magnitude (OOM) while preserving perceptual quality.

The VAE operates on the simple but powerful principle that not all pixels are equally important. The predecessors to VAE from traditional machine learning (ML) include mathematical concepts for dimensionality reduction like principal component analysis (PCA) (*https://oreil.ly/IEGmA*) and t-SNE. Much of the information in raw video is redundant, neighboring pixels often have similar colors, large areas might be uniform backgrounds, and fine details that humans don't perceive can be safely discarded. By learning a compact latent representation, each spatial dimension is often reduced by a constant factor. This reduction by the VAE enables efficient modeling without sacrificing visual fidelity.

In practice, the VAE is trained separately on a large corpus of video data to learn how to compress and reconstruct frames with minimal perceptual loss. Once trained, its weights are typically frozen during generative model training, allowing the diffusion or flow-based model to focus exclusively on learning dynamics in latent space.

Figure 3-1 illustrates the step by step process of ingesting a 256 × 256 video frame sequence and transforming it into compact latent space. The symmetry between encoding and decoding paths illustrates the bidirectional design, ensuring that information compressed into the latent space can be faithfully reconstructed. The dashed region labeled *Latent space* in the figure represents where all generative dynamics occur (Diffusion, Flow, ODE, etc.), emphasizing that the expensive generative modeling happens entirely in this compressed representation.

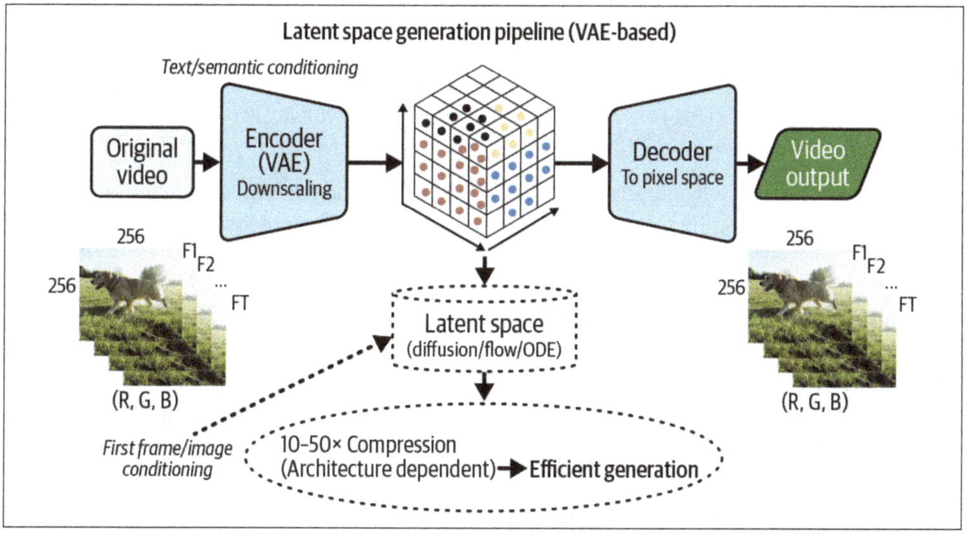


*Figure 3-1. Latent space compression enables efficient generation spatial while preserving perceptual structure*

## Understanding 3D Convolutions for Video VAE

Before examining the VAE implementation, we need to understand why video VAEs typically rely on 3D convolutions and why their kernel strategies differ from those used in other areas of the video generation pipeline. The encoder's role isn't to model motion or long-range temporal dynamics but rather to compress video efficiently while preserving temporal coherence.

2D convolutions process frames independently, like reading individual photographs without understanding their sequence. Each frame is filtered separately, capturing spatial features but missing temporal relationships. This independence breaks the temporal structure that video requires.

3D convolutions add temporal dimension awareness, but different kernel shapes serve different purposes. In video, VAE kernels are chosen to avoid mixing information across time while reducing spatial resolution.

A VAE-specific kernel strategy would work like this:

- (1, 3, 3) kernels extract spatial features while preserving temporal independence. This kernel is perfect for VAE compression where we want to reduce spatial resolution without temporal blur.
- (1, 4, 4) kernels with stride (1, 2, 2) enable spatial downsampling while maintaining temporal resolution. This downsampling is essential for VAE's spatial compression goal.

Now let's examine the implementation of the VAE encoder. The following code shows a complete video VAE encoder that handles the progressive downsampling through 3D convolutions. This implementation is designed to process video data efficiently while maintaining temporal consistency across frames. We'll build it step by step, starting with the architecture setup.

### Architecture setup and progressive downsampling

The encoder uses a series of 3D convolutional layers with increasing channel dimensions and spatial downsampling. Notice how the kernel sizes are carefully chosen: (1, 3, 3) and (1, 4, 4) ensure that temporal dimension is preserved while spatial dimensions are reduced. This is crucial. We want to maintain the temporal resolution while compressing spatial information:

```
# VAE Encoder implementation for video compression
import torch
import torch.nn as nn
import torch.nn.functional as F

class VideoVAEEncoder(nn.Module):
    def __init__(self, in_channels=3,
                 latent_channels=4, base_channels=128):
        super().__init__()
        # Progressive downsampling through 3D convolutions
        # kernel_size=(1,h,w) - '1' preserves time!
        self.conv1 = nn.Conv3d(
            in_channels, base_channels,
            kernel_size=(1, 3, 3),
            stride=(1, 1, 1),
            padding=(0, 1, 1)
        )
        self.conv2 = nn.Conv3d(
            base_channels, base_channels*2,
            kernel_size=(1, 4, 4),
            stride=(1, 2, 2),  # 2x downsample
            padding=(0, 1, 1)
        )
        self.conv3 = nn.Conv3d(
            base_channels*2, base_channels*4,
```

```
            kernel_size=(1, 4, 4),
            stride=(1, 2, 2),  # 4x total
            padding=(0, 1, 1)
        )
        self.conv4 = nn.Conv3d(
            base_channels*4, base_channels*4,
            kernel_size=(1, 4, 4),
            stride=(1, 2, 2),  # 8x total
            padding=(0, 1, 1)
        )

        # Project to latent distribution parameters
        self.conv_mu = nn.Conv3d(
            base_channels*4, latent_channels,
            kernel_size=(1, 3, 3), padding=(0, 1, 1)
        )
        self.conv_logvar = nn.Conv3d(
            base_channels*4, latent_channels,
            kernel_size=(1, 3, 3), padding=(0, 1, 1)
        )

        # Normalization for training stability
        self.norm = nn.GroupNorm(
            num_groups=32, num_channels=base_channels*4
        )
```

Think of this progressive downsampling like creating a movie summary. Instead of removing scenes (temporal compression), we simplify the visual details in each scene (spatial compression). A 256 × 256 frame becomes a 32 × 32 "sketch" that captures essential information but uses far less memory.

#### Forward pass and reparameterization trick

The forward pass progressively compresses the video through our convolutional layers, then uses the reparameterization trick to enable gradient flow through sampling:

```
    def forward(self, x):
        # x shape: [batch, channels, frames, height, width]

        # Encode through convolutional layers
        h = F.relu(self.conv1(x))
        h = F.relu(self.conv2(h))  # 2x downsample
        h = F.relu(self.conv3(h))  # 4x downsample
        h = F.relu(self.conv4(h))  # 8x downsample
        h = self.norm(h)

        # Get distribution parameters
        mu = self.conv_mu(h)
        logvar = self.conv_logvar(h)

        # Reparameterization trick for sampling
        std = torch.exp(0.5 * logvar)
```

```
        eps = torch.randn_like(std)
        z = mu + eps * std

        return z, mu, logvar
```

The key innovation here is the reparameterization trick. Instead of directly sampling from the latent distribution (which would break gradient flow), we sample from a standard normal distribution and transform it using the learned mean (`mu`) and variance (`logvar`). This mechanism is specific to variational autoencoders and allows gradients to flow through the sampling operation during training runs.

#### Deterministic inference path

For inference, we often want deterministic results rather than stochastic sampling. The `encode_to_latent` method provides reproducible results by leveraging a deterministic encoding path that returns just the mean of the latent distribution:

```
    def encode_to_latent(self, x):
        # For inference, just return the mean
        h = F.relu(self.conv1(x))
        h = F.relu(self.conv2(h))
        h = F.relu(self.conv3(h))
        h = F.relu(self.conv4(h))
        h = self.norm(h)
        mu = self.conv_mu(h)
        return mu
```

This deterministic path is typically used during video generation when we need consistent, reproducible results. By using only the mean of the distribution, we avoid the randomness that comes from sampling, ensuring that the same input always maps to the same latent representation.

The Latte implementation uses a pretrained VAE from Stable Diffusion rather than training its own VAE. This reuse significantly reduces development time and leverages a proven compression model that's demonstrated strong perceptual performance. The example implementation in this section provides intuition for how a VAE operates internally, while production systems often favor proven pretrained components.

## Video Tokenization: From Pixels to Patches

Once we have our video in latent space, we need to further structure it for transformer processing. This is where *video tokenization* comes in—the process of dividing each frame into a grid of patches, creating discrete tokens that transformers can process. This seemingly simple operation is actually a profound transformation that bridges the gap between the continuous nature of visual data and the discrete, sequential processing that transformers excel at.

To understand why tokenization is necessary, consider the fundamental mismatch between video data and transformer architectures. Video is inherently continuous, colors blend smoothly, objects have soft boundaries, and motion flows fluidly between frames. Transformers, on the other hand, were originally designed for discrete sequences like words in a sentence. Each word is a distinct unit with clear boundaries, and transformers learn relationships between these discrete tokens. Video tokenization resolves this mismatch by imposing a discrete structure on continuous visual data.

Imagine you're trying to describe a painting over the phone. You can't transmit the continuous brushstrokes directly, so instead you might divide the painting into a grid and describe each square: "Top-left is mostly blue sky with wisps of white clouds, next square has the peak of a mountain..." This grid-based description is exactly what video tokenization does: it creates a systematic way to break down continuous visual information into discrete, describable units.

The process begins with our latent video representation from the VAE, which has already compressed each frame from 256 × 256 × 3 to 32 × 32 × 4 dimensions. Now we further divide each 32 × 32 latent frame into non-overlapping patches. With a typical patch size of 2 × 2, we get 16 × 16 = 256 patches per frame. For a 16-frame video, this yields 16 × 256 = 4,096 total tokens, a manageable sequence length for transformer processing.

The choice of patch size is a critical design decision that affects both model performance and computational requirements. Smaller patches (like 1 × 1) preserve more spatial detail but create longer sequences that are computationally expensive to process. Larger patches (like 4 × 4 or 8 × 8) create shorter, more manageable sequences but may lose fine-grained spatial information. The 2 × 2 patch size used in Latte strikes a balance: it's small enough to capture local details while keeping sequence lengths tractable.

Figure 3-2 illustrates this tokenization process in detail, showing how a sequence of latent frames is systematically divided into patches, creating a three-dimensional grid of tokens. Notice how each patch maintains its spatial position within its frame and its temporal position across frames. This structure is crucial: it preserves the spatiotemporal relationships that the model needs to understand video content.

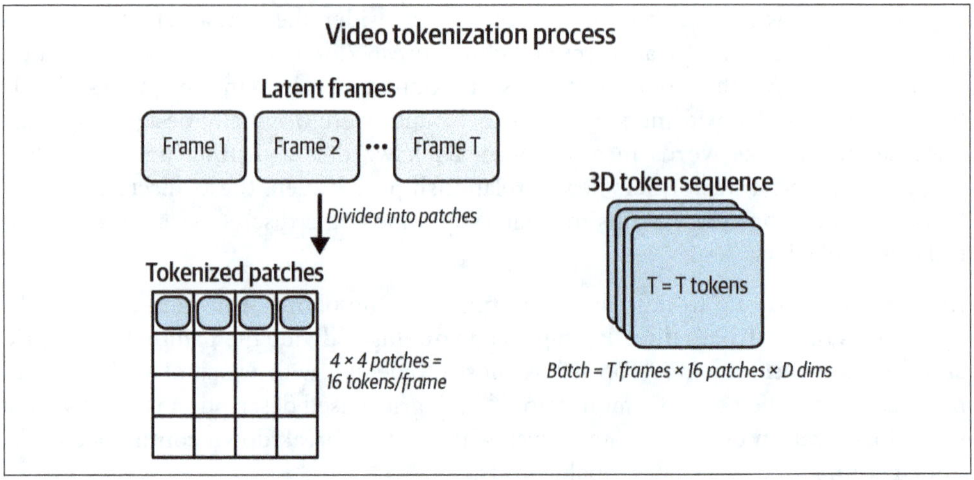


*Figure 3-2. Video tokenization divides latent frames into patches, creating a 3D grid of tokens*

## Patch Embedding and Positional Encoding

With our video tokenized into patches, we now need to transform these patches into rich representations that capture both their content and their position in space and time. This happens through two complementary processes: patch embedding and positional encoding.

*Patch embedding* is a learnable linear transformation that projects each latent patch from its raw pixel values into a high-dimensional embedding space. This transformation is crucial because it gives the model enough "room" to encode complex semantic information about each patch. A small 2 × 2 latent patch may contain part of an object, a shadow boundary, or a texture transition. Figure 3-3 illustrates the patch embedding process where patches are flattened into vectors and then transformed with learnable parameters into patch-based embedding, which can be processed by our attention heads.

Once we transform raw patches into learnable parameters, we move to positional encoding. Positional encoding adds spatial and temporal awareness to these embeddings. Latte uses a dual encoding scheme, spatial positions tell each patch where it is within a frame (top left, center, etc.), while temporal positions indicate which frame the patch belongs to. This dual encoding is essential for the model to understand both the structure within frames and the progression across time.

The following implementation combines both patch embedding and dual positional encoding. We'll build it in three parts: initialization, positional encoding setup, and the forward pass.

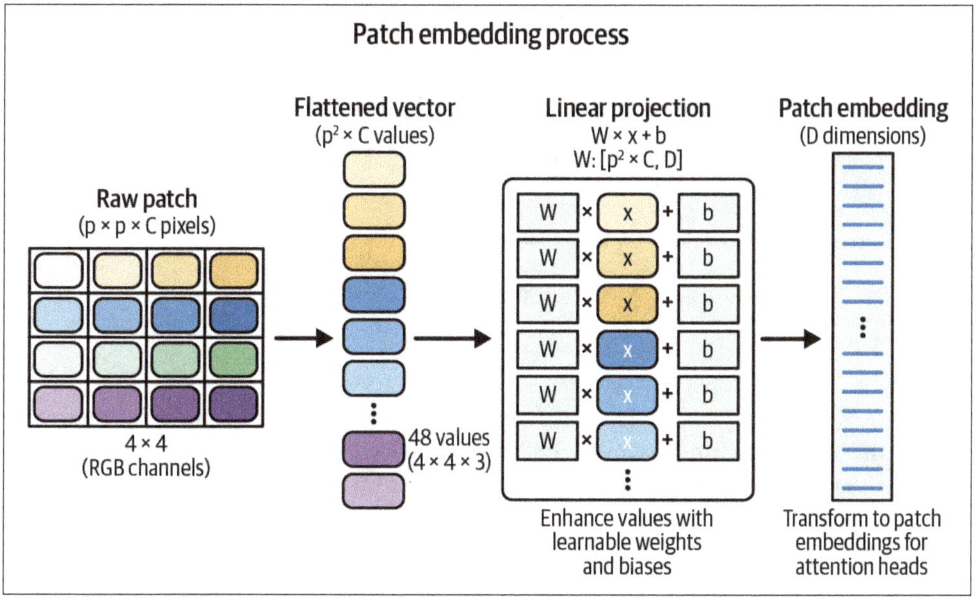


*Figure 3-3. Raw patches transformed with learnable weights and biases into patch embeddings*

### Module initialization and architecture

First, we set up the patch embedding module with its projection layer and dual positional encodings:

```
# Patch embedding with dual positional encoding
import torch
import torch.nn as nn
import numpy as np

class VideoPatchEmbed(nn.Module):
    def __init__(self, patch_size=2, in_channels=4,
                 embed_dim=768, num_frames=16,
                 image_size=32):
        super().__init__()
        self.patch_size = patch_size

        # Calculate total patches
        self.num_patches_per_frame = (
            (image_size // patch_size) ** 2
        )
        self.num_patches = (
            self.num_patches_per_frame * num_frames
        )

        # Linear projection: patches → embeddings
        patch_dim = in_channels * patch_size * patch_size
```

```
        self.proj = nn.Linear(patch_dim, embed_dim)

        # Dual positional encodings
        self.spatial_pos_embed = nn.Parameter(
            torch.zeros(1,
                        self.num_patches_per_frame,
                        embed_dim)
        )
        self.temporal_pos_embed = nn.Parameter(
            torch.zeros(1, num_frames, embed_dim)
        )

        # Initialize with sinusoidal patterns
        self._init_pos_encoding()
```

Notice how we separate spatial and temporal positional encodings. This separation allows the model to understand "*where in the frame*" independently from "*which frame in the sequence*," crucial for video understanding.

### Sinusoidal position encoding (intuition)

We introduce sinusoidal positional encoding here as a simple baseline to build intuition for positional representations. Sinusoidal encodings have a useful property: they allow the model to generalize to sequence lengths not seen during training.

Keep in mind that sinusoidal position encoding is to gain intuition on the requirements for encoding position as a smooth function. In Chapter 5, we will introduce Rotary Position Embedding (RoPE), which encodes position by rotating query and key vectors in attention space and is used in more recent video generation frameworks:

```
    def _init_pos_encoding(self):
        # Sinusoidal encoding for position
        def get_sincos_encoding(n_position, d_hid):
            # Create position angle vectors
            def get_position_angle_vec(position):
                return [
                    position / np.power(10000,
                                        2 * (hid_j // 2) / d_hid)
                    for hid_j in range(d_hid)
                ]

            # Build sincos table
            sincos_table = np.array([
                get_position_angle_vec(pos_i)
                for pos_i in range(n_position)
            ])

            # Apply sin to even indices
            sincos_table[:, 0::2] = np.sin(
                sincos_table[:, 0::2]
```

```
        )
        # Apply cos to odd indices
        sincos_table[:, 1::2] = np.cos(
            sincos_table[:, 1::2]
        )

        return torch.FloatTensor(
            sincos_table
        ).unsqueeze(0)

    # Initialize spatial positions
    self.spatial_pos_embed.data.copy_(
        get_sincos_encoding(
            self.num_patches_per_frame,
            self.spatial_pos_embed.shape[-1]
        )
    )

    # Initialize temporal positions
    self.temporal_pos_embed.data.copy_(
        get_sincos_encoding(
            self.temporal_pos_embed.shape[1],
            self.temporal_pos_embed.shape[-1]
        )
```

The sinusoidal pattern creates unique signatures for each position. The alternating sin/cos on even/odd dimensions ensures that nearby positions have similar encodings, while distant positions are easily distinguishable.

#### Forward pass: From videos to token sequences

The forward method in Latte performs the reshaping needed to convert latent video frames into a sequence of embedded patches with positional information:

```
def forward(self, x):
        # x shape: [batch, channels, frames, height, width]
        B, C, T, H, W = x.shape
        assert H % self.patch_size == 0 and W % self.patch_size == 0

        # Reshape into patches
        x = x.reshape(B, C, T, H // self.patch_size, self.patch_size,
                      W // self.patch_size, self.patch_size)
        x = x.permute(0, 2, 3, 5, 4, 6, 1).reshape(
            B, T * (H // self.patch_size) * (W // self.patch_size),
            C * self.patch_size * self.patch_size
        )

        # Apply linear projection
        x = self.proj(x)  # [B, T*num_patches_per_frame, embed_dim]

        # Add dual positional encoding
        x = x.reshape(B, T, -1, x.shape[-1])
```

```python
        # Add spatial position to each frame
        x = x + self.spatial_pos_embed.unsqueeze(1)

        # Add temporal position across frames
        x = x + self.temporal_pos_embed.unsqueeze(2)

        # Flatten back to sequence
        x = x.reshape(B, -1, x.shape[-1])

        return x
```

The elegance of this implementation lies in how it handles the reshaping operations. The forward method carefully reshapes the input video into patches, applies the linear projection, then reshapes again to separate temporal and spatial dimensions for adding the appropriate positional encodings. The final reshape flattens everything back into a sequence of tokens ready for transformer processing.

### Building toward attention

At this point, the foundation of our video generation model has been built. We have established three critical components:

*VAE compression*
: Reducing computational requirements

*Video tokenization*
: Structuring the data for transformer processing

*Patch embedding with positional encoding*
: Creating rich, spatially and temporally aware representations

With this foundation in place, we're ready to introduce the mechanisms that will process these tokens: attention.

## Attention Mechanisms: Understanding Relationships in Space and Time

With our video data properly encoded and positioned, we now face the core challenge of video generation: understanding the complex relationships between different parts of the video. A cat walking across a room involves spatial relationships (the cat's parts must stay connected) and temporal relationships (the cat must move smoothly). Latte addresses this challenge by separating these concerns through alternating spatial and temporal attention blocks.

## What Is Attention?

In ML, *attention* describes a model's ability to understand how elements relate to one another. While the concept existed in early neural-network research, it wasn't until Google's seminal paper "Attention Is All You Need" (*https://oreil.ly/wCeen*) that many in the field recognized its true potential. The paper revealed that attention can act as a form of intelligence compression, allowing models to dynamically focus on the most relevant parts of their input rather than treating every piece of data equally. As mentioned in Chapter 1, the attention mechanisms inside of the transformer architecture function similarly to the cortical tissue, providing a method for learning and comprehension on various modalities including voice, video, text, and so on.

In the context of video, we focus on two complementary forms of attention: spatial attention and temporal attention.

Imagine you're directing a stage play. Spatial attention is like *blocking*, ensuring actors are positioned correctly in each scene. Temporal attention is like *rehearsing transitions*, making sure actors move smoothly from one position to the next. By alternating between these two types of direction, you create a performance that's both visually coherent and dynamically fluid.

## Spatial Attention: Coherence Within Frames

*Spatial* attention is responsible for understanding relationships between patches within individual frames. When generating a video of a cat, spatial attention ensures that the cat's ears connect properly to its head, its tail follows naturally from its body, and it sits appropriately on the surface below it. This mechanism processes each frame independently, allowing for massive parallelization during training and inference. It's like having dozens of photo analysts working on different images simultaneously.

The multihead design of spatial attention is particularly powerful. Each attention head can specialize in different types of relationships: one might focus on object boundaries, another on textures, and another on color consistency. By combining insights from multiple heads, the model builds a comprehensive understanding of spatial structure. It's similar to having specialists in color, shape, texture, and semantics all analyzing the image simultaneously.

Figure 3-4 illustrates the spatial attention mechanism in action. On the left, we see how a single patch (marked as "Query") attends to all other patches within the same frame, with line thickness representing attention strength. The center panel shows the input tokens, the Query-Key-Value system (Q,K,V), the multihead processing pipeline, and how patch tokens are transformed through parallel attention heads and then concatenated to form the final spatial representation. On the right, a heat map of attention weights visualizes the relationships between patches: darker regions indicate stronger attention, highlighting which areas of the frame most influence the model's focus across the image.

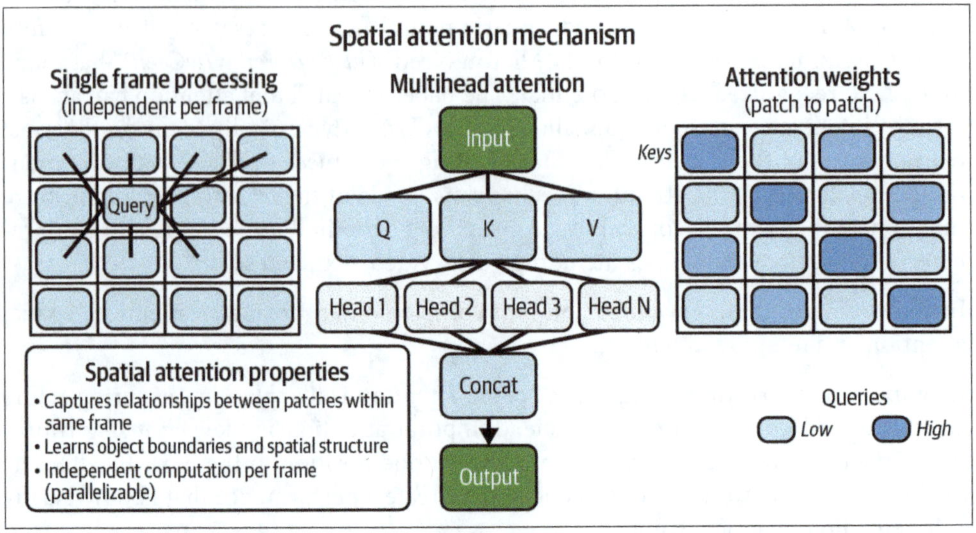


*Figure 3-4. Spatial attention processes relationships within individual frames through specialized multihead attention*

> In the Query-Key-Value (Question-Answer-Content System), each patch asks questions (Q), provides lookup keys (K), and offers content (V)—like a networking event where everyone has a business card, expertise, and questions to ask.
>
> Mathematically, the model heads apply three learned linear transformations per input:
>
> $$Q = XW_Q, K = XW_K, V = XW_V$$
>
> X is the patch embedding, and each W is a learned weight matrix.

## Temporal Attention: Continuity Across Frames

Whereas spatial attention ensures each frame is coherent, *temporal* attention is responsible for smooth, consistent motion across frames. This mechanism looks at the same spatial position across different time steps, tracking how each patch location evolves. It's this mechanism that ensures that a bouncing ball follows a realistic trajectory, a walking person maintains consistent gait, and objects don't randomly teleport or change appearance.

The temporal attention mechanism in Latte processes each spatial position independently across time. This means it can efficiently track multiple independent motions—for example, a bird flying while a car drives by without confusing the elements of the frame sequence. Each spatial location has its own *timeline* that temporal attention helps maintain.

Figure 3-5 illustrates how temporal attention tracks motion across frames. Notice how each spatial position maintains its own attention pattern across time, allowing the model to follow multiple independent motions simultaneously. The attention weights reveal motion trajectories where stronger attention between frames indicates continuous motion, and weaker attention suggests static regions or scene changes.

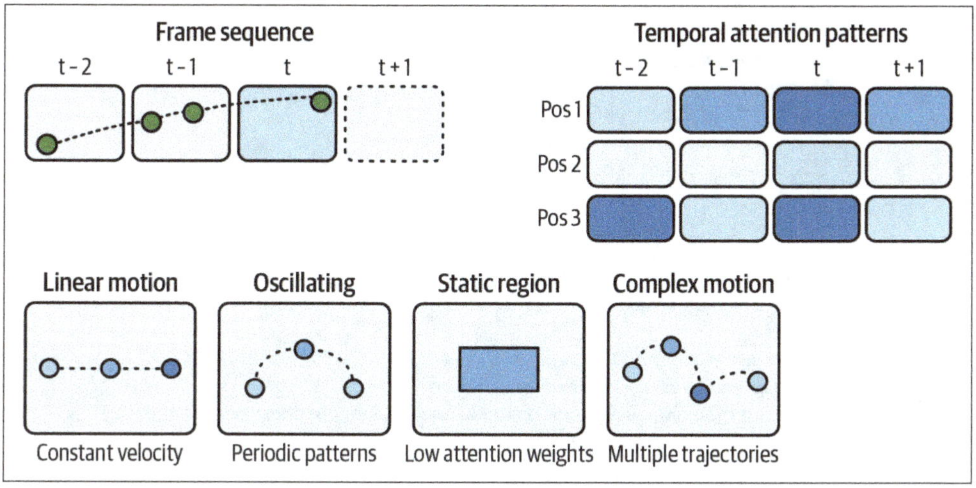


*Figure 3-5. Temporal attention tracks each spatial position across frames independently*

The following code implements both temporal and spatial attention blocks. The key insight in the temporal attention implementation is the reshaping strategy: we group patches by their spatial position across all frames, allowing the attention mechanism to track how each location evolves over time. The optional causal masking ensures that during autoregressive generation, each frame only attends to previous frames, maintaining the temporal causality of video.

First, let's implement the temporal attention block that handles relationships across frames:

```
# Temporal attention block implementation
import torch
import torch.nn as nn
import torch.nn.functional as F

class TemporalAttentionBlock(nn.Module):
    """Temporal dimension - how frames relate to each other"""
```

```
    def __init__(self, dim, num_heads=8, num_frames=16,
                 num_patches_per_frame=256, causal=False):
        super().__init__()
        self.num_heads = num_heads
        self.num_frames = num_frames
        self.num_patches_per_frame = num_patches_per_frame
        self.causal = causal # for autoregressive generation
        self.scale = (dim // num_heads) ** -0.5

        # Multi-head attention components
        self.qkv = nn.Linear(dim, dim * 3, bias=False)
        self.proj = nn.Linear(dim, dim)
        self.norm = nn.LayerNorm(dim)

        # Create causal mask if needed
        if causal:
            self.register_buffer(
                "causal_mask",
                torch.tril(torch.ones(num_frames, num_frames))
            )

    def forward(self, x, text_embed=None):
        # x shape: [batch, num_patches_total, dim]
        B, N, C = x.shape

        # Reshape to separate temporal and spatial dimensions
        # Group patches by spatial position across frames
        x = x.reshape(B, self.num_frames, self.num_patches_per_frame, C)
        # [B, num_patches_per_frame, num_frames, C]
        x = x.permute(0, 2, 1, 3)
        x = x.reshape(B * self.num_patches_per_frame, self.num_frames, C)

        # Apply layer norm and save for residual
        shortcut = x
        x = self.norm(x)
```

The temporal attention block groups patches by their spatial position and computes attention across time. This means each spatial location attends to the same location across all frames, learning how that region evolves temporally. Now let's see how the attention computation works:

```
# Compute Q, K, V
        qkv = self.qkv(x).reshape(
            B * self.num_patches_per_frame, self.num_frames,
            3, self.num_heads, C // self.num_heads
        )
        qkv = qkv.permute(2, 0, 3, 1, 4)
        q, k, v = qkv[0], qkv[1], qkv[2]

        # Compute attention scores
        attn = (q @ k.transpose(-2, -1)) * self.scale
```

```
        # Apply causal mask if needed (for autoregressive generation)
        if self.causal:
            mask_value = -torch.finfo(attn.dtype).max
            mask = self.causal_mask[:self.num_frames, :self.num_frames]
            mask = mask.reshape(1, 1, self.num_frames, self.num_frames)
            attn = attn.masked_fill(mask == 0, mask_value)

        # Apply softmax and attention
        attn = F.softmax(attn, dim=-1)
        x = (attn @ v).transpose(1, 2).reshape(
            B * self.num_patches_per_frame, self.num_frames, C
        )

        # Project and add residual
        x = self.proj(x)
        x = shortcut + x

        # Reshape back to original format
        x = x.reshape(B, self.num_patches_per_frame, self.num_frames, C)
        x = x.permute(0, 2, 1, 3)  # [B, num_frames, num_patches_per_frame, C]
        x = x.reshape(B, N, C)

        return x
```

The causal mask in temporal attention is particularly important for video generation. When generating videos autoregressively, we need to ensure that future frames don't influence past frames. The mask enforces this constraint by setting attention weights to negative infinity for future positions, effectively preventing information flow backward in time.

Now let's implement the complementary spatial attention block that ensures coherence within each frame. Temporal attention asks, "how does this patch evolve over time?" Meanwhile, spatial attention addresses a complementary question: "how does this patch relate to other patches in the same frame?"

```
class SpatialAttentionBlock(nn.Module):
    """Spatial dimension - how patches relate within a frame"""

    def __init__(self, dim, num_heads=8, num_frames=16):
        super().__init__()
        self.num_heads = num_heads
        self.num_frames = num_frames
        self.scale = (dim // num_heads) ** -0.5

        self.qkv = nn.Linear(dim, dim * 3, bias=False)
        self.proj = nn.Linear(dim, dim)
        self.norm = nn.LayerNorm(dim)

    def forward(self, x):
        # x shape: [batch, num_patches_total, dim]
```

```
        B, N, C = x.shape
        patches_per_frame = N // self.num_frames

        # Reshape to process each frame independently
        x = x.reshape(B * self.num_frames, patches_per_frame, C)

        # Standard multi-head self-attention
        shortcut = x
        x = self.norm(x)

        qkv = self.qkv(x).reshape(
            B * self.num_frames, patches_per_frame,
            3, self.num_heads, C // self.num_heads
        )
        qkv = qkv.permute(2, 0, 3, 1, 4)
        q, k, v = qkv[0], qkv[1], qkv[2]

        # Attention computation
        attn = (q @ k.transpose(-2, -1)) * self.scale
        attn = F.softmax(attn, dim=-1)

        x = (attn @ v).transpose(1, 2).reshape(
            B * self.num_frames, patches_per_frame, C
        )
        x = self.proj(x)
        x = shortcut + x

        # Reshape back to full sequence
        x = x.reshape(B, N, C)
        return x
```

The implementation shows the complementary nature of spatial and temporal attention. The `TemporalAttentionBlock` reshapes data to group by spatial position, while `SpatialAttentionBlock` reshapes to process each frame independently. This reshaping strategy is computationally efficient and allows both mechanisms to operate on the same data representation without interference.

## The Alternating Block Architecture

One of Latte's key architectural ideas is the alternating pattern of spatial and temporal blocks. Rather than trying to process all relationships simultaneously (which would be computationally prohibitive), the model alternates between spatial and temporal processing: spatial block, temporal block, spatial block, temporal block, and so on, repeated across the network.

This design reduces computational complexity from:

$$O(T^2 \times H^2 \times W^2)$$

to:

$$O(T \times H^2 \times W^2 + T^2 \times H \times W)$$

This is a substantive improvement that makes high-resolution video generation tractable in practice.

Each alternation refines the video representation further. Early blocks establish coarse structure and motion, middle blocks add details and smooth transitions, and later blocks refine subtle visual and temporal nuances. The process resembles a sculptor alternating between shaping the overall form and refining specific features, where each pass makes the work more complete.

> We separate spatial and temporal attention blocks here for clarity. Production implementations often achieve the same alternation through reshaping operations with `` `einops.rearrange` ``, resulting in code that is more concise but less transparent. Production code typically prioritizes efficiency over readability; in this example, understanding takes precedence over terseness.

The number of alternating blocks is a crucial hyperparameter. Too few blocks, and the model lacks capacity to generate complex videos. Too many, and training becomes unstable and computationally expensive. Most successful implementations use between 12 and 24 alternating blocks.

Table 3-1 shows the different Latte model variants, illustrating how model size scales with the number of blocks and hidden dimensions. Our implementation follows the base (B) configuration, which provides a good balance between quality and computational requirements. More recent models mentioned in Chapter 2 have billions of parameters. For learning purposes, we will begin with the foundational elements of Latte and work our way toward the state of the art (SOTA).

*Table 3-1. Latte architecture variants*

| Model | Blocks | Parameters | Hidden dim | Heads | Use case |
|---|---|---|---|---|---|
| Latte-S | 12 | 84M | 384 | 6 | Fast prototyping, limited resources |
| Latte-B | 12 | 151M | 768 | 12 | Balanced performance, standard choice |
| Latte-L | 24 | 459M | 1024 | 16 | High quality, longer videos |
| Latte-XL | 28 | 674M | 1152 | 16 | Maximum quality, research |

To understand why Latte's alternating architecture is so effective, let's compare the computational complexity of different attention strategies (Table 3-2).

*Table 3-2. Attention mechanism computational comparison*

| Attention type | Processes | Complexity | Memory usage | Purpose |
|---|---|---|---|---|
| Spatial | Within each frame | $O(H^2W^2) \times T$ | ~4 GB for 256 × 256 | Visual coherence, object structure |
| Temporal | Across frames | $O(T^2) \times HW$ | ~1 GB for 16 frames | Motion consistency, trajectories |
| Cross | Video ↔ Text | $O(HWT \times L)$ | ~2 GB for 77 tokens | Semantic alignment, conditioning |
| Alternating | Spatial + Temporal | $O(H^2W^2T + T^2HW)$ | ~5 GB total | Both, efficiently combined |
| Full 3D | All at once | $O((HWT)^2)$ | ~256 GB (!) | Theoretically optimal, practically impossible |

The attention mechanisms form the computational core of our video generation model. Spatial attention ensures visual coherence within frames, temporal attention maintains consistency across time, and the alternating architecture efficiently combines both. This interplay of attention mechanisms enables Latte-style models to generate videos that are both visually coherent and temporally smooth.

> The memory savings from alternating attention (Table 3-2) become critical when training at scale. Chapter 4 will show how these efficiencies are leveraged using techniques like gradient checkpointing and mixed-precision training.

At this stage, our attention mechanisms understand how to process and relate video information, but the model still doesn't know how to generate. It's like having a painter who understands composition and color theory but hasn't learned the techniques of applying paint to canvas.

This is where diffusion enters the picture. Diffusion models take a seemingly paradoxical approach to generation: we teach the model to generate by first teaching it to destroy. By gradually adding noise to videos until they become pure static and then learning how to reverse that process, we obtain a generative framework that is both mathematically grounded and remarkably effective. Creation, in this case, emerges from the systematic reversal of destruction.

# The Diffusion Process: From Noise to Video

With our architecture in place, we now introduce the generative process itself: diffusion. This is where the magic with diffusion happens, transforming pure random noise into coherent, high-quality video. The diffusion process is counterintuitive but powerful: we train the model to reverse a corruption process, teaching it to remove noise iteratively until a clean video emerges.

> While diffusion excels at restoring structure, it treats motion implicitly. The model learns to denoise individual states, and temporal coherence emerges as a side effect rather than an explicit objective. In later sections, we will revisit this assumption and introduce *flow matching*, which models motion directly as a continuous trajectory rather than as repeated denoising.

Imagine you have a perfect ice sculpture that slowly melts into a puddle of water. If you could reverse this process, starting with the puddle and gradually freezing it back into the exact sculpture, you'd have mastered generation. The diffusion process works similarly: it learns to reverse the gradual addition of noise, transforming static into structured video.

## Forward and Reverse Processes

The diffusion framework consists of two processes: forward and reverse. The *forward* process gradually adds Gaussian noise to clean video data over T timesteps, eventually transforming it into pure noise. This process is fixed and simple, just adding increasing amounts of noise according to a predefined schedule.

The *reverse* process is where learning happens. The model learns to predict and remove the noise at each timestep, gradually recovering the clean video. During *training*, we know exactly how much noise was added, so we can supervise this learning. During *generation*, the model applies this learned denoising process to pure noise, revealing the generated video step by step.

Figure 3-6 visualizes both the forward and reverse diffusion processes. The top row shows the forward process during training: how clean video gradually becomes pure noise through the controlled addition of Gaussian noise. The bottom row illustrates the reverse process during generation: how the trained model iteratively removes noise to reveal the generated video. The small graph on the right shows the noise schedule, which controls how quickly noise is added or removed at each step. This schedule is crucial for balancing generation quality with computational efficiency.

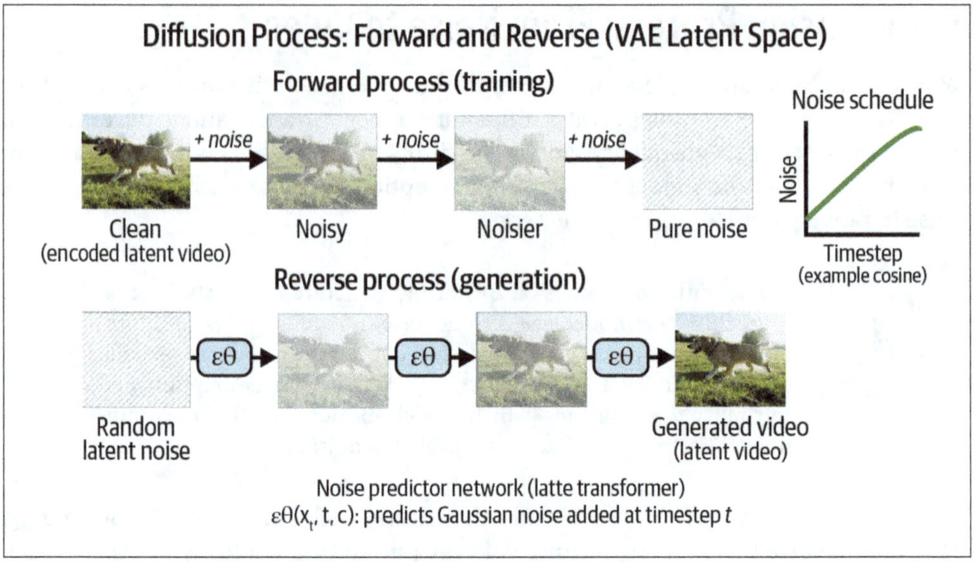


*Figure 3-6. The forward process adds noise during training, while the reverse process removes it during generation*

## Noise Prediction and Scheduling

At each denoising step, diffusion models do not predict the clean video directly. Instead, the model is trained to predict the noise that was added at that timestep. This parameterization has proven more stable in practice: by estimating the noise component, the model can incrementally remove corruption and recover structure.

Diffusion models rely on a predefined noise schedule that controls how strongly noise is injected during training and how it is removed during generation. While different schedules exist, the essential idea is that time indexes the degree of corruption rather than representing motion or dynamics directly.

The following code implements a minimal diffusion training loop. This baseline illustrates the core mechanics shared by most diffusion models: sampling random timesteps, adding noise according to a schedule, predicting that noise with a conditioned model, and optimizing a mean squared error objective.

> This objective is intentionally simple. Its purpose is to establish a stable baseline for generative modeling in latent space. In later sections, we will revisit the role of time in this process and show how alternative objectives replace noise prediction with explicit modeling of dynamics over time.

The following `DiffusionTrainer` class implements this loop, from noise sampling through the optimization step:

```
# Diffusion training loop implementation
import torch
import torch.nn.functional as F
from tqdm import tqdm

class DiffusionTrainer:
    def __init__(self, model, noise_scheduler, optimizer, device='cuda'):
        self.model = model
        self.noise_scheduler = noise_scheduler
        self.optimizer = optimizer
        self.device = device

    def train_step(self, batch):
        # batch contains: latent_video, text_embeddings
        latent_video = batch['latent_video'].to(self.device)
        text_embed = batch['text_embed'].to(self.device)
        batch_size = latent_video.shape[0]

        # Sample random timesteps for each video in batch
        timesteps = torch.randint(
            0, self.noise_scheduler.num_timesteps,
            (batch_size,), device=self.device
        ).long()

        # Sample noise to add to the latents
        noise = torch.randn_like(latent_video)

        # Add noise to the latent videos according to the noise schedule
        noisy_latents = self.noise_scheduler.add_noise(
            latent_video, noise, timesteps
        )

        # Predict the noise with the model
        noise_pred = self.model(
            noisy_latents,
            timesteps,
            encoder_hidden_states=text_embed
        )

        # Calculate MSE loss between predicted and actual noise
        loss = F.mse_loss(noise_pred, noise)

        # Backpropagation
        self.optimizer.zero_grad()
        loss.backward()

        # Gradient clipping for stability
        torch.nn.utils.clip_grad_norm_(self.model.parameters(), max_norm=1.0)
```

```
        self.optimizer.step()

        return loss.item()
```

The training step randomly samples timesteps for each video, adds corresponding noise levels, and optimizes the model to predict that noise. Despite its simplicity, this objective forms the foundation of diffusion-based generation and provides a useful point of comparison for more expressive generative formulations.

> Diffusion models learn to generate data by reversing a controlled noise corruption process. The implementation shown here focuses on the essential training loop: add noise at random timesteps and train the model to predict and remove it.
>
> Production systems often extend this foundation with faster samplers, improved parameterizations, and additional training refinements. These changes improve efficiency and quality, but the core denoising principle remains the same.

## Adaptive Conditioning with AdaLN

*Adaptive layer normalization* (AdaLN) is a conditioning mechanism that allows external information (like text prompts, class labels, diffusion timesteps, or continuous time embeddings) to dynamically modulate the internal features at each layer of the network. Unlike traditional conditioning methods that add or concatenate conditioning vectors, AdaLN directly adjusts the normalization parameters themselves, providing fine-grained, layer-level control over how information is processed and transformed.

Imagine a professional audio mixer where each channel has its own EQ and gain controls. Conditioning signals act like the sound engineer's instructions: *Make the bass deeper, brighten the highs, add warmth to the mids.* AdaLN translates these high-level directions into specific knob adjustments for each layer of the network, fine-tuning how features are amplified, dampened, or rebalanced across the entire model.

> While originally introduced in the context of diffusion-based denoising, AdaLN remains equally effective when the model is trained to predict continuous trajectories, as it provides a general mechanism for time- and condition-aware modulation at every layer.

In the context of the diffusion transformer (DiT), this adaptive conditioning becomes especially powerful. Not all denoising steps are equal. Early in the process, when the video is still dominated by noise, the model must first establish the global structure, broad spatial layouts, and coarse temporal relationships that give the video coherence. Later, as the video becomes clearer, the model needs to shift its attention to fine-grained refinements like lighting, texture, and subtle motion continuity.

AdaLN enables this timestep-aware behavior by allowing the model to adjust its internal processing based on how far along it is in the generation process. The same mechanism applies whether the model is trained with discrete diffusion steps or continuous-time objectives.

The parameters that drive these modulations are typically generated by a small multi-layer perceptron (MLP) that takes the timestep embedding as input. This MLP is trained jointly with the main model, learning to produce the appropriate modulation signals for each layer and generation step. Together, this system creates a continuous dialogue between the generation schedule and the model's internal representations.

In the broader generative framework, this coordination is key. The generative network provides stability, the schedule defines the pace and direction of generation, and AdaLN introduces adaptability, enabling each layer to respond intelligently to the evolving signal. This orchestration of stability, control, and adaptability is what allows models like Latte (*https://oreil.ly/RQ-64*) and other modern generative architectures to produce remarkably coherent, high-quality videos.

The original "Scalable Diffusion Models with Transformers" (*https://oreil.ly/KlYSb*) paper outlines why AdaLN was foundational to successfully moving off of legacy backbones like the U-Net onto transformer-based architectures.

# Conditioning and Control: From Text to Video

The final piece of our implementation brings everything together with purpose: conditioning the generation process on text descriptions and other semantic signals. Without conditioning, our model would generate random videos. With it, we can control what videos are generated, transforming text prompts into visual sequences. This section implements the mechanisms that bridge language and vision.

Think of conditioning as giving directions to an artist. Without directions, they might paint anything. But when you say, "Paint a sunset over mountains with eagles flying," you've constrained their creativity in a useful way. The artist still has freedom in how to interpret your words, but the core elements you requested will appear in the painting.

## Text Encoding with T5

The journey from text to video begins with understanding language. Latte uses the T5 (Text-to-Text Transfer Transformer) encoder, chosen for its strong ability to model compositional language structure and long-range dependencies. Unlike image-focused encoders like CLIP, T5 is designed to capture grammatical relationships, temporal structure (*first... then...*), and compositional meaning across detailed descriptions.

The text encoding process transforms your prompt into a sequence of high-dimensional embeddings that capture not just the words but their relationships and meanings. *A cat playing piano* becomes a rich representation that encodes the subject (cat), the action (playing), the object (piano), and their relationships.

While different architectures may employ alternative language encoders, the mechanism that integrates text into video generation remains largely the same.

Figure 3-7 illustrates the complete text-to-video conditioning pipeline. Text prompts are tokenized and encoded into embeddings that serve as keys and values in cross-attention layers, while video features act as queries. This mechanism allows semantic guidance to be injected into every transformer block. While shown here with a text encoder, the same integration pattern applies to other conditioning signals such as first-frame image embeddings.

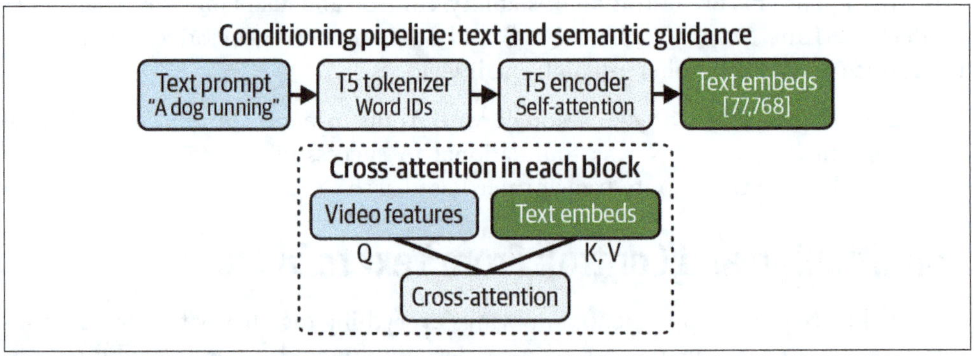


*Figure 3-7. Semantic conditioning via cross-attention*

## Cross-Attention Integration

Text embeddings guide the generation process through cross-attention mechanisms embedded in every transformer block. In cross-attention, video patches form queries that attend to the text embeddings serving as keys and values. This allows each patch to selectively focus on relevant parts of the text description.

For example, patches that will become the cat attend strongly to *cat* embeddings, while patches forming the piano focus on *piano* information. This selective attention ensures that generated videos accurately reflect the text prompt while maintaining visual coherence.

The following implementation shows how cross-attention bridges text and video domains. The `CrossAttention` class demonstrates the asymmetric nature of this mechanism. Video features become queries, while text embeddings provide keys and values. The `LatteTransformerBlock` shows how all attention types (spatial, temporal, and cross) combine with AdaLN conditioning to form a complete processing unit. This modular design allows each component to be optimized independently while working together seamlessly.

First, let's implement the cross-attention mechanism that connects video features with text embeddings:

```
# Cross-attention implementation for text conditioning
import torch
import torch.nn as nn
import torch.nn.functional as F

class CrossAttention(nn.Module):
    def __init__(self, dim, context_dim=768, num_heads=8):
        super().__init__()
        self.num_heads = num_heads
        self.scale = (dim // num_heads) ** -0.5

        # Separate projections for Q (from video) and K,V (from text)
        self.to_q = nn.Linear(dim, dim, bias=False)
        self.to_k = nn.Linear(context_dim, dim, bias=False)
        self.to_v = nn.Linear(context_dim, dim, bias=False)

        self.proj = nn.Linear(dim, dim)
        self.norm = nn.LayerNorm(dim)
        self.context_norm = nn.LayerNorm(context_dim)

    def forward(self, x, context):
        # x: video features [batch, num_patches, dim]
        # context: text embeddings [batch, seq_len, context_dim]

        B, N, C = x.shape

        # Normalize inputs
        shortcut = x
        x = self.norm(x)
        context = self.context_norm(context)

        # Create queries from video features
        q = self.to_q(x).reshape(B, N, self.num_heads, C // self.num_heads)
        q = q.permute(0, 2, 1, 3)  # [B, heads, N, head_dim]

        # Create keys and values from text embeddings
        k = self.to_k(context).reshape(
            B,
            -1,
            self.num_heads,
            C // self.num_heads,
        )
        k = k.permute(0, 2, 1, 3)  # [B, heads, seq_len, head_dim]
```

```
        v = self.to_v(context).reshape(
            B,
            -1,
            self.num_heads,
            C // self.num_heads
        )
        v = v.permute(0, 2, 1, 3)  # [B, heads, seq_len, head_dim]
```

The cross-attention mechanism creates a bridge between visual and textual modalities. Each video patch queries the text to understand which words are relevant to it. For example, patches containing a cat will attend strongly to the word *cat* in the prompt. Let's see how the attention computation brings these modalities together:

```
        # Compute attention scores: Q @ K^T
        attn = (q @ k.transpose(-2, -1)) * self.scale
        attn = F.softmax(attn, dim=-1)

        # Apply attention to values: attn @ V
        out = (attn @ v).transpose(1, 2).reshape(B, N, C)

        # Project and add residual
        out = self.proj(out)
        out = shortcut + out

        return out
```

Now let's build the complete transformer block that orchestrates all attention mechanisms together with adaptive conditioning:

> The following transformer block illustrates one representative way of combining spatial attention, semantic conditioning, and temporal modeling. Variants of this ordering exist across implementations, but the underlying principles remain consistent.

```
class LatteTransformerBlock(nn.Module):
    """Complete transformer block with spatial, temporal, and cross attention"""
    def __init__(self, dim, num_heads=8, num_frames=16,
                 context_dim=768, use_adaln=True):
        super().__init__()
        self.use_adaln = use_adaln

        # Attention layers
        self.spatial_attn = SpatialAttentionBlock(dim, num_heads, num_frames)
        self.temporal_attn = TemporalAttentionBlock(dim, num_heads, num_frames)
        self.cross_attn = CrossAttention(dim, context_dim, num_heads)

        # Feed-forward network
        self.ffn = nn.Sequential(
            nn.LayerNorm(dim),
            nn.Linear(dim, dim * 4),
```

```
            nn.GELU(),
            nn.Linear(dim * 4, dim)
        )

        # AdaLN modulation (if enabled)
        if use_adaln:
            self.adaln = AdaLN(dim)

    def forward(self, x, timestep_embed, text_embed):
        # Apply AdaLN modulation if enabled
        if self.use_adaln:
            x = self.adaln(x, timestep_embed)

        # Spatial attention within frames
        x = self.spatial_attn(x)

        # Cross-attention with text
        x = self.cross_attn(x, text_embed)

        # Temporal attention across frames
        x = self.temporal_attn(x)

        # Feed-forward network
        x = x + self.ffn(x)

        return x
```

One common sequencing applies spatial attention first (establishing visual coherence), followed by cross-attention (semantic grounding), temporal attention (consistency across frames), and a feed-forward network (capacity expansion). The AdaLN mechanism adapts all of this based on the noise level:

```
class AdaLN(nn.Module):
    """Adaptive Layer Normalization for timestep conditioning"""
    def __init__(self, dim, timestep_dim=256):
        super().__init__()
        self.norm = nn.LayerNorm(dim, elementwise_affine=False)

        # MLP to generate scale and shift from timestep
        self.timestep_mlp = nn.Sequential(
            nn.SiLU(),
            nn.Linear(timestep_dim, dim * 2)
        )

    def forward(self, x, timestep_embed):
        # Generate scale (gamma) and shift (beta) from timestep
        adaln_params = self.timestep_mlp(timestep_embed)
        adaln_params = adaln_params.unsqueeze(1)  # Add sequence dimension
        gamma, beta = adaln_params.chunk(2, dim=-1)

        # Apply adaptive normalization
        x = self.norm(x)
```

```
        x = (1 + gamma) * x + beta

        return x

# Example usage in full model:
# blocks = nn.ModuleList([
#     LatteTransformerBlock(dim=768, num_heads=8, num_frames=16)
#     for _ in range(12)  # 12 alternating blocks
# ])
```

> As an advanced technique, production Latte uses AdaLN-Zero, which adds learnable gating (`gate_msa`, `gate_mlp`) that starts at zero. This ensures the model begins training as a simple identity function, improving stability. I show the core AdaLN here; the zero initialization is a training trick, not a conceptual change.

The complete `LatteTransformerBlock` implementation in the last code example illustrates a representative way of combining spatial attention, semantic conditioning, temporal modeling, and adaptive modulation within a video generation transformer. Spatial attention establishes coherence within each frame, ensuring objects maintain consistent appearance. Cross-attention then grounds visual features in the text description, allowing specific regions to align with semantic concepts. Temporal attention propagates these aligned features across frames, maintaining consistency over time.

AdaLN modulates all of these operations based on the current noise level, applying stronger conditioning early in generation when structure must be established and more subtle refinement later as fine details emerge. While implementations may vary in ordering and emphasis, this sequence captures the core principles that enable Latte-style models to generate videos that are both visually coherent and semantically aligned.

## Classifier-Free Guidance

*Classifier-free guidance* (CFG), introduced in the original "Classifier-Free Diffusion Guidance" paper (*https://oreil.ly/n4guz*), improves adherence to text prompts by amplifying the difference between conditional and unconditional predictions. During training, the model occasionally sees empty text prompts, enabling unconditional generation. During inference, the model is run twice: once with the text prompt and once without.

The final prediction combines both:

$$\tilde{\varepsilon} = \varepsilon(\varnothing) + w \times (\varepsilon(text) - \varepsilon(\varnothing))$$

Here, *w* is the guidance scale controlling the strength of conditioning.

CFG is an inference-time technique rather than a core architectural component. Its role is to sharpen conditioning and improve prompt adherence, not to define the underlying generative dynamics.

# Latte Model Component Integration

Imagine constructing a car, building the engine (VAE compression), assembling the transmission (attention mechanisms), installing the fuel system (diffusion), and adding the steering wheel (conditioning). Once these parts exist, we need to wire everything together and connect the engine to the transmission, link the fuel system, attach the steering, and create a vehicle that actually drives.

This section implements the wiring that makes Latte functional. We assemble timestep embeddings that indicate where the model is in the generation process, integrate the text encoder that transforms prompts into semantic guidance, connect all attention mechanisms into a unified architecture, and define the output path that converts latent predictions back into video frames. This wiring reflects a diffusion-based generation pipeline and will serve as a useful baseline as we explore alternative formulations.

## Timestep Embedding: Encoding the Diffusion Schedule

The diffusion process operates over a fixed number of timesteps, but the model needs more than just the integer timestep. It needs a rich representation that captures where it is in the generation process. The timestep embedding process transforms a scalar timestep into a high-dimensional vector that allows the model to adapt its behavior based on where it is in the schedule.

Consider the difference between a late timestep and an early one. Near the start of generation, the input is dominated by noise and the model must establish coarse structure: *this will be a cat, not a car.* Near the end, the video is nearly complete and the model must refine fine details: *add whisker texture, smooth the fur.* A learned embedding can represent these semantic differences in a way a raw integer cannot.

> We reuse the same sinusoidal encoding strategy from positional embeddings, applying it to timesteps instead of spatial positions. This provides two useful properties:
>
> *Smooth interpolation*
> : Nearby timesteps receive similar embeddings, enabling the model to generalize across the training schedule.
>
> *Extrapolation capability*
> : Models trained with one number of steps can often be sampled with fewer steps at inference.

## Text Encoder: From Prompts to Embeddings

Previously, we showed how cross-attention uses text embeddings. However, we haven't shown how to generate them. The text encoder transforms natural language prompts into the embedding vectors that guide generation. This is where language meets vision, where "*a cat playing piano*" becomes a mathematical representation that the model can interpret.

Latte uses a T5 encoder, chosen for its understanding of complex language structure compared to vision-focused encoders like CLIP. T5 excels at parsing grammatical relationships ("*first the cat jumps, then it lands*"), understanding temporal structure, and handling detailed descriptions up to 77 tokens in length.

# Putting It All Together: The Generation Pipeline

With all components implemented, we can now describe the complete generation pipeline:

*Text encoding*
: The user's prompt is tokenized and encoded by T5 into embedding vectors.

*Initialization*
: Random noise is sampled in the latent space as the starting point.

*Iterative denoising*
: For each timestep from T to 0:

  - The noisy latents and timestep embeddings are inputted into the model.
  - Text embeddings provide conditioning via cross-attention.
  - Spatial and temporal attention blocks process relationships.
  - AdaLN modulates processing based on noise level.
  - The model predicts noise to remove.
  - Noise is subtracted to get a cleaner latent.

*Decoding*
: The final latent is decoded by the VAE into video frames.

*Output*
: The generated video matching the text description is produced.

> Diffusion-based pipelines can be accelerated using sampling strategies that skip timesteps, trading a small amount of quality for significant speed improvements. These techniques improve efficiency without changing the underlying training objective.

Text conditioning transforms our video generation model from a random generator into a controllable creative tool. Language encoders capture semantic intent; cross-attention injects that intent throughout the model; and classifier-free guidance sharpens alignment between prompts and outputs.

## Summary

In this chapter, we've implemented a complete diffusion-based generation model using the Latte architecture. We began by building the foundation with VAE compression and video tokenization, creating an efficient representation space for processing. We then introduced spatial and temporal attention mechanisms that capture complex structure across frames and conditioning mechanisms that connect language with visual generation.

Diffusion provides a stable and expressive foundation for generation, transforming noise into structured video through iterative refinement. Text conditioning adds control, allowing human intent to guide the generative process.

Together, these components form a strong baseline for modern video generation. With this implementation complete, we're ready to move to Chapter 4, where we'll explore training these models on video datasets, configuring optimization strategies, and building systems capable of supporting production-quality training.

CHAPTER 4

# Training Video Generation Models

*Learning objective:* In this chapter, you'll build on your implementation of the Latte architecture and learn how to create progressive training pipelines that transform your model into a production-ready video generation system.

In Chapter 3, you implemented the complete Latte architecture, from VAE compression and patch embedding through spatial and temporal attention blocks to the diffusion process and text conditioning. Now we'll transform that architecture into a functioning video generation model through a systematic training loop.

Training video generation models requires more than just feeding data through your architecture. As mentioned in previous chapters, the temporal dimension introduces unique challenges: datasets are massive, memory constraints are severe, and optimization is delicate. Building on Chapter 3, and leveraging Latte's (*https://oreil.ly/g5Ijl*) training approach as our guide, we'll build a progressive pipeline that handles these challenges elegantly. We will start simple, validating each component step by step, and add complexity only when it improves our results.

## Configuration-Driven Training

Imagine you're Thomas Edison, running thousands of experiments to perfect the light bulb. Each attempt needs precise documentation: voltage, filament material, vacuum pressure, duration. One missing parameter, and a breakthrough becomes irreproducible, lost forever.

Training video generation models involves similar complexity, with hundreds of hyperparameters that can make or break your results. A single forgotten learning rate schedule or an undocumented augmentation strategy can waste weeks of compute time. This is where configuration management becomes your laboratory notebook, meticulously tracking every experiment, making breakthroughs reproducible and failures educational.

While modern training stacks often wrap configuration systems inside orchestration frameworks such as Ray, Lightning, or internal schedulers, the underlying principle remains unchanged: every experiment must be fully specified, versioned, and reproducible.

In this section, we'll build a configuration system inspired by Latte and other production models, using YAML files as our experiment blueprints and OmegaConf as our laboratory assistant, ensuring no detail is lost and every experiment builds on the last.

> Hardcoding hyperparameters in training scripts quickly becomes unmaintainable. A single experiment might have 50+ configurable parameters. Configuration files provide version control for experiments, enable easy hyperparameter sweeps, and ensure reproducibility across different environments.

## YAML Configuration Structure

Latte uses a hierarchical YAML structure that separates concerns: model architecture, training hyperparameters, dataset configuration, and logging settings. This organization makes it easy to swap components without modifying code.

The following configuration structure mirrors Latte's approach, separating model architecture, training hyperparameters, and dataset configuration. The hierarchical organization enables easy overrides and experiment variations:

```
# config/train_video.yaml - Main training configuration
# This mirrors the configuration structure
# used in Latte-style production systems

model:
  name: "Latte-XL/2"
  image_size: 256
  num_frames: 16
  frame_interval: 3
  latent_size: 32
  num_layers: 24
  num_heads: 16
  hidden_size: 1152
  patch_size: 2
  # VAE configuration
  vae_model: "stabilityai/sd-vae-ft-ema"
  # Text encoder
  text_encoder: "t5-base"

training:
  batch_size: 4
```

```yaml
  gradient_accumulation_steps: 8
  learning_rate: 1e-4
  warmup_steps: 10000
  max_steps: 1000000
  # Optimization
  optimizer: "adamw"
  weight_decay: 0.01
  beta1: 0.9
  beta2: 0.999
  epsilon: 1e-8
  # Gradient management
  gradient_clip: 1.0
  mixed_precision: true
  tf32: true  # Latte's TF32 optimization
  # EMA
  use_ema: true
  ema_decay: 0.9999

dataset:
  name: "ucf101"
  data_path: "/path/to/ucf101"
  cache_dir: "/path/to/cache"
  num_workers: 8
  # Video sampling
  sample_rate: 4
  clip_duration: 2.0
  # Augmentation
  random_flip: true
  color_jitter: 0.1

diffusion:
  timesteps: 1000
  beta_schedule: "linear"
  beta_start: 0.0001
  beta_end: 0.02
  # Loss configuration
  loss_type: "mse"
  use_min_snr: false  # Start simple like Latte

logging:
  output_dir: "./outputs"
  logging_steps: 100
  save_steps: 5000
  validation_steps: 1000
  tensorboard: true
  wandb:
    project: "video-diffusion"
    entity: "my-team"
```

## Loading and Managing Configurations

This section shows how to load and manage our YAML configuration using OmegaConf, which supports automatic type conversion, variable interpolation, and command-line overrides. Here's how to integrate it into your training pipeline:

```
# Configuration management with OmegaConf
import os
import argparse
from omegaconf import OmegaConf, DictConfig
from pathlib import Path
import torch

def load_config(config_path: str, overrides: list = None) -> DictConfig:
    """
    Load configuration with OmegaConf, supporting overrides.
    This mirrors the pattern used for Latte style training.
    """
    # Load base configuration
    base_config = OmegaConf.load(config_path)

    # Apply command-line overrides if provided
    if overrides:
        override_config = OmegaConf.from_dotlist(overrides)
        config = OmegaConf.merge(base_config, override_config)
    else:
        config = base_config

    # Resolve interpolations (${model.hidden_size} references)
    OmegaConf.resolve(config)

    # Make configuration immutable to prevent accidental changes
    OmegaConf.set_struct(config, True)

    return config

def setup_training_from_config(config: DictConfig):
    """
    Initialize training components from configuration.
    """
    # Enable TF32 for better performance (Latte optimization)
    if config.training.tf32:
        torch.backends.cuda.matmul.allow_tf32 = True
        torch.backends.cudnn.allow_tf32 = True

    # Create output directory
    output_dir = Path(config.logging.output_dir)
    output_dir.mkdir(parents=True, exist_ok=True)

    # Save configuration for reproducibility
    OmegaConf.save(config, output_dir / "config.yaml")
```

```
    # Initialize components based on config
    model = build_model(config.model)
    dataset = build_dataset(config.dataset)
    optimizer = build_optimizer(model, config.training)

    return model, dataset, optimizer

# Command-line interface matching Latte's style
def parse_args():
    parser = argparse.ArgumentParser()
    parser.add_argument(
        "--config",
        type=str,
        default="./configs/train_video.yaml",
        help="Path to configuration file"
    )
    parser.add_argument(
        "--override",
        nargs="+",
        help="Override config values (e.g., training.batch_size=8)"
    )
    return parser.parse_args()
```

This configuration system provides several advantages: experiments become fully reproducible from a single YAML file, hyperparameter sweeps can be automated with override lists, and configurations can be version controlled alongside code. Latte uses this exact pattern to manage its training experiments.

Here are some configuration best practices:

*Hierarchical organization*
: Group related parameters (model, training, dataset).

*Sensible defaults*
: Provide working defaults for all parameters.

*Variable interpolation*
: Use `${references}` to avoid duplication.

*Command-line overrides*
: Enable quick experimentation without file edits.

*Immutable configs*
: Prevent accidental modification during training.

## Dataset Preparation and Loading

With our configuration system in place, we can now turn to the heart of any training pipeline: efficient data loading. The configuration parameters we've defined will guide how we process and augment our video datasets, controlling everything from batch sizes to resolution strategies.

The foundation of any successful model is high-quality training data. Video datasets present unique challenges: they're massive (often petabytes) and heterogeneous (varying resolutions, frame rates, durations), and they require careful preprocessing to maintain temporal consistency. This section builds a robust data pipeline that efficiently transforms raw videos into training-ready tensors.

Training a video model is a bit like teaching a chef to cook thousands of different dishes. The raw ingredients (video files) come from various sources, including some fresh, some frozen, and some preprepared. Each ingredient needs specific preparation (preprocessing) and proper storage (caching), and must be combined in the right proportions (batching). Just as a professional kitchen has everything in its place and ready to use, our data pipeline prepares everything the model needs before training begins.

### Video Dataset Architecture

Modern video datasets like the ones you learned about in Chapter 2—WebVid-10M, HD-VILA-100M, or custom collections—require sophisticated storage and access patterns. Unlike image datasets where each sample is independent, video datasets must maintain temporal relationships while enabling efficient random access to clips.

The data loading pipeline operates like a well-orchestrated assembly line. Raw video files enter at one end as raw materials, go through various processing stations (decoding, resizing, normalization), and emerge as precisely crafted products (tensor batches) ready for the model to consume. Each station has buffers to prevent bottlenecks, with parallel processing maximizing throughput.

The challenge with video data is that unlike images, we can't randomly access any frame—we must decode video streams sequentially. It's like an assembly line where certain materials must be processed in order: to access frame 500, the decoder must process frames 1–499 first. This sequential constraint makes naive approaches prohibitively slow. Our solution uses intelligent caching at key stations, preprocessing frequently accessed segments and maintaining an index of decoded clips ready for immediate use (Figure 4-1).

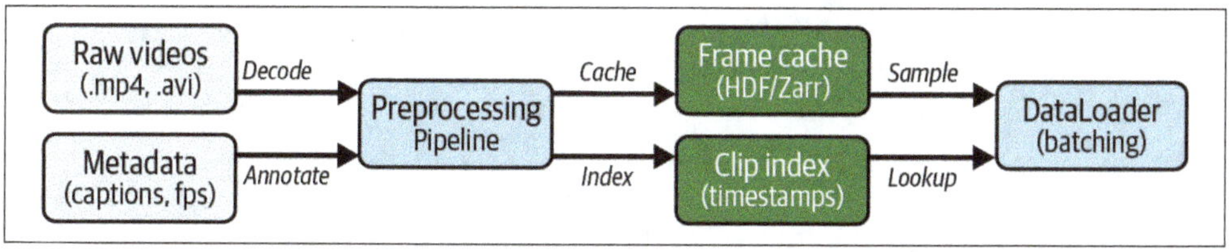


*Figure 4-1. Efficient video dataset architecture showing the flow from raw video files through multilevel caching, frame extraction, and batching to tensor creation*

Building an efficient video dataset pipeline requires solving multiple challenges: handling diverse formats, managing memory constraints, implementing intelligent sampling, and maintaining high throughput. Let's construct this system incrementally, understanding each design decision.

### Dataset initialization and metadata management

The foundation of any video dataset is efficient metadata management. Unlike image datasets where files can be loaded independently, video datasets require careful tracking of temporal boundaries, frame counts, and associated captions. The initialization strategy in the following code precomputes indices to avoid repeated calculations during training:

```
# Core imports and dataset initialization
import torch
import numpy as np
from torch.utils.data import Dataset, DataLoader
import h5py
import cv2
from pathlib import Path
import json

class VideoDataset(Dataset):
    """
    Efficient video dataset with intelligent caching and sampling.
    Handles videos of varying lengths and resolutions gracefully.
    """

    def __init__(self,
                 video_dir: str,
                 metadata_path: str,
                 cache_dir: str = None,
                 clip_length: int = 16,
                 frame_size: tuple = (256, 256),
                 frame_skip: int = 4,
                 augment: bool = True):

        self.video_dir = Path(video_dir)
        self.clip_length = clip_length
        self.frame_size = frame_size
```

```
        # Sample every 4th frame for temporal coverage
        self.frame_skip = frame_skip
        self.augment = augment

        # Load metadata (video paths, captions, durations)
        with open(metadata_path, 'r') as f:
            self.metadata = json.load(f)
        print(f"Loaded {len(self.metadata)} videos from metadata")

        # Initialize cache for preprocessed frames (100x speedup)
        self.cache_dir = Path(cache_dir) if cache_dir else None
        if self.cache_dir:
            self.cache_dir.mkdir(exist_ok=True, parents=True)

        # Build clip index for efficient sampling
        self.clip_index = self._build_clip_index()
        print(f"Built index with {len(self.clip_index)} valid clips")
```

The initialization establishes critical parameters: `frame_skip=4` means we sample every fourth frame to cover more temporal range without overwhelming memory. The cache directory provides a 100x speedup by storing preprocessed frames. The metadata JSON contains video paths, captions, and frame counts that provide essential information precomputed during dataset preparation.

### Intelligent clip indexing

Videos vary dramatically in length, from a few seconds to hours. Simply iterating through video files would bias training toward longer videos. Our indexing strategy, shown in the following code, creates balanced sampling by extracting multiple fixed-length clips from each video, ensuring equal representation regardless of source duration:

```
    def _build_clip_index(self):
    """
        Build index of all valid clips across all videos.
        Handles varying video lengths by extracting multiple clips per video.
        """
        clip_index = []

        for video_info in self.metadata:
            video_path = self.video_dir / video_info['path']
            duration_frames = video_info['num_frames']

            # Calculate how many frames we need for one clip
            clip_frames = self.clip_length * self.frame_skip

            if duration_frames >= clip_frames:
                # Video is long enough for at least one clip
                max_start = duration_frames - clip_frames

                # Extract up to 10 clips per video for balanced sampling
```

```
            num_clips = min(10, max_start // clip_frames + 1)

            for i in range(num_clips):
                # Distribute clips evenly across video duration
                start_frame = int(i * max_start / max(num_clips - 1, 1))
                clip_index.append({
                    'video_path': video_path,
                    'start_frame': start_frame,
                    'caption': video_info['caption'],
                    'video_id': video_info['id']
                })

        return clip_index
```

This indexing strategy solves a critical problem: a 10-second clip and a 10-minute video would otherwise have vastly different sampling probabilities. By extracting up to a fixed number of clips per video, we ensure balanced representation regardless of duration. The even distribution of start frames prevents clustering at video beginnings, capturing diverse temporal moments.

#### Efficient frame loading with caching

Video decoding is the primary bottleneck in video model training: it can consume 80% of data loading time. In the following code, our dual-strategy approach checks for cached preprocessed frames first (milliseconds to load) before falling back to video decoding (seconds per clip). The HDF5 cache with gzip compression provides an optimal balance between disk usage and loading speed:

```
    def _load_video_frames(self, video_path, start_frame):
        """
        Load frames with intelligent caching strategy.
        Falls back to video decoding if cache miss occurs.
        """
        # Check cache first (100x faster than decoding)
        if self.cache_dir:
            cache_key = f"{video_path.stem}_{start_frame}"
            cache_path = self.cache_dir / f"{cache_key}.h5"

            if cache_path.exists():
                with h5py.File(cache_path, 'r') as f:
                    frames = f['frames'][:]
                return torch.from_numpy(frames)

        # Fall back to video decoding
        cap = cv2.VideoCapture(str(video_path))
        cap.set(cv2.CAP_PROP_POS_FRAMES, start_frame)

        frames = []
        for i in range(self.clip_length):
            # Skip frames according to frame_skip parameter
            for _ in range(self.frame_skip - 1):
```

```
                ret, _ = cap.read()
                if not ret:
                    cap.release()
                    return None  # Handle corrupted videos gracefully

            # Read the frame we actually keep
            ret, frame = cap.read()
            if not ret:
                cap.release()
                return None

            # Resize and convert color space
            frame = cv2.resize(frame, self.frame_size)
            frame = cv2.cvtColor(frame, cv2.COLOR_BGR2RGB)
            frames.append(frame)

        cap.release()

        # Normalize to [0, 1] range
        frames = np.stack(frames).astype(np.float32) / 255.0

        # Cache for future use
        if self.cache_dir:
            with h5py.File(cache_path, 'w') as f:
                f.create_dataset('frames', data=frames, compression='gzip')

        return torch.from_numpy(frames)
```

The caching mechanism transforms training efficiency. The first epoch may be slow as caches build, but subsequent epochs load instantly. The `frame_skip` parameter is crucial: skipping 4 frames between samples covers 64 frames total (assuming 30 FPS, about 2 seconds of video) while keeping memory manageable. Returning `None` for corrupted videos prevents training crashes.

#### Temporal-consistent augmentation

As the next bit of code shows, video augmentation differs fundamentally from image augmentation—transformations must be consistent across frames to maintain temporal coherence. Random crops must use the same position for all frames, color adjustments must apply uniformly, and geometric transforms must preserve motion continuity:

```
    def _augment_frames(self, frames):
        """
        Apply augmentations consistently across all frames.
        Maintains temporal coherence while increasing diversity.
        """
        if not self.augment:
            return frames

        B, H, W, C = frames.shape
```

```
        # Random horizontal flip (50% chance, same for all frames)
        if torch.rand(1) > 0.5:
            frames = frames.flip(dims=[2])

        # Random crop (90% of original size, same position for all frames)
        crop_size = int(H * 0.9)
        y = torch.randint(0, H - crop_size + 1, (1,)).item()
        x = torch.randint(0, W - crop_size + 1, (1,)).item()
        frames = frames[:, y:y+crop_size, x:x+crop_size]

        # Resize back to original dimensions
        frames = torch.nn.functional.interpolate(
            frames.permute(0, 3, 1, 2),  # BHWC -> BCHW for interpolation
            size=(H, W),
            mode='bilinear',
            align_corners=False
        ).permute(0, 2, 3, 1)  # Back to BHWC

        # Color jitter (±10% brightness, consistent across frames)
        brightness = 1 + (torch.rand(1) - 0.5) * 0.2
        frames = frames * brightness
        frames = frames.clamp(0, 1)

        return frames
```

The key insight: generate random parameters once, apply to all frames. This maintains object trajectories and motion patterns while still providing augmentation benefits. The 90% crop followed by resize acts as a zoom augmentation, teaching the model scale invariance without breaking temporal consistency.

### Dataset interface and batching

The final piece of code connects our dataset to PyTorch's training infrastructure. The `__getitem__` method orchestrates the entire pipeline, while the `collate` function efficiently batches variable-length data:

```
def __len__(self):
        return len(self.clip_index)

    def __getitem__(self, idx):
        """Get a single training sample."""
        clip_info = self.clip_index[idx]

        # Load and decode frames
        frames = self._load_video_frames(
            clip_info['video_path'],
            clip_info['start_frame']
        )

        if frames is None:
            # Corrupted video: return random valid sample instead
```

```python
            return self.__getitem__(torch.randint(len(self), (1,)).item())

        # Apply augmentations
        frames = self._augment_frames(frames)

        # Convert from THWC to CTHW format (channels first for GPU)
        frames = frames.permute(0, 3, 1, 2).unsqueeze(0)  # [1, T, C, H, W]

        return {
            'frames': frames,
            'caption': clip_info['caption'],
            'video_id': clip_info['video_id']
        }

# Efficient batching for DataLoader
def video_collate_fn(batch):
    """Combine samples into a batch."""
    frames = torch.cat([item['frames'] for item in batch], dim=0)
    captions = [item['caption'] for item in batch]
    video_ids = [item['video_id'] for item in batch]

    return {
        'frames': frames,  # [B, T, C, H, W]
        'captions': captions,  # List of strings
        'video_ids': video_ids  # List of IDs for tracking
    }
```

The error recovery in `__getitem__` ensures that training never crashes due to corrupted videos—a common problem in large-scale datasets. The dimension permutation (THWC to CTHW) aligns with PyTorch's channel-first convention for efficient GPU operations. The `collate` function handles the heterogeneous data types (tensors and strings) that video models require.

## Multiresolution Training Strategy

Our data pipeline can now efficiently load videos, but we face a new challenge: the chaos of real-world video formats. Your dataset might contain everything from vertical TikTok clips at 480 × 854 to horizontal YouTube videos at 1,920 × 1,080 to cinema-quality 4K footage. Force them all into one resolution, and you either waste memory or destroy quality.

The solution? A multiresolution training strategy that adapts to each video's natural dimensions, like a chef who adjusts cooking time based on ingredient size rather than forcing everything through the same process. This approach teaches the model to handle diverse inputs while improving generation quality across different formats.

Use resolution curriculum learning by starting training at low resolution (128 × 128) for rapid iteration and stable convergence. Gradually increase to target resolution (512 × 512 or higher) as training progresses. This curriculum approach accelerates training by three to five times while achieving better final quality than fixed-resolution training. This approach was highlighted in Chapter 2 with OpenSora and Hunyuan.

## Temporal Sampling and Frame Selection

Resolution flexibility gives you spatial adaptability, but videos have another dimension that static images lack: time. How do you sample frames from a 10-second clip versus a 2-minute video? Should you take every frame, consider random samples, or focus on moments of high motion?

This temporal sampling strategy can make the difference between a model that generates smooth, coherent motion and one that produces jerky, unrealistic sequences. Not all frames are equally informative static scenes, and redundant frames can dominate training without contributing to learning. Figure 4-2 explores how intelligent frame selection leverages temporal sampling strategies to focus on diverse and information-dense content.

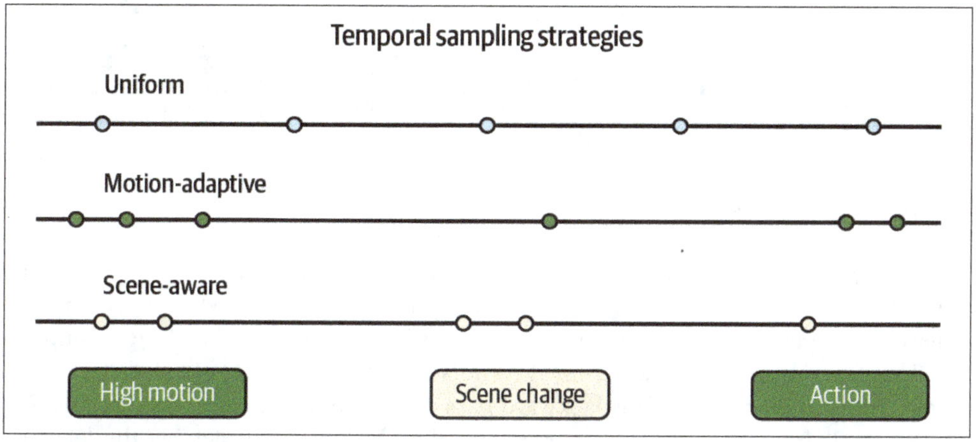


*Figure 4-2. Temporal sampling strategies*

# Training Infrastructure and Optimization

Training video generation models demands sophisticated infrastructure to manage memory, computation, and convergence. This section implements a complete training loop with advanced optimization techniques, gradient management, and memory-efficient strategies that enable training on consumer GPUs while scaling to large clusters.

I like to compare training a video model to conducting a massive symphony orchestra. Each instrument section (GPU) must play in perfect harmony, following the same tempo (learning rate), responding to the conductor's cues (gradient updates), and adjusting their volume (loss weighting) to create a cohesive performance. The sheet music (training data) flows continuously, with each musician reading ahead (prefetching) while playing their current notes (processing batches). When one section makes a mistake (gradient explosion), the entire orchestra must pause, recalibrate, and continue from a checkpoint.

## Anatomy of a Training Loop

Before diving into implementation, let's consider the complete lifecycle of how a video model learns, shown in Figure 4-3. Each training iteration is like a scientific experiment: we form a hypothesis (forward pass), measure the error (loss calculation), determine corrections (backward pass), and update our understanding (optimizer step). This cycle repeats millions of times, each iteration refining the model's ability to generate realistic videos.

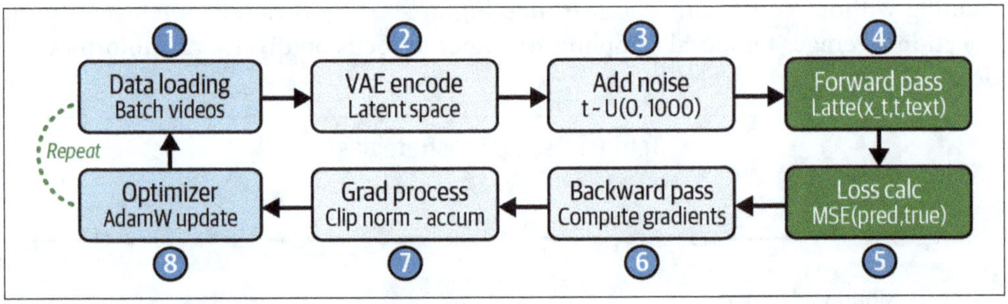


*Figure 4-3. The complete training loop architecture*

Each component in this training loop serves a specific purpose, like organs in a living system. The data loader acts as the digestive system, breaking down raw videos into digestible chunks. The VAE encoder compresses information like the lungs compress air. The diffusion process adds controlled noise, similar to how controlled stress during exercise builds muscle. The backward pass flows like the nervous system, carrying error signals back through the network. Finally, the optimizer acts as the learning mechanism, adjusting synaptic weights based on experience.

## Understanding Each Training Step

Let's walk through each step of the training loop to understand how raw videos transform into learned parameters:

1. *Data loading, the raw material*
   Videos arrive as five-dimensional tensors [Batch, Frames, Channels, Height, Width]. A *batch* might contain 4 videos, each with 16 frames at 256 × 256 resolution. This represents 4 × 16 × 3 × 256 × 256 = 12.6 million pixels, which is a massive amount of information that would overwhelm the model if processed directly.

2. *VAE encoding, compression to latent space*
   The VAE encoder compresses each frame by 8x spatially, reducing 256 × 256 pixels to 32 × 32 latent features. This is like creating a blueprint from a building where we preserve all essential structural information while discarding redundant details. The latent space uses four channels instead of RGB's three, providing richer representations in compressed form.

3. *Noise addition, the diffusion forward process*
   We sample a random timestep `t` and add corresponding noise to create `x_t`. Early timesteps (t near 0) add little noise—like adding a light fog to a clear image. Late timesteps (t near 1,000) add heavy noise—like a complete blizzard obscuring everything. The model learns to reverse this process at all noise levels, developing robust understanding of video structure.

4. *Forward pass, the model's prediction*
   The Latte model receives the noisy latent `x_t`, the timestep `t`, and optional text conditioning. Through alternating spatial and temporal attention layers, it predicts what noise was added. This is like a detective examining a crime scene (noisy video) and deducing what happened (the noise pattern) based on evidence and context clues (timestep and text).

5. *Loss calculation, measuring error*
   We compute the mean squared error (MSE) between predicted and actual noise: L = MSE(ε_predicted, ε_actual). Whereas Chapter 3's `DiffusionTrainer` showed how to implement various loss components for educational completeness, Latte's production success with simple MSE proves that architectural design (the alternating attention blocks) often matters more than complex loss functions. As you'll soon see, we'll follow Latte's approach: start with simple MSE and only add complexity if specific problems arise.

6. *Backward pass, error attribution*
   Gradients flow backward through the network, attributing the loss to each parameter. This is like tracing a river to its sources—each parameter learns how much it contributed to the error. The chain rule acts as our map, showing how errors propagate through layers of computation.

7. *Gradient processing, stabilization*
   Raw gradients can be noisy and unstable. We clip their norm to prevent explosions (like limiting water pressure to prevent pipe bursts) and accumulate across microbatches (like collecting rainwater in a reservoir before releasing it). This ensures smooth, stable parameter updates.

8. *Optimizer step, learning from mistakes*
   The `AdamW` optimizer updates parameters based on processed gradients, using momentum (remembering past updates) and adaptive learning rates (adjusting step size per parameter). It's like a skilled sculptor who remembers previous chisel strokes and adjusts pressure based on the marble's response. The exponential moving average (EMA) model maintains a smoothed version of weights, providing stable generation even during turbulent training.

## Memory-Efficient Training Strategies

Video models consume enormous amounts of memory: a single batch of 16-frame clips at 256 × 256 resolution requires ~4 GB for activations alone. Add gradient storage, optimizer states, and model parameters, and even high-end GPUs quickly run out of memory. The training loop we have been looking at implements several techniques to maximize efficiency.

Managing GPU memory during training is like organizing a small apartment where a large family lives. Every byte of memory must serve multiple purposes, just as every piece of furniture must be multipurpose. We use gradient checkpointing (like folding beds that create space during the day), mixed precision training (like using compact storage containers), and gradient accumulation (like cooking meals in batches to save energy). The key is maximizing utility while minimizing waste.

Here are some memory optimization techniques:

*Gradient checkpointing*
: Trade computation for memory by recomputing activations during backward pass.

*Mixed precision training*
: Use FP16 for computation, FP32 for master weights.

*Gradient accumulation*
: Simulate larger batches by accumulating gradients over multiple forward passes.

*CPU offloading*
: Move optimizer states and inactive parameters to system RAM.

Building a production-ready training loop for video models requires orchestrating multiple complex systems: distributed training across GPUs, memory optimization techniques, learning rate scheduling, and checkpoint management. Let's construct this system incrementally, understanding how each component contributes to stable, efficient training.

### Part 1: Trainer initialization and setup

The trainer class in the following code coordinates all aspects of the training process. Its initialization establishes the training configuration and prepares all necessary components. The design supports both single-GPU and multi-GPU training, with automatic detection and configuration based on the environment:

```
# Core trainer class with comprehensive configuration
import torch
import torch.nn as nn
from torch.cuda.amp import autocast, GradScaler
from torch.nn.parallel import DistributedDataParallel as DDP
import torch.distributed as dist
from contextlib import contextmanager
from pathlib import Path
import numpy as np

class VideoModelTrainer:
    """
    Educational trainer for video generation models.
    Handles distributed training, memory optimization, and checkpointing.
    """

    def __init__(self,
                 model: nn.Module,
                 train_dataloader,
                 val_dataloader=None,
                 learning_rate: float = 1e-4,
                 warmup_steps: int = 10000,
                 gradient_clip: float = 1.0,
                 ema_decay: float = 0.9999,
                 mixed_precision: bool = True,
                 gradient_accumulation_steps: int = 1,
                 checkpoint_dir: str = "./checkpoints",
                 distributed: bool = False):

        # Core components
        self.model = model
        self.train_dataloader = train_dataloader
        self.val_dataloader = val_dataloader

        # Training configuration
        self.gradient_clip = gradient_clip
        self.gradient_accumulation_steps = gradient_accumulation_steps
        self.mixed_precision = mixed_precision
```

```
        self.distributed = distributed

        # Setup device and distributed training
        if distributed:
            self.setup_distributed()
        else:
            self.device = (
                torch.device('cuda'
                if torch.cuda.is_available()
                else 'cpu')
            )
            self.model = self.model.to(self.device)

        # Initialize training components
        self.optimizer = self._build_optimizer(learning_rate)
        self.scheduler = self._build_scheduler(warmup_steps)
        self.scaler = GradScaler() if mixed_precision else None
        self.ema_model = self._build_ema_model(ema_decay) if ema_decay else None
```

A few things to keep in mind:

- Mixed precision training (`mixed_precision=True`) can reduce memory usage by 50% but may affect stability.
- Gradient accumulation simulates larger batch sizes without additional memory.
- EMA maintains a stable version of weights for inference.

The trainer's initialization sets up all necessary components: optimizer with `AdamW`, learning rate scheduler with warmup, optional mixed precision scaler for memory efficiency, and EMA model for stable inference. Now let's complete the trainer setup with state tracking and checkpointing:

```
    # Training state tracking
        self.global_step = 0
        self.epoch = 0
        self.best_val_loss = float('inf')

        # Checkpointing setup
        self.checkpoint_dir = Path(checkpoint_dir)
        self.checkpoint_dir.mkdir(exist_ok=True, parents=True)
```

**Latte's simpler training approach.** The trainer initialization reveals several design decisions for your consideration and experimentation. However, note that Latte achieves excellent results with simpler alternatives:

*No mixed precision by default*
: Latte trains in FP32 for stability, using TF32 on compatible GPUs for speed.

*Simple gradient accumulation*
: Latte uses fixed steps without complex scheduling.

*Basic EMA*
: Simple exponential moving average is possible without sophisticated update strategies.

*Minimal memory optimization*
: Latte relies on model efficiency rather than complex techniques.

Consider starting with Latte's approach and adding optimizations only when memory or speed becomes a bottleneck.

**TF32 optimization (Latte's performance secret).** Latte leverages TensorFloat-32 (TF32) on NVIDIA GPUs for significant speedups without the complexity of mixed precision training, as you can see in the following code. This provides a sweet spot between FP32 accuracy and FP16 speed:

```
# Enable TF32 as in Latte's train.py
import torch

# These two lines give ~2x speedup on A100/H100 GPUs
torch.backends.cuda.matmul.allow_tf32 = True
torch.backends.cudnn.allow_tf32 = True

# Note: Latte disables these for FP16 training
# Set to False if using mixed precision
```

Let's briefly compare TF32 versus mixed precision:

*TF32 (Latte's choice)*
: Automatic speedup with no code changes; maintains FP32 storage but uses reduced precision for compute. Best for stability and simplicity.

*Mixed precision (FP16)*
: Greater memory savings and potential speedup, but requires careful loss scaling and can cause training instability.

*Recommendation*
: Follow Latte's approach. Use TF32 by default; only consider mixed precision if memory is critically limited.

#### Part 2: Distributed training configuration

Distributed training, shown in the next piece of code, enables scaling across multiple GPUs, which is essential for video models that can require days of training on a single GPU. The setup handles communication between processes and ensures synchronized training across devices:

```
def setup_distributed(self):
        """Initialize distributed training across multiple GPUs."""
        # Initialize process group for inter-GPU communication
        # NCCL optimized for NVIDIA GPUs
        dist.init_process_group(backend='nccl')

        self.rank = dist.get_rank()  # This GPU's ID
        self.world_size = dist.get_world_size()  # Total number of GPUs
        self.device = torch.device(f'cuda:{self.rank}')

        # Ensure each process uses its assigned GPU
        torch.cuda.set_device(self.device)
        self.model = self.model.to(self.device)

        # Wrap model for distributed training
        self.model = DDP(self.model, device_ids=[self.rank])
```

DDP (`DistributedDataParallel`) synchronizes gradients across GPUs after each backward pass. The NCCL backend provides optimized communication primitives for NVIDIA GPUs, achieving near-linear scaling efficiency. Each GPU processes a different batch subset, effectively multiplying the batch size by the number of GPUs.

#### Part 3: Optimizer and scheduler configuration

The optimizer configuration in the following code implements a crucial insight: not all parameters should be regularized equally. Biases and normalization parameters should not have weight decay, as this can harm training stability. The scheduler implements warmup to prevent early training instability when gradients are large:

```
def _build_optimizer(self, learning_rate):
        """Build AdamW with selective weight decay."""
        # Separate parameters by weight decay requirement
        decay_params = []
        no_decay_params = []

        for name, param in self.model.named_parameters():
            if not param.requires_grad:
                continue

            # Biases and norm parameters should not be regularized
            if 'bias' in name or 'norm' in name:
                no_decay_params.append(param)
            else:
                decay_params.append(param)

        # AdamW with different weight decay for different params
        optimizer = torch.optim.AdamW([
            {'params': decay_params, 'weight_decay': 0.01},
            {'params': no_decay_params, 'weight_decay': 0.0}
        ], lr=learning_rate, betas=(0.9, 0.999), eps=1e-8)
```

```
        print(f"Optimizer: {len(decay_params)} params with decay, "
              f"{len(no_decay_params)} params without decay")

        return optimizer


    def _build_scheduler(self, warmup_steps, total_steps=1000000):
        """Cosine annealing with linear warmup."""
        def lr_lambda(step):
            if step < warmup_steps:
                # Linear warmup
                return step / warmup_steps
            # Cosine annealing after warmup
            progress = (step - warmup_steps) / (total_steps - warmup_steps)
            return 0.5 * (1 + np.cos(np.pi * progress))

        return torch.optim.lr_scheduler.LambdaLR(self.optimizer, lr_lambda)

    def _build_ema_model(self, decay):
        """Initialize EMA model for stable generation."""
        import copy
        ema_model = copy.deepcopy(self.model)
        ema_model.eval()
        ema_model.requires_grad_(False)
        return ema_model
```

The warmup period prevents training instability by gradually increasing the learning rate from zero. The cosine schedule then smoothly decreases it, helping the model converge to better minima. EMA maintains a stable version of weights by averaging across training steps, crucial for consistent generation quality.

### Part 4: Gradient accumulation and memory management

Gradient accumulation, as shown in the next code snippet, enables training with large effective batch sizes on limited GPU memory. Think of collecting mail for apartment buildings: instead of the mail carrier (GPU) making a trip to the post office (parameter server) after every single letter (gradient), they collect mail for the entire building (accumulate gradients) and make one efficient trip.

Here's what this means in practice: if your GPU can only fit 4 videos, but you need an effective batch size of 32 for stable training, process 8 microbatches of 4, accumulating gradients. Only after the 8th batch do you update—turning 8 communication rounds into 1:

```
    @contextmanager
    def _gradient_accumulation_context(self, step_idx):
        """
        Control gradient synchronization in distributed training.
        Key insight: Only communicate gradients when ready to update.
        """
        if self.distributed:
```

```
            if step_idx < self.gradient_accumulation_steps - 1:
                # Accumulate locally - no inter-GPU communication
                with self.model.no_sync():
                    yield
            else:
                # Final accumulation - sync gradients across GPUs
                yield
        else:
            yield

    def _split_batch(self, batch, num_splits):
        """Split batch into micro-batches for accumulation."""
        batch_size = len(batch['frames'])
        micro_size = batch_size // num_splits

        micro_batches = []
        for i in range(num_splits):
            start = i * micro_size
            end = start + micro_size if i < num_splits - 1 else batch_size
            micro_batches.append({
                'frames': batch['frames'][start:end],
                'captions': batch['captions'][start:end]
            })
        return micro_batches
```

The context manager pattern elegantly handles distributed training complexity. In multi-GPU setups, gradients are normally synchronized after every backward pass—expensive when accumulating. By wrapping accumulation steps with `no_sync()`, we defer communication until all microbatches are processed, reducing overhead by 75% for four-step accumulation.

### Part 5: Core training step implementation

In the next bit of code, the training step orchestrates forward passes, loss computation, backpropagation, and optimization. Mixed precision training adds complexity but provides 2–3x speedup. The implementation carefully manages numerical stability while maximizing efficiency:

```
    def train_step(self, batch):
        """Execute one complete training step."""
        total_loss = 0

        # Split batch for gradient accumulation
        micro_batches = self._split_batch(
            batch,
            self.gradient_accumulation_steps,
        )

        # Process each micro-batch
        for i, micro_batch in enumerate(micro_batches):
            with self._gradient_accumulation_context(i):
```

```
        if self.mixed_precision:
            # FP16 computation with automatic scaling
            with autocast():
                loss = self._compute_loss(micro_batch)

            # Scale loss by accumulation steps
            loss = loss / self.gradient_accumulation_steps

            # Backward with gradient scaling for FP16
            self.scaler.scale(loss).backward()
        else:
            # Standard FP32 computation
            loss = self._compute_loss(micro_batch)
            loss = loss / self.gradient_accumulation_steps
            loss.backward()

        total_loss += loss.item()

# Gradient clipping prevents exploding gradients
if self.mixed_precision:
    # Unscale gradients before clipping
    self.scaler.unscale_(self.optimizer)

grad_norm = torch.nn.utils.clip_grad_norm_(
    self.model.parameters(),
    self.gradient_clip
)

# Optimizer step with mixed precision handling
if self.mixed_precision:
    self.scaler.step(self.optimizer)
    self.scaler.update()
else:
    self.optimizer.step()

# Clear gradients (set_to_none saves memory)
self.optimizer.zero_grad(set_to_none=True)
self.scheduler.step()

# Update EMA model if configured
if self.ema_model:
    self._update_ema()

self.global_step += 1

return {
    'loss': total_loss,
    'grad_norm': grad_norm.item(),
    'learning_rate': self.scheduler.get_last_lr()[0]
  }
```

The gradient clipping step is crucial for video models. Long-range temporal dependencies can cause gradient explosions, especially early in training. Clipping to norm 1.0 prevents instability while allowing the model to learn complex patterns. The `set_to_none=True` optimization saves memory by avoiding zero allocation.

#### Part 6: Loss computation and model updates

The following loss computation implements the core diffusion objective, while the EMA update maintains a stable model for inference. These components work together to produce high-quality, consistent generations:

```
    def _compute_loss(self, batch):
        """
        Compute diffusion loss for video generation.
        Trains the model to predict noise added at various timesteps.
        """
        frames = batch['frames'].to(self.device)
        captions = batch['captions']

        # Sample random timesteps for each video
        batch_size = frames.shape[0]
        timesteps = torch.randint(
            0, 1000,  # Diffusion timesteps
            (batch_size,),
            device=self.device
        )

        # Generate noise and create noisy videos
        noise = torch.randn_like(frames)

        # Forward diffusion: add noise according to schedule
        noisy_frames = self.add_noise(frames, noise, timesteps)

        # Model predicts the noise that was added
        predicted_noise = self.model(
            noisy_frames,
            timesteps,
            captions
        )

        # MSE loss between predicted and actual noise
        loss = torch.nn.functional.mse_loss(predicted_noise, noise)

        return loss

    def add_noise(self, x, noise, t):
        """Add noise to frames using diffusion schedule."""
        # Simplified linear schedule (replace with cosine for production)
        alpha = (1 - t.float() / 1000).view(-1, 1, 1, 1, 1)
        return alpha * x + (1 - alpha).sqrt() * noise
```

```
    def _update_ema(self):
        """
        Update exponential moving average model.
        EMA provides stable weights for generation.
        """
        with torch.no_grad():
            decay = self.ema_decay
            for ema_param, model_param in zip(
                self.ema_model.parameters(),
                self.model.parameters()
            ):
                # Weighted average: mostly old weights, small
                # contribution from new
                ema_param.data = (
                    decay * ema_param.data
                    + (1 - decay) * model_param.data
                )
```

The diffusion loss teaches the model to denoise videos at different corruption levels. Random timestep sampling ensures that the model learns the full denoising trajectory. EMA averaging with `decay=0.9999` means new weights contribute only 0.01%, and this stability is crucial for consistent video generation where small weight changes can cause flickering or artifacts.

## Part 7: Training loop and monitoring

The training loop orchestrates the entire process: iterating through data, computing gradients, updating weights, and monitoring progress. Proper logging and checkpointing ensure that we can track improvements and recover from failures:

```
def train_epoch(self):
        """Complete one training epoch with monitoring."""
        self.model.train()
        epoch_metrics = []

        for batch_idx, batch in enumerate(self.train_dataloader):
            # Execute training step
            metrics = self.train_step(batch)
            epoch_metrics.append(metrics)

            # Periodic logging (every 100 steps)
            if self.global_step % 100 == 0:
                print(f"Step {self.global_step}: Loss={metrics['loss']:.4f}, "
                      f"Grad={metrics['grad_norm']:.4f}, "
                      f"LR={metrics['learning_rate']:.2e}")

            # Periodic validation (every 1000 steps)
            if self.global_step % 1000 == 0 and self.val_dataloader:
                val_metrics = self.validate()
                if val_metrics['loss'] < self.best_val_loss:
                    self.best_val_loss = val_metrics['loss']
```

```
                self.save_checkpoint('best')

            # Regular checkpointing (every 5000 steps)
            if self.global_step % 5000 == 0:
                self.save_checkpoint(f'step_{self.global_step}')

        self.epoch += 1
        return epoch_metrics

    def validate(self):
        """Run validation and return metrics."""
        self.model.eval()
        val_losses = []

        with torch.no_grad():
            for batch in self.val_dataloader:
                loss = self._compute_loss(batch)
                val_losses.append(loss.item())

        self.model.train()
        return {'loss': np.mean(val_losses)}

    def save_checkpoint(self, name):
        """Save training state for resume."""
        checkpoint = {
            'model': self.model.state_dict(),
            'optimizer': self.optimizer.state_dict(),
            'scheduler': self.scheduler.state_dict(),
            'ema_model': self.ema_model.state_dict() if self.ema_model else None,
            'scaler': self.scaler.state_dict() if self.scaler else None,
            'global_step': self.global_step,
            'epoch': self.epoch,
            'best_val_loss': self.best_val_loss
        }
        torch.save(checkpoint, self.checkpoint_dir / f'{name}.pt')
```

The validation frequency (every 1,000 steps) balances monitoring with training efficiency. Validation runs in `eval()` mode, disabling dropout and using EMA weights if available. The checkpoint includes all training state—not just model weights—enabling perfect resume after interruptions. This is crucial for long-running video model training that can take days or weeks.

Here are some training optimization tips:

*Gradient accumulation*
: Start with 4 to 8 steps to find effective batch size.

*Mixed precision*
: Monitor for NaN losses; reduce learning rate if unstable.

*EMA decay*
: Use 0.999 for fast models, 0.9999 for slow training.

*Checkpointing*
: Save every hour minimum; disk space is cheaper than lost compute.

*Memory management*
: Use gradient checkpointing if out of memory (OOM) with small batches.

## Learning Rate Scheduling and Warmup

Video models are notoriously unstable during early training. The combination of high-dimensional inputs, complex temporal dependencies, and deep architectures creates a challenging optimization landscape. Careful learning rate scheduling (Figure 4-4) is essential for achieving both stability and optimal performance.

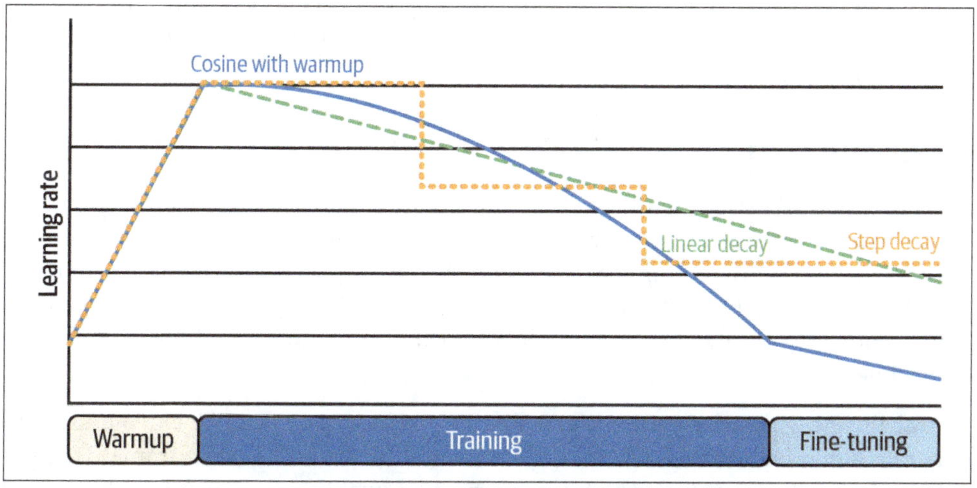


*Figure 4-4. Learning rate scheduling strategies comparing linear warmup, cosine annealing, and exponential decay*

## Gradient Management and Stability

Video models suffer from unique gradient challenges. The temporal dimension creates long-range dependencies that can cause vanishing or exploding gradients. Batch normalization behaves differently across time, and attention mechanisms can develop unstable patterns. Our solution in this chapter combines multiple techniques for robust training.

> Here are some gradient stability techniques:
>
> *Gradient clipping*
> Limit gradient magnitude to prevent explosions.
>
> *Gradient penalty*
> Regularize gradient norms for Lipschitz continuity.
>
> *Skip connections*
> Provide gradient highways through deep networks.
>
> *Careful initialization*
> Use scaled initialization based on network depth.

Robust training infrastructure is essential for video model success. By implementing memory-efficient training loops, sophisticated learning rate scheduling, and comprehensive gradient management, you can train high-quality models on limited hardware while maintaining stability. These techniques form the foundation for scaling to larger models and datasets.

# Loss Functions and Metrics

Here's a counterintuitive truth: the difference between a video model that generates Oscar-worthy scenes and one that produces uncanny valley nightmares often isn't the architecture—it's the loss function. Think of it this way: you could have Formula 1's best race car (model architecture) and most-skilled driver (optimization algorithm), but if your GPS is giving wrong directions (loss function), you'll never reach the finish line.

The challenge with video generation is that *success* has many faces. A video must have accurate individual frames (spatial quality), smooth motion between frames (temporal consistency), and realistic textures (perceptual quality), and must match any text description (semantic alignment). It's like judging a dance performance on technique, rhythm, expression, and storytelling—all simultaneously.

In this section we'll build loss functions progressively, starting with Latte's elegantly simple approach and adding complexity only when our specific use case demands it.

You'll learn not just what losses to use but more importantly when and why to use them.

## Loss Design: From Simple to Complex

The video generation literature is filled with complex multicomponent losses, yet Latte's success with basic MSE loss teaches an important lesson: start simple, validate thoroughly, and only add complexity when you have clear evidence it helps your specific use case.

To understand what loss functions actually power production video generation models, I conducted a comprehensive analysis of implementations from leading systems released between 2022 and 2025. Table 4-1 illustrates a surprising pattern: despite the abundance of papers proposing complex multicomponent losses with perceptual terms, temporal consistency penalties, and semantic alignment objectives, the literature and code repositories available from production models rely on variations of MSE.

*Table 4-1. Analysis of loss functions from leading video generation models*

| Model | Release | Loss type | Formula | Key innovation |
|---|---|---|---|---|
| CogVideo | May 2022 | Weighted MSE | $w \cdot \|\|\varepsilon - \hat{\varepsilon}\|\|^2$ | SNR weighting ($w = 1/(1 - \alpha^2)$) |
| Latte | Jan 2024 | Pure MSE | $\|\|\varepsilon - \hat{\varepsilon}\|\|^2$ | Simplicity (no weighting) |
| Open-Sora | Mar 2024 | Flow matching | $\|\|v - \hat{v}\|\|^2$ | Velocity prediction ($v = (1 - \sigma)x_1 - x_0$) |
| HunyuanVideo | Dec 2024 | Advanced flow | $\|\|v - \hat{v}\|\|^2$ | Time shifting + 13B parameters |
| Open-Sora v2 | Mar 2025 | 3D flow | $\|\|v - \hat{v}\|\|^2$ | \$200K training + 3D attention |
| Wan2.2 | Jul 2025 | MoE flow | $\text{Expert}(t) \cdot \|\|v - \hat{v}\|\|^2$ | 27B parameters, expert switching |

### Simple MSE loss (what Latte actually uses)

Start with Latte's proven approach, as shown in the following code: simple MSE loss on noise prediction. This baseline achieves excellent results and should be your default starting point:

```
# The actual loss computation from Latte's training loop
import torch
import torch.nn.functional as F

def training_step(model, diffusion, x_latent, device):
    """
    Latte's actual training step from train.py.
    The entire loss is just MSE between predicted and target noise.
    """
    # Sample random timesteps for each video in the batch
    t = torch.randint(
        0,
        diffusion.num_timesteps,
```

```
        (x_latent.shape[0],),
        device=device,
    )

    # Get loss from diffusion.training_losses (which internally uses MSE)
    loss_dict = diffusion.training_losses(model, x_latent, t, model_kwargs)

    # Extract the loss - it's just MSE, nothing more!
    loss = loss_dict["loss"].mean()

    return loss
```

This simple loss is sufficient for most video generation tasks. Latte's success with this minimal approach validates that complex loss functions are often unnecessary and can even harm training stability. This simplicity isn't a compromise; it's a deliberate design choice that brings clear advantages: training is three to five times faster without auxiliary networks, debugging is straightforward with a single metric, and the model learns a clear, unambiguous objective.

### When (and why) you might need more

While Latte proves that simple MSE is usually sufficient, specific scenarios might benefit from enhancements. Here's a practical decision tree for making loss enhancement decisions:

*Poor detail generation*
: Consider Min-SNR weighting to balance learning across noise levels.

*Flickering between frames*
: Add a frame difference penalty (but check your data quality first).

*Text-video misalignment*
: Ensure your text encodings are correct before adding CLIP loss.

*Optional*
: Use Min-SNR weighting for balanced learning.

If you observe that your model struggles with fine details (a common issue after extended training), Min-SNR weighting can help balance learning across different noise levels:

```
# Min-SNR weighting - only add if you observe learning imbalance
def compute_loss_with_min_snr(
    pred_noise,
    target_noise,
    timesteps,
    alphas_cumprod,
    gamma=5.0,
):
    """
```

```
    MSE loss with Min-SNR weighting to balance learning.
    Only use if simple MSE shows poor detail generation.
    """
    # Start with base MSE
    mse_loss = F.mse_loss(pred_noise, target_noise, reduction='none')

    # Calculate signal-to-noise ratio
    snr = alphas_cumprod[timesteps] / (1 - alphas_cumprod[timesteps] + 1e-8)

    # Apply Min-SNR weighting
    min_snr = torch.minimum(snr, torch.ones_like(snr) * gamma)
    weight = min_snr / snr

    # Weight the loss
    weighted_loss = mse_loss * weight.view(-1, 1, 1, 1, 1)

    return weighted_loss.mean()
```

Interestingly, this Min-SNR approach is exactly what CogVideo pioneered in 2022, two years before Latte proved you could achieve similar results without it. The evolution continued: Open-Sora (March 2024) switched to flow matching for better motion dynamics, then Wan2.2 (July 2025) added mixture of experts on top. Yet all these "advanced" approaches still use MSE at their core—they change what they're predicting (noise versus velocity) or how they weight it.

## Scaling and Distributed Training

Training video generation models presents a unique scaling challenge: the need to process massive amounts of high-dimensional data (videos are 4D tensors!) while maintaining model weights that can reach tens of billions of parameters. The solution is *distributed training*. Before we dive into Latte's approach, let's look at the fundamental parallelism strategies that power modern AI training:

*Data parallelism (DP)*
: Each GPU holds a complete copy of the model but processes different batches of data. Think of it as multiple identical kitchens cooking different dishes from the same recipe. This is what Latte uses: it's simple and effective, and scales linearly with GPU count.

*Model parallelism (MP)*
: The model is split across GPUs, with each GPU holding only part of the layers. Imagine a factory assembly line where each station handles specific components. This is necessary when models exceed single-GPU memory (like HunyuanVideo's 13B parameters).

*Pipeline parallelism (PP)*
: This combines time and space efficiency by having different GPUs process different microbatches through different model segments simultaneously. It's like a car factory where multiple cars are at different stages of assembly. PP is often combined with MP for maximum efficiency.

*3D parallelism*
: This is the ultimate scaling strategy, combining all three approaches. This strategy is used by massive models like Wan2.2's 27B parameters, where data is distributed, the model is sharded, and computation is pipelined across potentially hundreds of GPUs.

Latte achieves state-of-the-art results using only simple data parallelism. This connects back to our configuration system from the beginning of the chapter; we leverage the same YAML file whether we have 1 or 100 GPUs. The data pipeline automatically shards across workers, each GPU receiving its unique subset of videos. The training loop needs just three additional lines for distributed support. This is the power of thoughtful design: complexity that scales without complicating.

## Data Parallelism (Latte Approach)

Latte demonstrates that straightforward PyTorch DDP (`DistributedDataParallel`) is sufficient for most video generation models. This approach avoids the complexity of model sharding or pipeline parallelism while scaling effectively to 8–16 GPUs. The key insight is that efficient model architecture (like Latte's) fits comfortably on a single GPU, making complex parallelism strategies unnecessary.

Why Latte leverages simple DDP:

*Efficient architecture*
: Latte's model fits on single GPU (8–24 GB VRAM).

*Standard PyTorch*
: No custom communication code or complex frameworks are required.

*Easy debugging*
: Each GPU runs identical code with different data.

*Linear scaling*
: Near-perfect speedup is available up to 8 GPUs in a single system.

The following code demonstrates the lightweight DDP configuration used by Latte:

```
# Latte's distributed setup from train.py
import torch.distributed as dist
from torch.nn.parallel import DistributedDataParallel as DDP

def setup_distributed():
    """Minimal distributed setup following Latte."""
    dist.init_process_group("nccl")
    rank = int(os.environ["RANK"])
    local_rank = int(os.environ["LOCAL_RANK"])
    device = torch.device("cuda", local_rank)
    torch.cuda.set_device(device)
    return rank, local_rank, device

# Usage in training
rank, local_rank, device = setup_distributed()
model = model.to(device)
model = DDP(model, device_ids=[local_rank])
```

## Advanced Parallelism

Latte's simple DDP approach works well because the model architecture is efficient. However, as models scale beyond Latte's elegant design—think HunyuanVideo's 13B parameters or Wan2.2's 27B mixture of experts—you'll need more sophisticated parallelism strategies.

Consider advanced approaches only in the following situations:

*Model doesn't fit on single GPU*
: When your model exceeds 24 GB VRAM even with gradient checkpointing

*Batch size of 1 still OOMs*
: When even a single sample overwhelms GPU memory

*Training time exceeds patience*
: When DDP scaling plateaus and months of training isn't acceptable

*Budget permits complexity*
: When you have engineering resources to debug distributed systems

Figure 4-5 illustrates the primary parallelism strategies and when each makes sense. Notice how Latte's approach (data parallel) remains the simplest and most efficient for models under ~10B parameters, while larger models like Wan2.2 require the complexity of 3D parallelism to train efficiently.

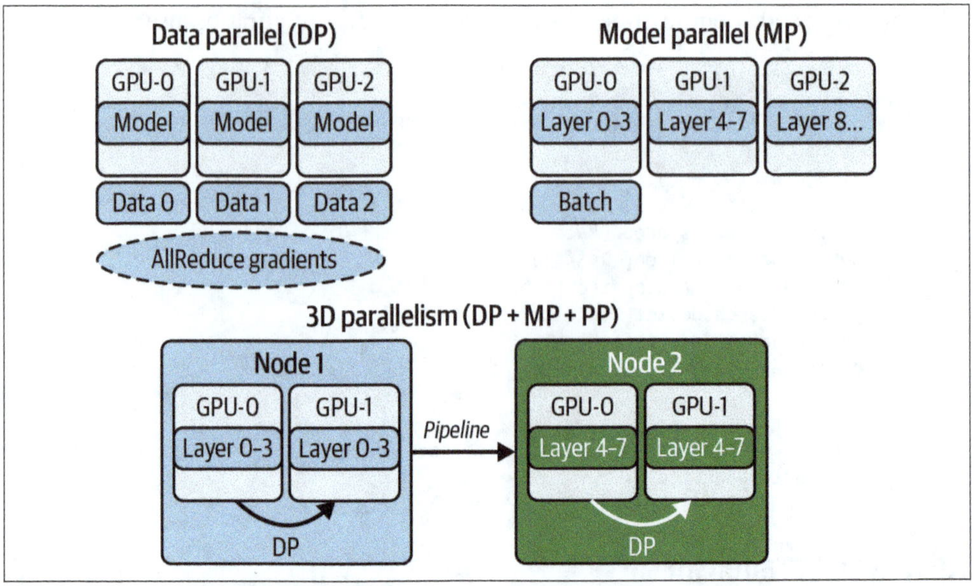


*Figure 4-5. Comparison of distributed training architectures*

## Practical Considerations

Beyond the parallelism strategy, successful distributed training requires attention to additional critical details that Latte handles elegantly:

*Communication—keep it simple*
: Latte uses NCCL's `AllReduce`, nothing fancy. No gradient compression, no asynchronous updates: just reliable gradient averaging. This simplicity means fewer bugs and easier debugging. The performance hit from "unoptimized" communication is negligible compared to the complexity cost of exotic optimizations.

*Checkpointing—save early, save often*
: Training can fail. GPUs crash, jobs time out, gradients explode. Latte saves full checkpoints (model, optimizer, scheduler, random state) every N steps. When training resumes, everything continues exactly where it left off. Simple strategy: keep the last three checkpoints, save to persistent storage, and resume automatically on failure.

## Summary

This chapter walked through the complete training pipeline for video generation models, from data loading to distributed scaling. You've seen how Latte's pragmatic choices—WebVid preprocessing, simple MSE loss, data-parallel training—achieve strong results without unnecessary complexity.

The key insight: production models succeed through engineering excellence, not algorithmic complexity. All the models the chapter analyzed (Latte, Open-Sora, HunyuanVideo, CogVideo, Wan2.2) use variations of MSE loss with careful weighting strategies. The differences lie in scale, data quality, and training stability, not exotic loss functions.

Key takeaways:

*Data matters most*
: Clean, diverse video data beats algorithmic tricks.

*Simple losses work*
: MSE with proper weighting handles video generation well.

*Start with data parallelism*
: Use complex distributed strategies only when necessary.

*Memory optimization is essential*
: Gradient checkpointing and mixed precision are nonnegotiable.

*Robustness over performance*
: Stable training beats fast training.

In Chapter 5 we'll explore fine-tuning strategies that adapt these foundation models to specific creative tasks. The solid training foundation we've built here enables the specialized applications that make video generation truly useful.

CHAPTER 5

# Fine-Tuning for Specific Video Tasks

*Learning objective:* In this chapter you'll look into fine-tuning methods leveraging the CogVideo model from Chapter 1. CogVideo provides an accessible and comprehensive fine-tuning framework developed by Tsinghua University, supporting both LoRA and supervised fine-tuning (SFT) with the necessary tooling required to specialize our model.

In Chapter 4 you focused on gaining intuition via training the Latte model; you configured experiments, implemented training loops, and distributed training across GPUs. This chapter bridges theory and practice. You'll explore *low-rank adaptation* (LoRA) for *parameter-efficient fine-tuning* (PEFT) that requires nominal 16–24 GB VRAM, and *supervised fine-tuning* (SFT) with DeepSpeed integration. Each technique provided includes discussion of environmental requirements, optimization strategies, and issues you may encounter.

Fine-tuning requirements vary dramatically by method and model type:

*LoRA*
: 16 GB (RTX 4080) to 24 GB (RTX 4090) VRAM, 30 minutes to 2 hours training

*SFT*
: 36 GB to 80 GB (A100/H100) VRAM, 2–12 hours training

*Multi-GPU*
: Near-linear scaling with DeepSpeed ZeRO optimization

## Fine-Tuning Methods

Video generation systems use two primary fine-tuning approaches, both integrated into CogVideo's implementation. LoRA enables rapid, memory-efficient adaptation by updating only 1–10% of parameters. SFT provides maximum flexibility by updating all parameters with sophisticated memory optimization. You will implement both using examples aligned with our learning from the previous chapters. Table 5-1 outlines the requirements for each model and resolution.

*Table 5-1. Requirements and resolution capabilities of sample models*

| Model | LoRA VRAM | SFT VRAM | Resolution |
|---|---|---|---|
| CogVideoX-2B | 16 GB | 36 GB | 49 × 480 × 720 |
| CogVideoX-5B | 24 GB | 42 GB | 49 × 480 × 720 |
| CogVideoX1.5-5B | 35 GB | 56 GB | 81 × 768 × 1360 |

### LoRA: Low-Rank Adaptation for Video Models

When CogVideo's team faced the challenge of personalizing their 5B parameter model for specific styles, they needed a solution that wouldn't require 80 GB GPUs for every user. They chose LoRA, which changed how we think about model adaptation. Fine-tuning by decomposing weight updates into low-rank matrices. Building on the attention mechanisms we implemented in Chapter 3, LoRA modifies only the query, key, and value projections. Instead of updating a full weight matrix W, LoRA learns two smaller matrices, A and B, where $W' = W + BA$, reducing trainable parameters by over 90% while maintaining quality in the process. CogVideo's implementation applies LoRA to the transformer's attention layers, achieving this efficiency.

Think of a *weight matrix* like a large spreadsheet with thousands of rows and columns containing the model's knowledge. When you fine-tune, you are essentially editing this spreadsheet and aligning the model toward the provided dataset.

LoRA's insight is most edits follow simple patterns. Imagine adjusting colors in a massive painting. Instead of repainting every pixel, you could describe the change as "make everything 20% warmer and 10% brighter." That's what LoRA does: it captures complex weight changes through simple, low-dimensional transformations.

Consider a weight matrix $W \in \mathbb{R}^{1024 \times 1024}$ containing 1 million parameters. LoRA decomposes updates into the following:

- Matrix $B \in \mathbb{R}^{1024 \times 16}$ (16,384 parameters)
- Matrix $A \in \mathbb{R}^{16 \times 1024}$ (16,384 parameters)
- Total: 32,768 parameters (97% reduction)

The key insight: W′ = W + BA still captures a significant amount of the adaptation quality because most fine-tuning changes lie in a low-dimensional subspace.

## How LoRA Works in CogVideo

CogVideo employs LoRA in the transformer's query, key, value, and output projections:

*Weight decomposition*
: $W \in \mathbb{R}^{d \times k} \rightarrow B \in \mathbb{R}^{d \times r} \times A \in \mathbb{R}^{r \times k}$ where $r << \min(d, k)$

*Rank selection*
: r = 16 for quick adaptation, r = 128 for quality

*Scaling factor*
: $\alpha/r$ where $\alpha = 32$ typically

*Memory savings*
: 2B model: 16 GB VRAM; 5B model: 24 GB VRAM

This achieves 90% or more of full fine-tuning quality with ~10% of the memory. Figure 5-1 illustrates the LoRA architecture, showing how low-rank matrices decompose weight updates and where they inject into the transformer's attention layers.

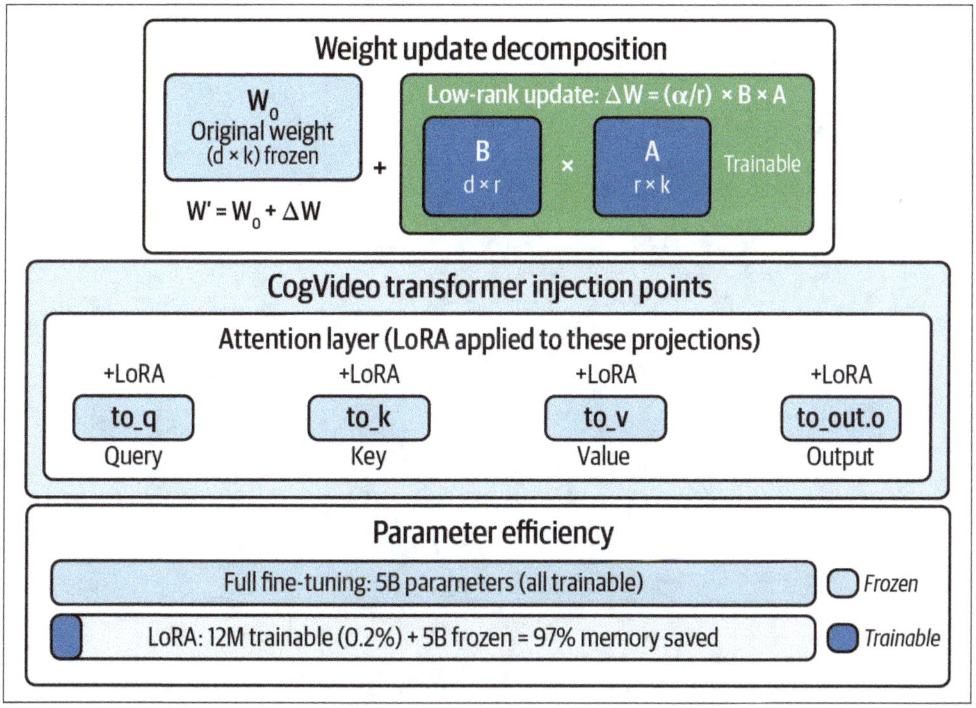


*Figure 5-1. LoRA: Low-rank adaptation architecture*

Let's explore the actual LoRA implementation from CogVideo's production codebase. The configuration class `CogVideoLoRAConfig` captures the settings the project found optimal across different model sizes and hardware constraints. Observe how the configuration targets specific attention layers (query, key, value, output projections)—these components are where adaptation happens most effectively:

```
# LoRA implementation based on CogVideo's production code
import torch
import torch.nn as nn
from diffusers import CogVideoXTransformer3DModel
from peft import LoraConfig, get_peft_model
import math

# CogVideo's LoRA configuration for efficient fine-tuning
class CogVideoLoRAConfig:
    """
    Production LoRA configuration used by CogVideo for different model sizes.
    These settings are proven to work across thousands of fine-tuning runs.
    """

    @staticmethod
    def get_lora_config(model_size: str = "2b", rank: int = 128):
        """Get LoRA configuration for CogVideo models.

        Args:
            model_size: "2b" for 2B model, "5b" for 5B model
            rank: LoRA rank (16 for fast, 128 for quality)

        Returns:
            LoraConfig object for PEFT library
        """

        # Target modules based on CogVideo's implementation
        target_modules = [
            "to_q",  # Query projection
            "to_k",  # Key projection
            "to_v",  # Value projection
            "to_out.0",  # Output projection
        ]

        # Configuration based on model size
        # Note: Repo default lora_alpha=64 (finetune/schemas/args.py:76)
        if model_size == "2b":
            # 2B model: Works on RTX 4080 (16GB)
            config = LoraConfig(
                r=rank,  # LoRA rank (default: 128)
                lora_alpha=64,  # Repo default: 64
                init_lora_weights=True,
                target_modules=target_modules,
            )
        elif model_size == "5b":
            # 5B model: Requires RTX 4090 (24GB)
```

```
        config = LoraConfig(
            r=rank,
            lora_alpha=64,  # Repo default: 64
            init_lora_weights=True,
            target_modules=target_modules,
        )
    else:
        raise ValueError(f"Unsupported model size: {model_size}")

    return config
```

With our LoRA configuration established, you need a way to apply these adapters to our base model. The next code block demonstrates CogVideo's approach to model modification and provides training configurations that are aligned toward documented production runs. Pay attention to the `apply_lora_to_model` function. This function is a simple wrapper around PEFT's functionality, but the real magic lies in the training configurations that follow. These settings represent the sweet spot between training speed and quality. Creating a grid search across all parameter space may be required for more advanced experimentation:

```
def apply_lora_to_model(transformer: CogVideoXTransformer3DModel,
                        lora_config: LoraConfig) -> nn.Module:
    """Apply LoRA to CogVideo transformer model.

    Args:
        transformer: Base CogVideoX transformer
        lora_config: LoRA configuration

    Returns:
        Model with LoRA adapters applied
    """
    # Apply PEFT (Parameter-Efficient Fine-Tuning) to model
    lora_model = get_peft_model(transformer, lora_config)

    # Print trainable parameters (typically 1-10% of total)
    lora_model.print_trainable_parameters()

    return lora_model

# CogVideo's training configuration
class CogVideoTrainingConfig:
    """Training configuration used by CogVideo."""

    # Model configurations
    model_configs = {
        "cogvideox-2b": {
            "learning_rate": 1e-4,
            "batch_size": 1,  # Per GPU
            "gradient_accumulation": 4,
            "mixed_precision": "fp16",
            "max_grad_norm": 1.0,
```

```
            "num_frames": 49,  # Must be 8N+1
            "height": 480,
            "width": 720,
        },
        "cogvideox-5b": {
            "learning_rate": 5e-5,
            "batch_size": 1,
            "gradient_accumulation": 8,
            "mixed_precision": "bf16",
            "max_grad_norm": 1.0,
            "num_frames": 49,
            "height": 480,
            "width": 720,
        },
        "cogvideox1.5-5b": {
            "learning_rate": 5e-5,
            "batch_size": 1,
            "gradient_accumulation": 16,
            "mixed_precision": "bf16",
            "max_grad_norm": 0.5,
            "num_frames": 81,  # Higher frame count
            "height": 768,
            "width": 1360,
        },
    }
```

### Common Pitfall: Rank Selection

Setting LoRA rank too high often provides no quality benefit but doubles memory usage and training time. Documented experiments show the following:

- Rank 16: 85% of full fine-tuning quality (30 minutes training)
- Rank 64: 92% of full fine-tuning quality (1 hour training)
- Rank 128: 95% of full fine-tuning quality (2 hours training)
- Rank 256: 96% of full fine-tuning quality (diminishing returns)

My recommendation is to start with rank = 16 and increase only if validation metrics significantly improve. Most style adaptations work well with rank = 32–64.

Now you come to the heart of the implementation: the actual training class that orchestrates everything. This `CogVideoLoRATrainer` class builds directly on the training infrastructure from Chapter 4. It extends the training loop we created, uses the same loss functions, and adds LoRA-specific optimizations. The class demonstrates several critical design decisions: component separation (VAE, text encoder, transformer), selective freezing (only the transformer gets LoRA adapters), and memory-efficient encoding.

In this code, the VAE and text encoder stay frozen during training, crucial for LoRA's efficiency. The trainer loads components but creates gradients only for LoRA parameters:

```
from diffusers import AutoencoderKLCogVideoX, DDPMScheduler
from transformers import T5EncoderModel
from typing import Dict
import torch.nn.functional as F

class CogVideoLoRATrainer:
    """Production LoRA trainer from CogVideo repository."""

    def __init__(self,
                 model_path: str,
                 output_dir: str,
                 rank: int = 128,
                 learning_rate: float = 2e-5):

        # Load base model components
        self.transformer = CogVideoXTransformer3DModel.from_pretrained(
            model_path, subfolder="transformer"
        )
        self.vae = AutoencoderKLCogVideoX.from_pretrained(
            model_path, subfolder="vae"
        )
        self.text_encoder = T5EncoderModel.from_pretrained(
            model_path, subfolder="text_encoder"
        )

        # Apply LoRA to transformer
        lora_config = CogVideoLoRAConfig.get_lora_config(
            model_size="2b", rank=rank
        )
        self.transformer = apply_lora_to_model(
            self.transformer, lora_config
        )

        # Freeze VAE and text encoder
        self.vae.requires_grad_(False)
        self.text_encoder.requires_grad_(False)

        # Setup optimizer (only LoRA parameters)
        lora_params = filter(
            lambda p: p.requires_grad,
            self.transformer.parameters()
        )
        self.optimizer = torch.optim.AdamW(
            lora_params, lr=learning_rate
        )

        # Initialize scheduler for noise addition
        self.scheduler = DDPMScheduler.from_pretrained(
            model_path, subfolder="scheduler"
```

```
        )

    def encode_video(self, video: torch.Tensor) -> torch.Tensor:
        """Encode video frames to latent space using VAE."""
        # video shape: [B, C, F, H, W]
        with torch.no_grad():
            latent = self.vae.encode(video).latent_dist.sample()
            latent = latent * self.vae.config.scaling_factor
        return latent
```

The next `training_step` method implements the core diffusion training loop adapted for LoRA. This is where theory meets practice: you encode videos to latent space, add noise according to the diffusion schedule, and train the model to predict that noise. The key insight is that only the LoRA parameters update during backpropagation, while the massive base model remains frozen. This single training step, repeated thousands of times, is all it takes to adapt a multibillion parameter model to new domains:

```
def training_step(self, batch: Dict) -> torch.Tensor:
        """Single training step with LoRA fine-tuning."""

        # Encode video to latent space
        video_latents = self.encode_video(batch["video"])

        # Encode text prompt
        prompt_embeds = self.text_encoder(
            batch["input_ids"]
        )[0]

        # Sample timestep for diffusion
        timesteps = torch.randint(
            0, 1000, (video_latents.shape[0],)
        ).to(video_latents.device)

        # Add noise to latents
        noise = torch.randn_like(video_latents)
        noisy_latents = self.scheduler.add_noise(
            video_latents, noise, timesteps
        )

        # Predict noise with LoRA-adapted transformer
        model_pred = self.transformer(
            hidden_states=noisy_latents,
            encoder_hidden_states=prompt_embeds,
            timestep=timesteps,
        ).sample

        # Compute loss
        loss = F.mse_loss(model_pred, noise)

        # Backward pass (only LoRA parameters update)
        loss.backward()
```

```
    # Gradient clipping for stability
    torch.nn.utils.clip_grad_norm_(
        self.transformer.parameters(), max_norm=1.0
    )

    # Optimizer step
    self.optimizer.step()
    self.optimizer.zero_grad()

    return loss
```

Figure 5-2 illustrates the complete LoRA training loop, showing how data flows through the model during each training step. Notice how the VAE and text encoder remain frozen, while only the LoRA adapter parameters receive gradient updates.

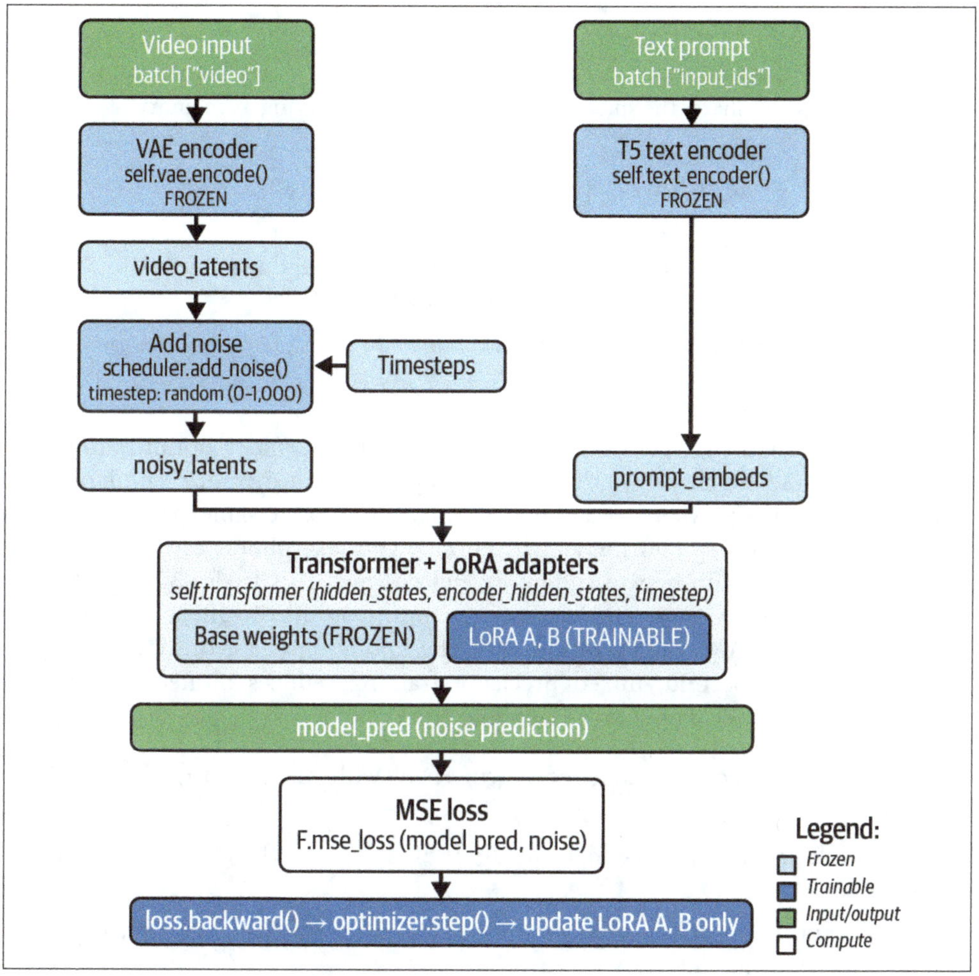


*Figure 5-2. LoRA training step flow*

## Supervised Fine-Tuning (SFT) with DeepSpeed

Although LoRA excels at efficient adaptation, some scenarios demand the full expressiveness of updating all model parameters. SFT provides maximum flexibility but faces a challenge: modern video models often exceed single-GPU memory. Enter DeepSpeed with its ZeRO (Zero Redundancy Optimizer) technology, Microsoft's solution that makes the impossible possible.

DeepSpeed ZeRO works like a perfectly coordinated restaurant kitchen. Imagine a team of chefs preparing an elaborate meal where no single kitchen has enough space for all ingredients and equipment. Traditional training is like every chef having a complete copy of everything redundant and wasteful.

> Here is the DeepSpeed workload distribution:
>
> *ZeRO Stage 1*
> Shares the spice racks (optimizer states), saving 4x memory
>
> *ZeRO Stage 2*
> Also shares prep work (gradients), achieving 8x savings
>
> *ZeRO Stage 3*
> Goes further, distributing even the ingredients (parameters) for Nx savings, where N is the number of GPUs
>
> The result: a 10-person team can prepare a meal requiring 10x the space of any single kitchen.

Beyond distribution strategies, SFT employs two critical memory-optimization techniques. First, gradient checkpointing trades computation for memory. Think of it like climbing a mountain where you must return by the exact same path; instead of remembering every step (storing all activations), you take photos only at waypoints and recompute the path between them during descent. This trades 30%–50% more computation time for 60%–80% memory savings. CogVideoX-5B, which normally requires 48 GB VRAM, fits in 24 GB with checkpointing enabled, though training takes 1.4x longer. Second, mixed precision training reduces numerical precision where it doesn't matter. Think of it like photo compression:

- fp32 (full precision) is like shooting in RAW with maximum quality but huge files.
- fp16 (half precision) is like high-quality JPEG images—99% of the quality at 50% the size.
- bf16 (brain float) offers even better dynamic range for the same size, making it ideal for video models.

The technique uses lower precision for most computations while keeping fp32 for critical operations like loss scaling and weight updates. The result of mixed precision is 2x memory savings, 2–3x speedup, with less than 1% quality loss.

> fp16 works on any GPU (RTX 20-series or newer), whereas bf16 requires Ampere architecture or newer (RTX 30-series, A100, H100).

Table 5-2 summarizes how each ZeRO stage trades memory against training speed.

*Table 5-2. Memory requirements and training speed by ZeRO stage*

| Configuration | ZeRO stage | Memory required | Training speed | Use case |
|---|---|---|---|---|
| Basic | ZeRO-1 | 36 GB | 1x (baseline) | Single A100, fast iteration |
| Balanced | ZeRO-2 + Gradient Checkpointing | 24 GB | 0.7x | CogVideoX-2B/5B on consumer GPUs |
| Maximum | ZeRO-3 + CPU Offload | 16 GB + System RAM | 0.3x | Large models on limited hardware |

> Practical recommendations:
>
> - Start with ZeRO-2 for most fine-tuning tasks—it provides the best balance of speed and memory efficiency.
> - Enable gradient checkpointing only when you hit memory limits—the speed penalty is significant.
> - Use bf16 mixed precision if your GPU supports it (Ampere or newer); otherwise, fp16.
> - CPU offloading (ZeRO-3) should be a last resort—training becomes 3–5x slower.

The following DeepSpeed configuration is the result of optimization experiments leveraged to maximize training efficiency on limited hardware. Each parameter requires tuning from bucket sizes that optimize communication overhead to gradient accumulation steps that balance memory usage with training stability. The configuration enables training a 5B parameter model on a single A100 GPU, something that would typically require 8x the memory without these optimizations:

```
# DeepSpeed configuration for CogVideo SFT
class DeepSpeedConfig:
    """Production DeepSpeed configurations for different hardware."""

    @staticmethod
    def get_zero2_config():
        """ZeRO-2: For single GPU with 36GB+ VRAM"""
```

```python
    return {
        "train_batch_size": "auto",
        "gradient_accumulation_steps": "auto",
        "gradient_clipping": 1.0,
        "zero_optimization": {
            "stage": 2,
            "offload_optimizer": {
                "device": "cpu",  # Offload to CPU
                "pin_memory": True
            },
            "allgather_partitions": True,
            "allgather_bucket_size": 2e8,
            "reduce_scatter": True,
            "reduce_bucket_size": 2e8,
            "overlap_comm": True,
            "contiguous_gradients": True
        },
        "fp16": {
            "enabled": True,
            "loss_scale": 0,
            "loss_scale_window": 1000,
            "initial_scale_power": 16,
            "hysteresis": 2,
            "min_loss_scale": 1
        }
    }
```

This DeepSpeed configuration represents the initial stages of optimization. In production, you'd also configure gradient checkpointing (trading computation for memory), activation checkpointing (storing only essential activations), and CPU offloading strategies. The beauty of CogVideo's implementation is that these complexities are abstracted away, and you can simply choose a configuration profile based on your hardware—the framework handles the rest.

## Choosing Between LoRA and SFT

The choice between LoRA and SFT depends on your specific requirements and resources available in your training environment. Table 5-3 adapted from CogVideo's documentation provides clear guidance on when to use each approach and the estimated time requirements for each approach.

*Table 5-3. LoRA versus SFT time estimates and decision support*

| Factor | Use LoRA | Use SFT |
|---|---|---|
| Dataset size | 100–1000 videos | 1000+ videos |
| Training time | 30 minutes to 2 hours | 2–12 hours |
| Hardware | RTX 4080/4090 | A100/H100 |
| Task switching | Easy | Fixed |
| Quality ceiling | 90%–95% | 100% |

## Decision Guide: When to Use Each Method

Choose LoRA when you have limited GPU memory (16–24 GB available) and need quick iteration cycles. This method excels when you need to maintain multiple styles or adaptations simultaneously—imagine serving personalized video styles for different users or brands. LoRA is perfect for training datasets with fewer than 1,000 examples and moderate domain shifts within the same general category. If you're serving multiple fine-tuned models in production and need to swap between them quickly, LoRA's small adapter weights make this process trivial.

Choose SFT when you have access to multiple GPUs or high-memory cards (40 GB+) and need absolute maximum quality. This approach is essential for significant domain shifts from the base model—think medical imaging or scientific visualization. When training on more than 10,000 examples or creating a new foundation model for your specific domain, SFT provides the flexibility to reshape the entire model. For production deployments where that final 5%–10% quality improvement justifies 10x more resources, SFT delivers the results.

> Start with LoRA for rapid prototyping and validation. It provides 90%–95% of full fine-tuning quality at 10% of the cost. Only invest in SFT after validating that the approach works and that extra 5%–10% quality improvement justifies the 10x increase in resources.

Now that I've covered the fundamental fine-tuning methods—LoRA for efficiency and SFT for maximum quality—we face a critical question: how do these techniques perform when the target domain differs dramatically from the training data? Medical imaging looks nothing like natural video, satellite footage has unique perspectives, and artistic styles require specialized understanding. "Common Fine-Tuning Issues" on page 146 explores how to bridge these domain gaps while preserving the model's core capabilities.

## Common Fine-Tuning Issues

This section covers five issues commonly encountered in fine-tuning.

### Issue 1: RuntimeError—Tensor Size Mismatch

Error: "The size of tensor a (45) must match the size of tensor b (44)."

Cause: CogVideo requires frames to follow 8N+1 pattern (9, 17, 25, 33, 41, 49, etc.)

Solution:

- Use resolution "17 × 384 × 384" for testing (17 frames)
- Use resolution "49 × 480 × 720" for production (49 frames)
- Calculate: frames = 8 × latent_frames + 1

### Issue 2: CUDA Out of Memory (OOM)

Error: "CUDA out of memory. Tried to allocate X GB."

Solutions (in order of effectiveness):

1. Enable gradient checkpointing: Add `--gradient_checkpointing`
2. Reduce batch size: set `batch_size=1`, increase `gradient_accumulation`
3. Lower precision: use fp16 instead of fp32
4. Reduce resolution: start with smaller frames/resolution
5. Use LoRA instead of SFT: 90% memory reduction
6. Clear cache between training and inference: `torch.cuda.empty_cache(); gc.collect()`

### Issue 3: Training Not Converging

Symptoms: Loss plateaus, generated videos are noisy or static

Common causes and fixes:

- Learning rate too high: start with 1e-5 for LoRA, 5e-6 for SFT
- Insufficient data: need at least 50–100 videos for style transfer
- Wrong alpha value: set `lora_alpha = lora_rank` for video models
- Dataset issues: check videos are properly normalized to [−1, 1]

## Issue 4: Mixed Precision Training Fails

Error: "Expected cuda:0 but got cuda:1" or NaN losses

Solutions:

- bf16 requirements: Requires Ampere GPUs (RTX 30-series, A100+)
- fp16 overflow: Add loss scaling: `--fp16_scale_tolerance 0.25`
- Gradient explosion: Set `--max_grad_norm 1.0`

## Issue 5: LoRA Weights Not Loading

Error: "Weights may not be valid" or no effect after loading

Validation steps:

1. Check file size: `adapter_model.bin` should be rank × target_modules × 4 bytes
2. Verify config: `adapter_config.json` must match training settings
3. Load order: base model first, then LoRA weights
4. Test with higher alpha: `lora_scale=2.0` during inference

# Domain Adaptation and Transfer Learning

Real-world video generation often involves domains far from the original training distribution. Medical imaging, satellite footage, underwater scenes, and microscopy videos have unique characteristics that general models struggle with. Domain adaptation techniques bridge this gap, transferring knowledge from source to target domains efficiently.

### Understanding domain shift

Domain shift is like an artist trained on oil paintings trying to work with watercolors. The fundamental skills transfer (composition, color theory, perspective), but the specific techniques need adaptation. The paint behaves differently, drying times change, and blending methods vary. The domain adaptation methods below teach the model these new "brush techniques" without forgetting the artistic fundamentals.

Common domain shifts in video present unique challenges. The shift from natural scenes to medical imaging, X-rays, MRIs, and ultrasounds requires understanding entirely different visual patterns and motion dynamics. Moving from photorealistic to animated styles demands learning artistic conventions and exaggerated physics. The scale shift from human-visible to microscopic cellular footage introduces novel motion patterns like Brownian motion and cell division. Even perspective changes, from ground-level to satellite or drone views, require relearning spatial relationships and movement patterns.

### Unsupervised domain adaptation

When labeled data in the target domain is scarce or expensive, unsupervised domain adaptation leverages unlabeled target videos to align the model's representations. This approach is particularly valuable in specialized fields where expert annotation is costly.

The following implementation demonstrates the elegance of adversarial domain adaptation, building on the feature extraction capabilities we developed in Chapter 3's attention mechanisms. The core idea is to train a feature extractor that "fools" a domain discriminator: if the discriminator can't tell which domain the features come from, then we've successfully learned domain-invariant representations.

We'll build this system piece by piece, starting with this code snippet, which illustrates the gradient reversal layer that makes the adversarial training possible:

```
# Domain adaptation framework for video models
import torch
import torch.nn as nn
import torch.nn.functional as F
from torch.autograd import Function
from torch.utils.data import DataLoader
import numpy as np

class GradientReversalFunction(Function):
    """Gradient reversal for adversarial domain adaptation"""

    @staticmethod
    def forward(ctx, x, lambda_):
        ctx.lambda_ = lambda_
        return x.view_as(x)

    @staticmethod
    def backward(ctx, grad_output):
        return grad_output.neg() * ctx.lambda_, None

class DomainDiscriminator(nn.Module):
    """Discriminator for adversarial domain adaptation"""

    def __init__(self, feature_dim: int, hidden_dim: int = 256):
        super().__init__()

        self.discriminator = nn.Sequential(
            nn.Linear(feature_dim, hidden_dim),
            nn.ReLU(),
            nn.Dropout(0.5),
            nn.Linear(hidden_dim, hidden_dim // 2),
            nn.ReLU(),
```

```
            nn.Dropout(0.5),
            nn.Linear(hidden_dim // 2, 1)
        )

    def forward(self, x: torch.Tensor, lambda_: float = 1.0):
        # Apply gradient reversal
        x = GradientReversalFunction.apply(x, lambda_)
        return self.discriminator(x)
```

This gradient reversal layer is deceptively simple but incredibly powerful. During the forward pass, it's invisible, just passing data through. But during backpropagation, it flips the sign of gradients, causing the feature extractor to maximize the domain discriminator's loss rather than minimize it. This adversarial dynamic is what drives domain alignment. Now let's build the complete domain adaptation architecture. This model combines several techniques: adversarial training through the discriminator, domain-specific batch normalization to handle different data distributions, and domain embeddings for explicit conditioning. Each component serves a specific purpose in achieving cross-domain performance:

```
class DomainAdaptationVideoModel(nn.Module):
    """Video model with domain adaptation capabilities"""

    def __init__(self,
                 base_model: nn.Module,
                 feature_dim: int,
                 num_domains: int = 2,
                 adaptation_method: str = 'adversarial'):
        super().__init__()

        self.base_model = base_model
        self.feature_dim = feature_dim
        self.num_domains = num_domains
        self.adaptation_method = adaptation_method

        # Domain discriminator for adversarial adaptation
        if adaptation_method == 'adversarial':
            self.domain_discriminator = DomainDiscriminator(feature_dim)

        # Domain-specific batch norm layers
        self.domain_bn = nn.ModuleList([
            nn.BatchNorm1d(feature_dim) for _ in range(num_domains)
        ])

        # Feature alignment layers
        self.alignment_proj = nn.Linear(feature_dim, feature_dim)

        # Domain embedding for conditioning
        self.domain_embed = nn.Embedding(num_domains, feature_dim)
```

This model sets up our domain adaptation infrastructure. Notice the domain-specific batch normalization layers: these are crucial because different domains often have vastly different feature statistics (think medical X-rays versus natural videos). By maintaining separate normalization statistics per domain while sharing all other weights, we get the best of both worlds: adaptation and parameter efficiency. The following methods show how features flow through this architecture. The `extract_features` method applies domain-specific normalization, while the `forward` method orchestrates the full pipeline including optional domain classification for adversarial training:

```
def extract_features(self, x: torch.Tensor, domain_id: int = None):
        """Extract features with optional domain-specific normalization"""
        features = self.base_model.encode(x)

        # Apply domain-specific batch normalization
        if domain_id is not None and domain_id < self.num_domains:
            B, T, D = features.shape
            features = features.reshape(B * T, D)
            features = self.domain_bn[domain_id](features)
            features = features.reshape(B, T, D)

        return features

def forward(self, x: torch.Tensor, domain_id: int = None,
                return_domain_loss: bool = False, lambda_: float = 1.0):
        # Extract features
        features = self.extract_features(x, domain_id)

        # Apply domain conditioning if available
        if domain_id is not None:
            domain_emb = self.domain_embed(torch.tensor(
                [domain_id],
                device=x.device,
            ))
            features = features + domain_emb.unsqueeze(1)

        # Generate video
        output = self.base_model.decode(features)

        if return_domain_loss and self.adaptation_method == 'adversarial':
            # Compute domain classification loss
            domain_pred = self.domain_discriminator(features.mean(
                dim=1),
                lambda_
            )
            return output, domain_pred

        return output
```

With our model architecture complete, we need a training procedure that balances two competing objectives: maintaining good performance on the source domain task while learning features that transfer to the target domain. The `DomainAdaptationTrainer` class manages this delicate balance. It coordinates data loading from both domains, computes the various loss components, and implements the training schedule that gradually increases adversarial strength:

```
class DomainAdaptationTrainer:
    """Trainer for domain adaptation of video models"""

    def __init__(self,
                 model: DomainAdaptationVideoModel,
                 source_loader: DataLoader,
                 target_loader: DataLoader,
                 optimizer: torch.optim.Optimizer,
                 device: str = 'cuda'):

        self.model = model
        self.source_loader = source_loader
        self.target_loader = target_loader
        self.optimizer = optimizer
        self.device = device

        # Loss functions
        self.task_criterion = nn.MSELoss()
        self.domain_criterion = nn.BCEWithLogitsLoss()

        # Training statistics
        self.global_step = 0
        self.epoch = 0
```

This implements a carefully orchestrated balance between three objectives: task performance (on the source domain), domain discrimination (distinguishing domains), and domain confusion (fooling the discriminator). The `lambda_schedule` is critical. Starting with low values allows the model to learn basic features before gradually enforcing domain invariance. Watch how the implementation handles the two data streams and computes separate losses for each objective:

```
def train_epoch(self, lambda_schedule: callable = None):
        """Train for one epoch with domain adaptation"""
        self.model.train()

        source_iter = iter(self.source_loader)
        target_iter = iter(self.target_loader)

        total_task_loss = 0
        total_domain_loss = 0

        for step in range(len(self.source_loader)):
            # Get lambda for gradient reversal
            if lambda_schedule:
```

```
        lambda_ = lambda_schedule(self.global_step)
    else:
        lambda_ = 2 / (1 + np.exp(-10 * self.global_step / 1000)) - 1

    # Load source batch
    try:
        source_batch = next(source_iter)
    except StopIteration:
        source_iter = iter(self.source_loader)
        source_batch = next(source_iter)

    # Load target batch
    try:
        target_batch = next(target_iter)
    except StopIteration:
        target_iter = iter(self.target_loader)
        target_batch = next(target_iter)

    # Move to device
    source_videos = source_batch['frames'].to(self.device)
    target_videos = target_batch['frames'].to(self.device)
```

Now we reach the crucial loss computation that makes domain adaptation work. This code block shows the interplay between three forces: the task loss (keeping the model good at its original job), the domain loss (training the discriminator to tell domains apart), and the gradient reversal (secretly training the feature extractor to confuse the discriminator). The balance weight of 0.1 for domain loss is empirically determined—too high and you lose task performance, too low and you don't achieve domain invariance:

```
# Forward pass for source domain (with task loss)
            source_output, source_domain_pred = self.model(
                source_videos, domain_id=0,
                return_domain_loss=True, lambda_=lambda_
            )

            # Forward pass for target domain (no task loss)
            _, target_domain_pred = self.model(
                target_videos, domain_id=1,
                return_domain_loss=True, lambda_=lambda_
            )

            # Task loss (only for source domain)
            task_loss = self.task_criterion(source_output, source_videos)

            # Domain classification loss
            source_domain_labels = torch.zeros(
                source_domain_pred.shape[0], 1
            ).to(self.device)
            target_domain_labels = torch.ones(
                target_domain_pred.shape[0], 1
            ).to(self.device)
```

```
            domain_loss = self.domain_criterion(
                source_domain_pred, source_domain_labels
            ) + self.domain_criterion(
                target_domain_pred, target_domain_labels
            )

            # Combined loss
            total_loss = task_loss + 0.1 * domain_loss

            # Backward pass
            self.optimizer.zero_grad()
            total_loss.backward()
            self.optimizer.step()

            # Update statistics
            total_task_loss += task_loss.item()
            total_domain_loss += domain_loss.item()
            self.global_step += 1

            if step % 100 == 0:
                print(f"Step {step}: Task Loss: {task_loss:.4f}, "
                      f"Domain Loss: {domain_loss:.4f}, Lambda: {lambda_:.3f}")

        self.epoch += 1
        return {
            'task_loss': total_task_loss / len(self.source_loader),
            'domain_loss': total_domain_loss / len(self.source_loader)
        }
```

#### Cross-domain video generation

Having established how to adapt models between domains, let's explore a related but distinct challenge: generating videos that translate content from one visual domain to another. Unlike domain adaptation, which aims for invariance, cross-domain generation explicitly leverages domain differences for creative purposes. Imagine converting real-world footage to animation style, or medical scans to simplified diagrams. This technique opens up fascinating possibilities for data augmentation and artistic expression. Figure 5-3 illustrates how cross-domain generation through shared latent space enables video translation between visual domains.

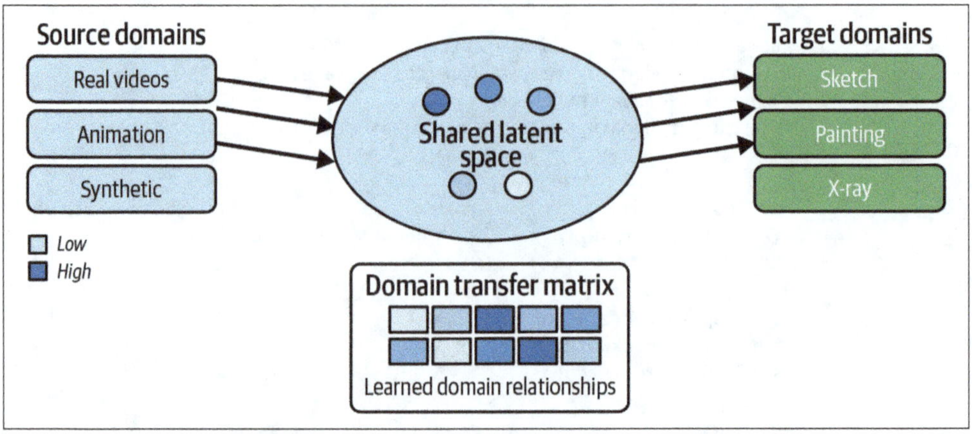

*Figure 5-3. Cross-domain video generation pipeline*

Domain adaptation enables video models to work effectively in new visual domains through adversarial training, feature alignment, and cross-domain generation. These techniques are essential for deploying models in specialized fields where training data differs significantly from general datasets.

# Few-Shot and Zero-Shot Video Generation

The fine-tuning methods we've explored so far—LoRA, SFT, and domain adaptation—all require substantial training data. But what happens when you need to generate videos of a rare animal species with only three reference clips? Or what if you need to create animations in a unique artistic style from a single example? This is where few-shot and zero-shot learning become essential. These techniques push the boundaries of generalization, enabling models to understand and generate novel concepts from minimal or even no direct training examples.

## Meta-Learning for Video Generation

Meta-learning fundamentally changes how we think about model training. Instead of optimizing for a specific task, we train the model to be good at learning new tasks quickly. Think of it as the difference between memorizing answers versus learning problem-solving strategies. For video generation, this means a model that can see five examples of a new animation style and immediately start generating videos in that style without full retraining. The following strategies have proven effective in production systems:

*MAML (model-agnostic meta-learning)*
: Finds initialization that adapts quickly

*Prototypical networks*
: Learns representative prototypes for each class

*Gradient-based adaptation*
: Fine-tunes with few examples using learned priors

*Memory-augmented models*
: Stores and retrieves relevant examples dynamically

## Compositional Video Generation

Humans effortlessly combine concepts they've never seen together. We can imagine a "purple elephant playing piano" even if we've never witnessed such a scene. Compositional video generation aims to replicate this ability. The key insight is that complex scenes decompose into simpler, reusable components: objects, actions, styles, and environments. By learning these components separately and understanding how they combine, models can generate an exponential variety of videos from a linear number of concepts. This is particularly powerful when combined with the LoRA adapters we discussed earlier where each adapter can specialize in a different component.

## Prompt Engineering and In-Context Learning

The rise of large language models has shown us that sufficiently large models can adapt to new tasks simply through clever prompting and no training required. Video generation models are beginning to exhibit similar capabilities. By carefully crafting text prompts, providing reference frames, or using attention manipulation techniques, we can guide models to generate highly specific outputs. This is the most accessible form of model adaptation, requiring no GPU resources or technical expertise, just creativity and understanding of how the model interprets inputs.

Effective video prompts combine multiple modalities: text descriptions, reference frames, motion sketches, and style examples. The key is providing sufficient context while allowing creative freedom. Techniques like prompt chaining, negative prompts, and attention weighting give fine-grained control over generation.

Few-shot and zero-shot techniques enable video models to generate novel content with minimal examples. Meta-learning provides rapid adaptation, compositional understanding enables concept combination, and prompt engineering offers gradient-free customization. These approaches dramatically expand the practical applicability of video generation models.

# Evaluation and Benchmarking Fine-Tuned Models

After investing time and resources into fine-tuning, how do you know if your model actually improved? Generic metrics like FID or IS tell only part of the story. A model fine-tuned for precise motion control might score poorly on diversity metrics but excel at trajectory accuracy. This section builds evaluation frameworks tailored to specific fine-tuning objectives, ensuring you measure what actually matters for your application.

## Task-Specific Evaluation Metrics

The evaluation framework below categorizes metrics by task type, recognizing that each application has unique success criteria. Motion control cares about physical accuracy, style transfer prioritizes artistic consistency, domain adaptation balances source performance with target quality, and general generation focuses on overall visual quality. By selecting appropriate metrics for your specific use case, you avoid the common pitfall of optimizing for the wrong objective. Figure 5-4 illustrates how these task-specific metrics aggregate into a comprehensive evaluation framework.

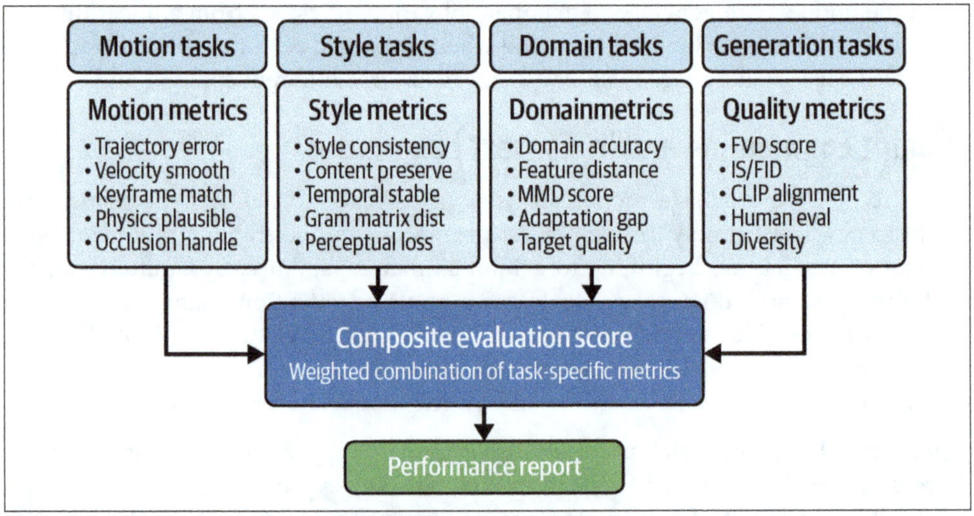


*Figure 5-4. Evaluation framework for fine-tuned video models across different task categories*

## Ablation Studies and Analysis

Understanding which components contribute to performance improvements is crucial for iterative model development. Ablation studies systematically remove or modify components to measure their impact, revealing insights about model behavior and optimization opportunities.

## Transfer Learning Effectiveness

Measuring how well fine-tuned models transfer to related tasks provides insights into their generalization capabilities. A model fine-tuned for cartoon animation should perform better on anime generation than a model fine-tuned for medical imaging.

Comprehensive evaluation of fine-tuned models requires task-specific metrics, systematic ablation studies, and transfer learning analysis. By implementing rigorous evaluation frameworks, we can quantify improvements, identify optimization opportunities, and ensure models meet application requirements.

# Practical Execution: Running Your First Fine-Tuning

Theory and architecture are essential, but nothing beats hands-on experience. This section provides concrete, runnable examples from CogVideo's repository that you can execute today. We'll walk through dataset preparation, configuration, and actual training commands that work on consumer hardware.

## Setting Up Your Environment

Before fine-tuning, you need the right environment. CogVideo requires the latest diffusers branch since the production code hasn't been merged to the main release yet. Here's the complete setup process:

```
# Clone and install the development version of diffusers
git clone https://github.com/huggingface/diffusers.git
cd diffusers
pip install -e .

# Clone CogVideo repository for fine-tuning scripts
git clone https://github.com/THUDM/CogVideo.git
cd CogVideo/finetune

# Install additional dependencies
pip install accelerate tensorboard transformers peft
pip install huggingface_hub

# For DeepSpeed (SFT only)
pip install deepspeed
```

## Preparing Your Dataset

CogVideo expects a specific dataset structure that's refreshingly simple. For a Disney cartoon fine-tuning example, here's what your dataset should look like:

```
# Dataset structure for Text-to-Video (T2V)
disney_dataset/
├── prompts.txt          # One prompt per line
├── videos/              # Directory containing .mp4 files
```

```
│   ├── scene_001.mp4
│   ├── scene_002.mp4
│   └── ...
└── videos.txt              # List of video filenames

# For Image-to-Video (I2V), add:
├── images/                 # Reference frames (optional)
│   ├── frame_001.png
│   └── ...
└── images.txt              # List of image filenames
```

Here's a practical example using the Disney Steamboat Willie dataset, which is publicly available and perfect for testing:

```
# Download sample dataset
huggingface-cli login
mkdir -p disney_dataset
hf download Wild-Heart/Disney-VideoGeneration-Dataset \
  --repo-type dataset \
  --local-dir disney_dataset

# Create file lists
cd disney_dataset
ls videos/*.mp4 > videos.txt
# Each video needs a corresponding prompt in prompts.txt
```

## LoRA Fine-Tuning: Quick Start

Let's start with LoRA fine-tuning on a single GPU. This configuration from CogVideo's production scripts trains in under two hours:

```
#!/bin/bash
# train_lora_4090.sh - LoRA training for RTX 4090 (24GB)

# Prevent tokenizer warnings
export TOKENIZERS_PARALLELISM=false

# Launch training with accelerate
accelerate launch train.py \
    --model_path "THUDM/CogVideoX-2B" \
    --model_name "cogvideox-t2v" \
    --model_type "t2v" \
    --training_type "lora" \
    --output_dir "./outputs/disney_lora" \
    --data_root "./disney_dataset" \
    --caption_column "prompts.txt" \
    --video_column "videos.txt" \
    --train_resolution "49x480x720" \
    --train_epochs 10 \
    --batch_size 1 \
    --gradient_accumulation_steps 4 \
    --mixed_precision "fp16" \
```

```
    --learning_rate 1e-4 \
    --rank 128 \
    --checkpointing_steps 100 \
    --seed 42
```

Monitor training progress with TensorBoard:

```
# In a separate terminal
tensorboard --logdir ./outputs/disney_lora/logs
```

## SFT with DeepSpeed: Maximum Quality

For full SFT, DeepSpeed enables training on consumer GPUs through memory optimization. This configuration works on a single RTX 4090 with CPU offloading:

```
# deepspeed_config.json - ZeRO-2 with CPU offload
{
    "train_batch_size": "auto",
    "gradient_accumulation_steps": "auto",
    "zero_optimization": {
        "stage": 2,
        "offload_optimizer": {
            "device": "cpu",
            "pin_memory": true
        },
        "allgather_partitions": true,
        "allgather_bucket_size": 2e8,
        "reduce_scatter": true
    },
    "fp16": {
        "enabled": true,
        "loss_scale": 0,
        "loss_scale_window": 1000
    }
}
```

With the config in place, launch training with the following `DeepSpeed` script:

```
#!/bin/bash
# train_sft_deepspeed.sh - SFT with DeepSpeed

accelerate launch --config_file accelerate_config.yaml train.py \
    --model_path "THUDM/CogVideoX-2B" \
    --training_type "sft" \
    --use_deepspeed \
    --deepspeed_config "./deepspeed_config.json" \
    --output_dir "./outputs/disney_sft" \
    --data_root "./disney_dataset" \
    --train_epochs 5 \
    --batch_size 1 \
    --gradient_accumulation_steps 8 \
    --learning_rate 5e-5
```

## Multi-GPU Training: Scaling Up

With multiple GPUs, training becomes significantly faster. CogVideo supports both DDP and DeepSpeed distribution strategies:

```
# For 8x DGX cluster
# accelerate_config_multi.yaml
compute_environment: LOCAL_MACHINE
distributed_type: MULTI_GPU
num_machines: 1
num_processes: 8
gpu_ids: all
mixed_precision: fp16

# Launch distributed training
accelerate launch --config_file accelerate_config_multi.yaml train.py \
    --model_path "THUDM/CogVideoX-5B" \
    --training_type "lora" \
    --rank 256 \
    --train_resolution "49x480x720" \
    --batch_size 2 \
    --gradient_accumulation_steps 1
```

## Inference with Fine-Tuned Models

After training, generate videos with your fine-tuned model:

```
from diffusers import CogVideoXPipeline
from diffusers import CogVideoXDPMScheduler
import torch

# Load base model
pipe = CogVideoXPipeline.from_pretrained(
    "THUDM/CogVideoX-2B",
    torch_dtype=torch.float16
).to("cuda")

# Load LoRA weights
pipe.load_lora_weights("./outputs/disney_lora/checkpoint-1000")

# Generate video
prompt = "Mickey Mouse steering a steamboat, black and white cartoon style"
video_frames = pipe(
    prompt=prompt,
    num_videos_per_prompt=1,
    num_frames=49,
    guidance_scale=6.0,
).frames[0]

# Save video
from diffusers.utils import export_to_video
export_to_video(video_frames, "mickey_steamboat.mp4", fps=8)
```

Training tips from production:

*Resolution matters*
: Start with lower resolution (480 × 720) for faster iteration.

*Frame count*
: Must be 8N + 1 (49, 81, 113); 49 frames is usually sufficient.

*Gradient accumulation*
: Simulate larger batches on limited VRAM.

*Validation frequency*
: Check quality every 100–200 steps to catch issues early.

*Cache management*
: CogVideo caches encoded latents. Delete cache if you modify data.

## Production Examples

Table 5-4 provides example configurations used to fine-tune CogVideo.

*Table 5-4. Sample fine-tuning examples*

| Use case | Dataset size | Method | Training time | Hardware |
|---|---|---|---|---|
| Cartoon style | 500 clips | LoRA r = 128 | 1.5 hours | 1x RTX 4090 |
| Medical imaging | 2,000 clips | SFT + DeepSpeed | 8 hours | 4x A100 40 GB |
| Game assets | 100 clips | LoRA r = 64 | 30 minutes | 1x RTX 4080 |
| Brand videos | 5,000 clips | SFT + ZeRO-3 | 12 hours | 8x RTX 4090 |

This guide helps you transform theory into action. With CogVideo's production scripts and the dataset examples, you can start fine-tuning within about an hour. Remember: start with LoRA for quick experiments, use your smallest dataset first, and scale up only when you've validated the approach. The configurations provided here are tested and will save you time on trial and error.

# Summary

This chapter shifted from theoretical fine-tuning to production methods used by leading video generation systems. You implemented CogVideo's LoRA and SFT approaches, complete with hardware requirements, training configurations, and optimization strategies. These aren't solely academic exercises; they're the exact techniques underlying modern video generation.

You learned that successful fine-tuning isn't about complex algorithms but practical engineering. LoRA delivers 90% quality with 10% of the resources, making it perfect for rapid iteration. SFT provides that final quality push when needed. CogVideo's framework, with DeepSpeed integration and memory optimization, makes both approaches accessible even on consumer hardware.

Key insights from this chapter:

*LoRA is the workhorse*
: 16–24 GB VRAM, 30 minutes to 2 hours of training, easy task switching

*SFT for production*
: When you need maximum quality and have the resources

*DeepSpeed enables everything*
: ZeRO optimization makes large models trainable

*Start simple*
: LoRA with rank 16–128 solves most problems

*Hardware reality*
: RTX 4090 for LoRA, A100 for SFT

The foundation built by combining Latte's architecture with CogVideo's fine-tuning provides a complete pipeline from training to deployment. Armed with production-tested fine-tuning methods, you are ready for Chapter 6, where we'll explore vision-language models and how they support multimodal learning.

CHAPTER 6

# Vision-Language Models for Video Understanding

*Learning objective:* In this chapter, you will learn the architecture and implementation of vision-language models (VLMs) for video understanding, including the three-component design (vision encoder, projector, language model), 3D positional encoding for spatiotemporal reasoning, and building practical video question-answering systems with fine-tuning capabilities.

Building on Chapter 5's fine-tuning techniques, we now tackle a complementary challenge: given a video, how can a model understand and reason about its contents? VLMs provide the answer, transforming video understanding into a language modeling problem. As discussed in Chapter 2, fully semantic understanding is an additional benefit to leveraging VLMs.

## From Generation to Understanding

If video *generation* is like painting from a description, video *understanding* is like art criticism that analyzes what's already there. The previous chapters taught you to create video from images and text; this chapter teaches you to extract meaning from video as text. These capabilities are complementary: generation creates content; understanding interprets it. Together, they form a complete loop for video AI applications.

### The Two Sides of Video AI

Consider two scenarios that illustrate the distinction between generation and understanding:

*Generation*

A filmmaker types "A golden retriever runs through autumn leaves in slow motion" into CogVideo. The model iteratively denoises random noise, guided by the text embedding, until it produces a coherent video matching the description. The input is text; the output is pixels.

*Understanding*

A security analyst uploads surveillance footage and asks, "At what time does the person in the red jacket enter the building?" A VLM processes the video frames, correlates visual features with the question, and responds, "The person in the red jacket enters at 02:34." The input is pixels plus text; the output is text.

These two capabilities are, as mentioned, complementary. Generation creates content; understanding interprets it. Together, they form a complete loop: we can generate videos, analyze what we've created, and use that analysis to inform further generation. Many emerging applications—from video editing assistants to autonomous video production pipelines—require both capabilities working in concert.

Real-world applications of video understanding span numerous domains:

*Video search*

Finding specific moments in large video archives based on natural language queries

*Accessibility*

Generating audio descriptions of video content for visually impaired users

*Content moderation*

Automatically detecting policy violations in uploaded videos

*Surveillance analysis*

Answering investigative queries about recorded footage

*Sports analytics*

Extracting structured data about plays, player positions, and game events

*Medical imaging*

Interpreting video from endoscopy, ultrasound, or surgical recordings

## The Paradigm Shift

The architectural approach to video understanding differs fundamentally from video generation. In Chapters 3 through 5, we worked with diffusion models that operate in continuous latent or pixel space, iteratively refining noisy representations toward clean outputs. VLMs take a different approach: they convert visual information into discrete tokens and process those tokens using the same autoregressive mechanisms that power large language models (LLMs). Figure 6-1 illustrates.

This paradigm shift has profound implications. Instead of learning to predict noise, VLMs learn to predict the next token in a sequence that contains both visual and textual information. The training objective is cross-entropy loss over vocabulary tokens, the same objective used to train GPT, LLaMA, and other language models. Video, in effect, becomes another "language" that the model reads.

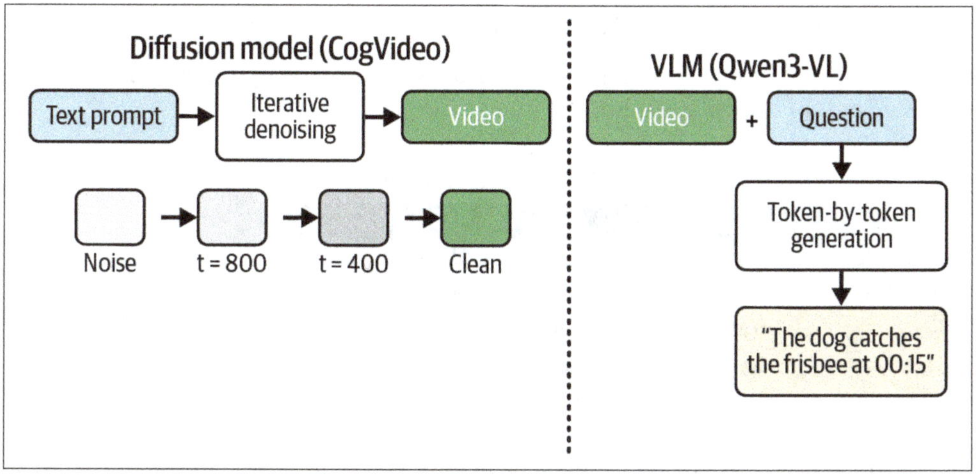


*Figure 6-1. Diffusion models (left) transform text into video through iterative denoising in pixel space while VLMs (right) transform video and questions into text through autoregressive token prediction*

Table 6-1 summarizes the key differences between these two paradigms.

*Table 6-1. Comparison of diffusion models and VLMs for video tasks*

| Aspect | Diffusion model (CogVideo) | VLM (Qwen3-VL) |
|---|---|---|
| Primary input | Text prompt | Video + text query |
| Output | Video frames (pixels) | Text response (tokens) |
| Core operation | Iterative denoising | Next-token prediction |
| Training signal | Noise prediction loss (MSE) | Cross-entropy loss |
| Inference steps | 20–50 denoising steps | Variable (until EOS token) |
| Output space | Continuous (latent/pixel) | Discrete (vocabulary tokens) |

Understanding this paradigm shift is essential for the remainder of this chapter. We are no longer working with denoising score matching or classifier-free guidance. Instead, we are working with vision encoders, projection layers, and causal language modeling—a different set of tools for a different task.

## Introducing Qwen3-VL

For this chapter, we will work with Qwen3-VL. At the time of this writing, Qwen3-VL is a state-of-the-art VLM, developed by Alibaba's Qwen team. I chose Qwen3-VL for several reasons: it offers strong video understanding performance, provides open model weights across multiple sizes, includes a well-documented fine-tuning framework, and demonstrates several architectural innovations worth studying.

The Qwen3-VL family spans a range of model sizes to accommodate different compute budgets, as shown in Table 6-2.

*Table 6-2. Qwen3-VL model variants and their typical use cases*

| Model | Parameters | Architecture | Typical use case |
|---|---|---|---|
| Qwen3-VL-2B | 2 billion | Dense | Edge deployment, mobile |
| Qwen3-VL-8B | 8 billion | Dense | Single GPU inference |
| Qwen3-VL-32B | 32 billion | Dense | High-quality production |
| Qwen3-VL-30B-A3B | 30B total, 3B active | MoE | Efficiency-optimized |
| Qwen3-VL-235B-A22B | 235B total, 22B active | MoE | Maximum capability |

The MoE (mixture of experts) variants use sparse activation, where only a subset of parameters are active for any given input. This allows larger total model capacity while keeping inference costs manageable.

Qwen3-VL introduces several architectural innovations that make it particularly effective for video understanding:

*Interleaved Multimodal Rotary Position Embedding (MRoPE)*
: A 3D positional encoding scheme that assigns separate position information for temporal (frame), height, and width dimensions. This enables precise spatiotemporal localization—the model knows not just that something appears in the video but exactly when and where.

*DeepStack*
: Multilevel feature fusion from the vision encoder, capturing both high-level semantics and fine-grained visual details.

*Text-timestamp alignment*
: Native support for temporal grounding, allowing the model to associate events with specific timestamps in the video.

*Long context support*
: Context windows up to 256K tokens (1M in some configurations), enabling analysis of lengthy videos without chunking.

By the end of this chapter, you will build a working video question-answering (Q&A) system using Qwen3-VL. You will understand how the model processes video input, how positional encoding enables spatiotemporal reasoning, and how to fine-tune the model for domain-specific video understanding tasks using the LoRA techniques introduced in Chapter 5.

This chapter culminates in a hands-on implementation of a video Q&A system capable of answering natural language questions about video content and providing temporal grounding ("When does X happen?"), spatial localization ("Where is Y in the frame?"), and fine-tuning on custom video datasets.

Before we begin, install the core dependencies. Inference on the 8B model requires 18 GB+ VRAM; for limited hardware, use 4-bit quantization:

```
pip install torch transformers accelerate qwen-vl-utils decord
pip install flash-attn --no-build-isolation # Optional
pip install peft # For fine-tuning later
```

Let's verify the environment by loading the model. This code establishes our foundation for everything that follows:

```
import torch
from transformers import AutoModelForImageTextToText, AutoProcessor

# Load model and processor
MODEL_ID = "Qwen/Qwen3-VL-8B-Instruct"
model = AutoModelForImageTextToText.from_pretrained(
    MODEL_ID,
    torch_dtype=torch.bfloat16,
    device_map="auto"
)
processor = AutoProcessor.from_pretrained(MODEL_ID)
print(
    f"Model loaded: "
    f"{sum(p.numel() for p in model.parameters()) / 1e9:.1f}B "
    f"parameters"
)
```

With the model loaded, the following section examines the architecture component by component, building your understanding alongside the code.

# VLM Architecture

A VLM combines three distinct components into a unified system capable of processing both visual and textual information. We will see how these components interact with each other and why each is necessary. This intuition provides the foundation for everything that follows in this chapter.

At a high level, the architecture follows a simple pattern: encode visual information, project it into a shared representation space, then process the combined visual and textual tokens through a language model. Each stage transforms the data, progressively converting raw pixels into the structured representations needed for language generation.

## The Three-Component Model

As illustrated in Figure 6-2, current VLM models consist of three primary components:

*Vision encoder*
: Converts images or video frames into sequences of visual feature vectors

*Projector (merger)*
: Transforms vision features into the embedding space expected by the language model

*Language model*
: Processes the combined visual and textual tokens to generate output text

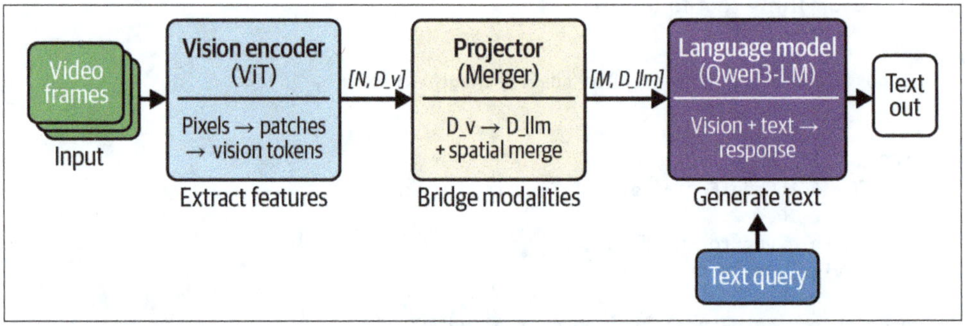


*Figure 6-2. The three-component VLM architecture*

This modular design offers several advantages. Each component can be pretrained independently on massive datasets: the vision encoder on image classification tasks, the language model on text corpora. The projector then learns to bridge these pretrained representations with comparatively little data. This transfer learning approach—connecting powerful pretrained models rather than training everything from scratch—is what makes VLMs practical to develop and deploy.

## Vision Encoder: Seeing the Video

The vision encoder's job is to transform raw pixels into a sequence of feature vectors that capture visual semantics. Modern VLMs universally use the vision transformer (ViT) architecture (Figure 6-3) for this purpose, applying the same attention mechanisms that power language models to visual data.

Think of the vision encoder like a museum curator preparing an exhibit. Rather than describing an entire painting in one breath, the curator might divide it into a grid of smaller sections and write detailed notes about each one: "upper left shows a stormy sky with purple clouds, center right contains a windswept tree." In a vision encoder, 256 individual descriptions (called *patch embeddings*) capture the essential visual information while making it digestible for further analysis.

The ViT processes images through a series of steps:

*Patch embedding*
: The input image is divided into fixed-size patches (typically 14 × 14 or 28 × 28 pixels). Each patch is flattened and linearly projected to create a patch embedding vector.

*Position encoding*
: Since transformers have no inherent notion of spatial order, position embeddings are added to encode each patch's location in the original image.

*Transformer layers*
: The sequence of patch embeddings passes through multiple transformer layers, where self-attention allows each patch to aggregate information from all other patches.

*Output features*
: The final layer produces a sequence of feature vectors, one per patch, representing the visual content.

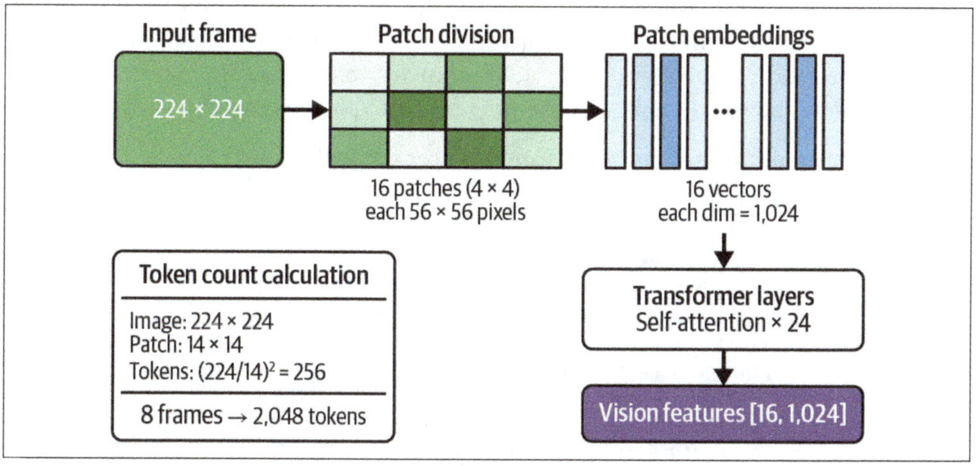


*Figure 6-3. ViT patch processing*

For video input, the vision encoder processes each frame independently, then concatenates the resulting feature sequences. An 8-frame video with 256 patches per frame produces 2,048 vision tokens, which is a substantial sequence that the downstream components must handle efficiently.

Qwen3-VL uses a patch size of 14 × 14 pixels and processes frames at variable resolutions based on the input image size. This flexibility allows the model to preserve fine details in high-resolution inputs while keeping token counts manageable for lower-resolution content:

```
# Conceptual token count for video processing
frame_height, frame_width = 224, 224
patch_size = 14
patches_per_frame = (
    (frame_height // patch_size)
    * (frame_width // patch_size) # 256
)
num_frames = 8
total_vision_tokens = patches_per_frame * num_frames  # 2,048
```

The vision encoder's output dimensionality (typically 1,024 or 1,280 for ViT variants) does not match the language model's embedding dimension. This mismatch motivates the next component: the projector.

## The Projector: Bridging Two Worlds

The *projector* serves a critical function: it transforms vision encoder outputs into representations compatible with the language model's embedding space. Without this bridge, the LLM would receive inputs in a format it was never trained to process.

Think of the projector as a translator between specialists who speak different technical languages. The vision encoder speaks in 1,024-dimensional "visual dialect," while the language model understands only 4,096-dimensional "language dialect." The projector translates between them, also merging adjacent patches to reduce token count.

The simplest projector architecture is a multilayer perceptron (MLP):

```
# Basic MLP projector
class Projector(nn.Module):
    def __init__(self, vision_dim, llm_dim):
        super().__init__()
        self.linear1 = nn.Linear(vision_dim, llm_dim)
        self.gelu = nn.GELU()
        self.linear2 = nn.Linear(llm_dim, llm_dim)

    def forward(self, vision_features):
        # vision_features: [batch, num_patches, vision_dim]
        x = self.linear1(vision_features)
        x = self.gelu(x)
        x = self.linear2(x)
        # output: [batch, num_patches, llm_dim]
        return x
```

However, directly projecting all vision tokens creates a problem: the sequence length becomes prohibitively long for the language model. Processing 2,048 vision tokens alongside text tokens strains memory and compute resources, especially for longer videos.

Qwen3-VL addresses this with a Patch Merger, which combines spatial projection with token reduction, as shown in Figure 6-4.

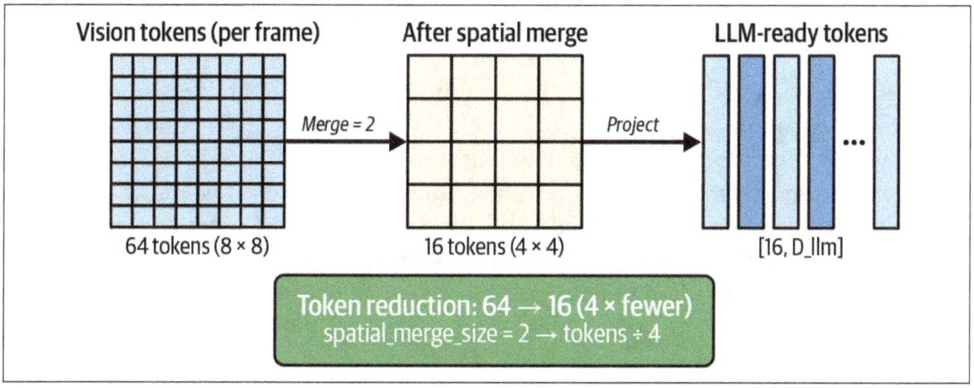


*Figure 6-4. The Patch Merger performs spatial pooling before projection*

The `spatial_merge_size` parameter controls how aggressively tokens are pooled. A merge size of 2 combines each 2 × 2 group of adjacent patches into a single token, reducing the token count by a factor of 4. This parameter trades off between visual detail preservation and computational efficiency:

```
# Merger with spatial pooling (simplified)
class Merger(nn.Module):
    def __init__(self, vision_dim, llm_dim, spatial_merge_size=2):
        super().__init__()
        self.merge_size = spatial_merge_size
        # Input dim multiplied by merge_size² because we concatenate
        # pooled patches
        merged_dim = vision_dim * (spatial_merge_size ** 2)
        self.mlp = nn.Sequential(
            nn.Linear(merged_dim, llm_dim),
            nn.GELU(),
            nn.Linear(llm_dim, llm_dim)
        )

    def forward(self, vision_features, grid_h, grid_w):
        # Reshape to spatial grid, pool adjacent patches, project
        # [batch, h*w, dim] -> [batch, h//m * w//m,
        # dim * m²] -> [batch, reduced, llm_dim]
```

For Qwen3-VL with `spatial_merge_size=2`, an 8-frame video that originally produced 2,048 vision tokens (256 per frame) is reduced to 512 tokens after merging—a

75% reduction that dramatically improves processing efficiency while retaining essential spatial information.

## The LLM: Reasoning Over Multimodal Tokens

The language model component is a standard autoregressive transformer, identical in architecture to text-only models like GPT or LLaMA. What makes it "multimodal" is not architectural changes but the content of its input sequence: projected vision tokens interleaved with text tokens.

Processing a video with questions is like reading an illustrated children's book aloud. The reader encounters picture pages, which correspond to vision tokens, and text pages, which correspond to text tokens, interleaved throughout. Special markers act like page headers, signaling when an illustration begins and ends, and helping the reader switch between looking mode and reading mode. The language model processes this combined sequence, interpreting both the visual content and the textual question to generate a coherent answer.

Qwen3-VL uses special tokens to mark the boundaries of visual content within the sequence, as shown in Table 6-3.

*Table 6-3. Special tokens used by Qwen3-VL to mark visual content boundaries*

| Token | ID | Purpose |
|---|---|---|
| <\|vision_start\|> | 151652 | Marks the beginning of visual content |
| <\|vision_end\|> | 151653 | Marks the end of visual content |
| <\|vision_pad\|> | 151654 | Padding within vision sequences |
| <\|image_pad\|> | 151655 | Placeholder for image tokens in text |
| <\|video_pad\|> | 151656 | Placeholder for video tokens in text |

These special tokens serve as markers that help the model distinguish between visual and textual content. During preprocessing, placeholder tokens in the text are replaced with the projected vision tokens before the sequence is passed to the transformer.

The LLM processes this mixed sequence using causal attention. Each token can attend to all previous tokens but not future ones. This structure enables autoregressive generation. The model predicts one token at a time, using all preceding context to inform each prediction.

## Token Sequence Construction

Understanding how the final input sequence is constructed clarifies how all three components work together. Consider Figure 6-5, where a user is asking about a video: "What is the dog doing?"

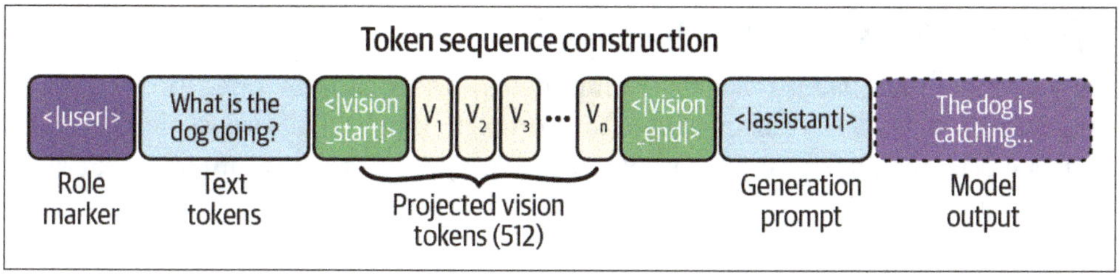


*Figure 6-5. Complete token sequence for a video Q&A query*

The sequence construction follows these steps:

1. *Template application*
   The conversation is formatted using a chat template that adds role markers (<|user|>, <|assistant|>) and structures the turn-taking.

2. *Placeholder insertion*
   Where video content should appear, a placeholder token (or series of tokens) is inserted.

3. *Vision processing*
   The video is processed through the vision encoder and projector, producing projected vision tokens.

4. *Token replacement*
   Placeholder tokens are replaced with the actual projected vision tokens, wrapped in <|vision_start|> and <|vision_end|> markers.

5. *Generation*
   The complete sequence is passed to the LLM, which generates response tokens autoregressively.

This sequence structure enables the model to condition its responses on both the visual content and the textual query. The attention mechanism allows every generated token to attend to all vision tokens, enabling rich visual reasoning.

> Attention patterns in vision-language models are hybrid during generation. Vision tokens attend to each other bidirectionally since they are part of the input context, while text tokens follow causal attention and can only attend to previous tokens. This allows the model to build a complete understanding of the visual content before generating any response tokens.

The architecture we have examined, consisting of a vision encoder, projector, and language model, provides the foundation for video understanding.

## Putting It Together: A VideoQA Class

Now that we understand all three components—the vision encoder, projector, and language model—we can encapsulate the complete pipeline in a reusable class. This `VideoQA` class wraps the model and processor and provides a clean interface for video Q&A:

```
from qwen_vl_utils import process_vision_info
from transformers import AutoModelForImageTextToText, AutoProcessor

class VideoQA:
    """A video question-answering system built on Qwen3-VL."""

    def __init__(self, model_name: str = "Qwen/Qwen3-VL-8B-Instruct"):
        self.model = AutoModelForImageTextToText.from_pretrained(
            model_name, torch_dtype=torch.bfloat16, device_map="auto")
        self.processor = AutoProcessor.from_pretrained(model_name)

    def ask(self, video_path: str, question: str, fps: float = 2.0,
            max_frames: int = 32, max_new_tokens: int = 512) -> str:
        """Ask a question about a video."""
        messages = [{"role": "user", "content": [
            {
                "type": "video",
                "video": video_path,
                "fps": fps,
                "max_frames": max_frames,
            },
            {"type": "text", "text": question}
        ]}]
        text = self.processor.apply_chat_template(
            messages,
            tokenize=False,
            add_generation_prompt=True,
        )
        image_inputs, video_inputs = process_vision_info(
            messages, image_patch_size=16
        )
        inputs = self.processor(
            text=[text],
            images=image_inputs,
            videos=video_inputs,
            padding=True,
            return_tensors="pt",
        ).to(self.model.device)
        with torch.no_grad():
            outputs = self.model.generate(
                **inputs, max_new_tokens=max_new_tokens
            )
        return self.processor.decode(
            outputs[0][inputs.input_ids.shape[1]:],
            skip_special_tokens=True,
```

```
    )

def describe(self, video_path: str, **kwargs) -> str:
    """Generate a description of the video."""
    return self.ask(
        video_path, "Describe what happens in this video.", **kwargs
    )

def find_event(self, video_path: str, event: str, **kwargs) -> str:
    """Find when a specific event occurs."""
    return self.ask(
        video_path,
        f"When does: {event}? Give timestamps in MM:SS.",
        **kwargs,
    )
```

The class encapsulates everything we've discussed: the `ask` method constructs the message `format`, processes vision inputs, builds the token sequence, and generates a response. These convenience methods describe and `find_event` provide common patterns:

```
# Usage example
qa = VideoQA()
response = qa.ask("cooking.mp4", "What dish is being prepared?")
print(response)

description = qa.describe("nature_documentary.mp4")
timestamp = qa.find_event("sports.mp4", "the goal is scored")
```

This `VideoQA` class demonstrates the power of the three-component architecture in action. But there's a critical detail we've glossed over: how does the model know the spatial and temporal position of each vision token? A patch from the top-left corner of frame 1 should be distinguishable from a patch at the bottom right of frame 8, yet so far we've treated all patches identically. The next section addresses this with Qwen3-VL's 3D positional encoding scheme, which gives the model precise awareness of where and when each visual element appears in the video.

## 3D Positional Encoding for Video

Transformers are permutation-invariant by default. Without positional information, they treat input as an unordered set of tokens. For text, this is handled with simple sequential positions such as token 1, token 2, and token 3. Video formatting introduces a more complex challenge. A vision token does not only have a position in a sequence; it has a position in 3D space and time. It belongs to a specific frame and has a location within that frame defined by height and width.

Qwen3-VL addresses this with a 3D positional encoding scheme called Interleaved-MRoPE. This approach assigns each vision token three separate position indices, one for each dimension, allowing the model to understand when and where visual information appears.

Consider what happens when a video is flattened into a sequence of tokens. An 8-frame video with 64 patches per frame, after spatial merging, produces 512 vision tokens. If we assign simple sequential positions such as 1 through 512, the model loses important structural information:

- Token 1 and token 65 may come from different frames but share the same spatial position.
- Token 1 and token 2 are adjacent in the sequence but may be far apart spatially.
- The model cannot distinguish between the top left of frame 1 and the bottom right of frame 8.

A useful analogy is addressing packages using only sequential numbers such as package 1, 2, or 512. There would be no way to know whether two packages are in the same building or in different cities. Video understanding has the same issue. A token might represent the top-left corner of frame 1, while another represents the bottom-right corner of frame 3. By assigning 3D coordinates, frame, row, and column, the model can distinguish spatial relationships from temporal ones, as illustrated in Figure 6-6.

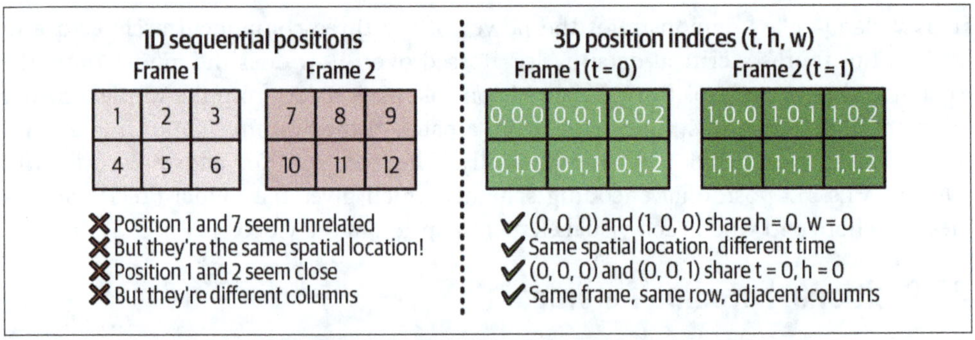


*Figure 6-6. The position problem: 1D sequential positions (left) lose spatiotemporal structure and 3D position indices (right) preserve the relationship between frame time (t), row position (h), and column position (w)*

This structural information is essential for video understanding tasks. When asked, "What moves from left to right?" the model needs to track how objects at specific spatial positions change across temporal positions. Without proper 3D position encoding, this kind of reasoning becomes impossible.

## Rotary Position Embedding (RoPE)

RoPE encodes position by rotating query and key vectors in attention, such that their dot product depends on relative position. Traditional position encoding stamps each token with a number badge; RoPE gives each token a compass rotated by a position-specific angle. When comparing tokens, the angle difference tells the model how far apart they are—and this naturally extends to longer sequences than seen during training.

## Extending to 3D: Temporal, Height, Width

Qwen3-VL extends RoPE to three dimensions by maintaining separate position indices for each axis. Every vision token receives three position values:

*t (temporal)*
: Which frame the token comes from

*h (height)*
: The row position within the frame

*w (width)*
: The column position within the frame

The embedding dimension is partitioned among these three axes. If the model has embedding dimension 4,096, it might allocate the following:

*Dimensions 0–1,023*
: Temporal position encoding

*Dimensions 1,024–2,559*
: Height position encoding

*Dimensions 2,560–4,095*
: Width position encoding

Like an orchestra assigning different frequency ranges to percussion (time), strings (pitch), and woodwinds (stereo position), Interleaved-MRoPE dedicates separate embedding dimensions to each axis. The model learns to "listen" to each dimension group independently. Figure 6-7 illustrates.

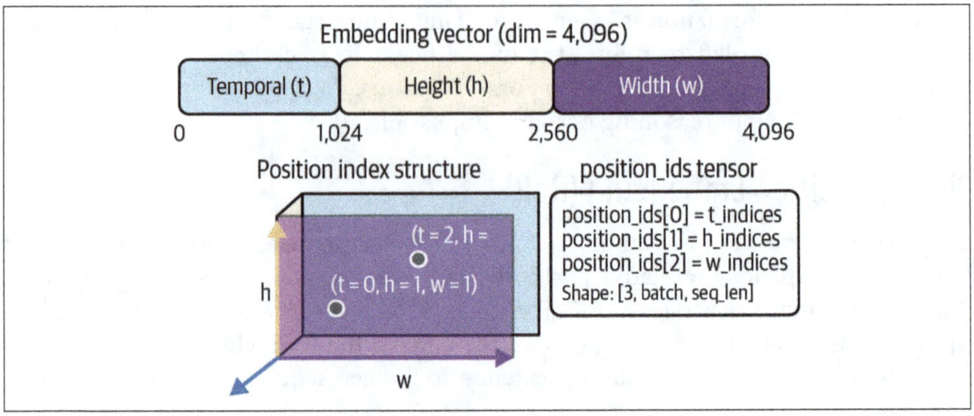


*Figure 6-7. 3D RoPE partitions the embedding dimension among temporal, height, and width axes*

This partitioning means that each axis has its own rotation frequencies applied to its portion of the embedding. The attention mechanism can then capture relationships along any axis: patches in the same row across different frames (temporal motion), patches in the same column across rows (vertical relationships), or any combination.

## Qwen3-VL's Interleaved-MRoPE Implementation

The Qwen3-VL codebase implements 3D position encoding in the `rope2d.py` module. The `get_rope_index_3` function constructs position indices for each vision token:

```
# From rope2d.py - Position index construction for Qwen3-VL
def get_rope_index_3(
    spatial_merge_size,
    input_ids,
    # [num_images, 3] - temporal, height, width for each image
    image_grid_thw,
    video_grid_thw,    # [num_videos, 3] - temporal, height, width for each video
    attention_mask
):
    """
    Construct 3D position indices for vision tokens.

    Returns position_ids of shape [3, batch_size, seq_len] where:
        position_ids[0] = temporal indices
        position_ids[1] = height indices
        position_ids[2] = width indices
    """
    position_ids = torch.ones(3, batch_size, seq_len, dtype=torch.long)

    for each video in batch:
        t, h, w = video_grid_thw[video_idx]
```

```
    # After spatial merging, grid dimensions are reduced
    llm_grid_t = t
    llm_grid_h = h // spatial_merge_size
    llm_grid_w = w // spatial_merge_size

    # Construct indices for each token in the video
    # t_index: [0,0,0,...,0, 1,1,1,...,1, 2,2,2,...,2, ...]
    t_index = torch.arange(llm_grid_t).view(-1, 1).expand(
        -1, llm_grid_h * llm_grid_w
    ).flatten()

    # h_index: [0,0,0,1,1,1,2,2,2, 0,0,0,1,1,1,2,2,2, ...]
    h_index = torch.arange(llm_grid_h).view(1, -1, 1).expand(
        llm_grid_t, -1, llm_grid_w
    ).flatten()

    # w_index: [0,1,2,0,1,2,0,1,2, 0,1,2,0,1,2,0,1,2, ...]
    w_index = torch.arange(llm_grid_w).view(1, 1, -1).expand(
        llm_grid_t, llm_grid_h, -1
    ).flatten()

    # Assign to position_ids at the vision token positions
    position_ids[0, batch_idx, vision_start:vision_end] = t_index
    position_ids[1, batch_idx, vision_start:vision_end] = h_index
    position_ids[2, batch_idx, vision_start:vision_end] = w_index

return position_ids
```

Let's trace through a concrete example. Consider a video with 4 frames, where each frame produces a 3 × 3 grid of patches after spatial merging (9 patches per frame, 36 total tokens), as illustrated in Figure 6-8.

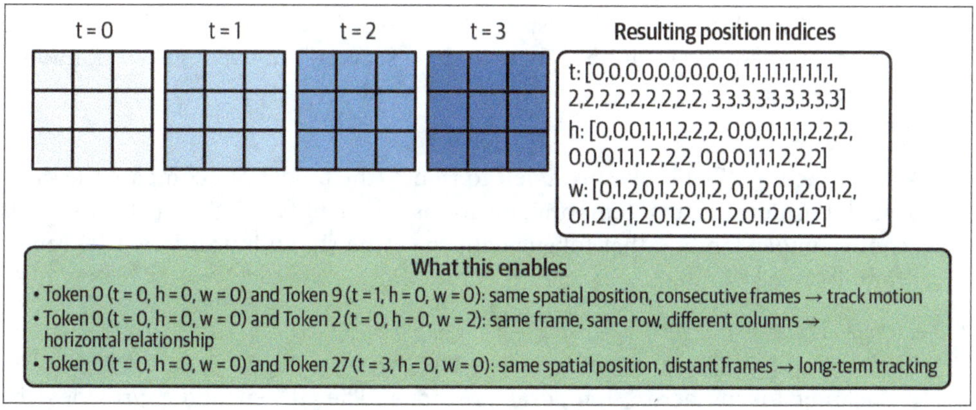


*Figure 6-8. Position index construction for a 4-frame video with 3 × 3 spatial grid*

## Timestamps Versus Frame Indices

Qwen3-VL introduces a subtle but important distinction from earlier models: it uses timestamps rather than simple frame numbers for temporal positions. This design choice accommodates videos with varying frame rates and enables precise temporal grounding in responses.

When processing a video sampled at 2 FPS, the temporal indices might represent actual seconds:

```
# Frame-based indexing (simpler models)
t_indices = [0, 1, 2, 3, 4, 5, 6, 7]  # Just frame numbers

# Timestamp-based indexing (Qwen3-VL)
t_indices = [0.0, 0.5, 1.0, 1.5, 2.0, 2.5, 3.0, 3.5]  # Actual seconds
```

This timestamp awareness enables the model to generate responses like "The event occurs at 00:02.5" rather than "The event occurs in frame 5"—a more natural and useful output for human users.

The 3D positional encoding system directly enables the video-understanding tasks we care about:

*Temporal grounding*
: When asked, "When does the person wave?" the model can identify which temporal positions contain the waving action and map those back to timestamps. Without temporal position encoding, the model would know that waving occurs but not when.

*Spatial localization*
: When asked, "Where is the ball in the last frame?" the model can identify which height and width positions correspond to the ball. The spatial position encoding enables it to describe locations ("bottom-left," "center") or even output bounding box coordinates.

*Motion tracking*
: When asked, ""What moves from left to right?" the model can compare the same spatial positions across temporal positions to identify motion patterns. This requires understanding that tokens with the same (h, w) but different (t) represent the same location across time.

*Object persistence*
: Understanding that an object in frame 1 is the same object in frame 8 requires correlating tokens across temporal positions. The 3D encoding provides the structural information needed for this correlation.

During training, position indices are computed dynamically based on each video's dimensions. The `get_rope_index_3` function is called during data preprocessing, and the resulting position IDs are passed to the model alongside input tokens. The model learns to use these positions through standard backpropagation—no special position-aware loss is needed.

## Extending VideoQA with Temporal Grounding

The 3D positional encoding enables precise temporal awareness. Let's extend our `VideoQA` class to leverage this capability, producing structured output with timestamps. First, we define a data structure to hold temporal segments:

```
import re
from dataclasses import dataclass
from typing import List

@dataclass
class TemporalSegment:
    """A time segment in a video."""
    start_time: str
    end_time: str
    description: str

    def to_seconds(self, time_str: str) -> float:
        parts = time_str.split(":")
        return (
            int(parts[0]) * 60
            + float(parts[1]) if len(parts) == 2 else float(time_str)
        )

    @property
    def duration(self) -> float:
        return self.to_seconds(self.end_time) - self.to_seconds(self.start_time)
```

Now we extend `VideoQA` to parse temporal grounding responses into structured segments:

```
class VideoQAWithGrounding(VideoQA):
    """Extended VideoQA with temporal grounding capabilities."""

    def ground_events(
        self,
        video_path: str,
        query: str,
        **kwargs,
    ) -> List[TemporalSegment]:
        """Find events and return structured temporal segments."""
        system_prompt = """Output events in this format:
[START_TIME-END_TIME] Description
Example: [00:05-00:12] A person enters the door
```

```
Use MM:SS format."""

        response = self.ask(
            video_path, query, system_prompt=system_prompt, **kwargs
        )

        segments = []
        pattern = r'\[(\d{2}:\d{2})-(\d{2}:\d{2})\]\s*(.+?)(?=\[|$)'
        for start, end, desc in re.findall(pattern, response, re.DOTALL):
            segments.append(
                TemporalSegment(start.strip(), end.strip(), desc.strip())
            )
        return segments

    def generate_timeline(
        self, video_path: str, **kwargs
    ) -> List[TemporalSegment]:
        """Generate a complete timeline of events."""
        return self.ground_events(
            video_path, "List all significant events with timestamps.", **kwargs
        )
```

This extension demonstrates the power of 3D positional encoding in action. The model uses its temporal awareness to identify when events occur:

```
qa = VideoQAWithGrounding()
timeline = qa.generate_timeline("lecture.mp4")

for segment in timeline:
    print(f"{segment.start_time} - {segment.end_time}: {segment.description}")

# Output:
# 00:00 - 00:15: Instructor introduces the topic
# 00:15 - 02:30: First concept explanation with slides
# 02:30 - 04:00: Live coding demonstration
# ...
```

With the architectural foundation complete—vision encoding, projection, language modeling, and 3D positional encoding—and our `VideoQA` classes ready to use, we now turn to the practical pipeline that ties these components together.

## Video Understanding Pipeline

We've examined the architectural components in isolation—vision encoder, projector, language model, and positional encoding. Now we trace the complete pipeline from a video file on disk to a generated text response. Understanding this end-to-end flow is essential for both using existing VLMs and debugging issues when they arise.

Before any neural network computation, raw video files must be transformed into the tensor format that the model expects. This preprocessing stage involves frame extraction, smart resizing, and normalization.

The first step is extracting frames from the video file. Qwen3-VL uses FPS-based sampling rather than uniform sampling, which better preserves temporal structure for videos of varying lengths:

```
def fetch_video(video_path, fps=2.0, min_frames=4, max_frames=None):
    """
    Extract frames from video at specified FPS.

    Args:
        video_path: Path to video file
        fps: Target frames per second for extraction
        min_frames: Minimum frames to extract (pad if needed)
        max_frames: Maximum frames to extract (subsample if exceeded)

    Returns:
        frames: Tensor of shape [num_frames, channels, height, width]
    """
    video = load_video(video_path)
    duration = video.duration
    native_fps = video.fps

    # Calculate frame indices based on target FPS
    num_frames = int(duration * fps)
    num_frames = max(num_frames, min_frames)
    if max_frames:
        num_frames = min(num_frames, max_frames)

    # Sample frames at regular intervals
    frame_indices = np.linspace(0, len(video) - 1, num_frames, dtype=int)
    frames = video[frame_indices]

    return frames
```

For a 10-second video sampled at 2 FPS, this produces 20 frames. The `min_frames` parameter ensures very short clips still provide enough temporal context, while `max_frames` prevents memory issues with long videos.

> The Qwen3-VL repository's `fetch_video` implementation supports multiple video decoding backends: decord (fastest, recommended), torchvision, and torchcodec. The backend is selected automatically based on availability. Set `FORCE_QWENVL_VIDEO_READER=decord` to enforce a specific backend.

Each frame must be resized to dimensions compatible with the vision encoder. Unlike simple resizing to a fixed resolution, Qwen3-VL uses something called *smart resize*, which preserves aspect ratio while respecting pixel budget constraints.

Smart resizing acts as a photo printer selecting the appropriate frame size. It can't fit a panoramic 4K image into a square frame without distortion. The algorithm determines the largest frame that naturally fits the photo, preserving proportions, staying within the pixel budget, and aligning dimensions with the patch grid:

```
def smart_resize(height, width, factor=28, min_pixels=None, max_pixels=None):
    """
    Resize dimensions to be divisible by factor while staying within
    pixel limits.
    Maintains aspect ratio and ensures total pixels fall within
    [min_pixels, max_pixels].
    """
    if min_pixels is None:
        min_pixels = 28 * 28 * 16    # ~12K pixels minimum
    if max_pixels is None:
        max_pixels = 28 * 28 * 576   # ~450K pixels maximum

    current_pixels = height * width

    # Scale down if exceeding maximum
    if current_pixels > max_pixels:
        scale = math.sqrt(max_pixels / current_pixels)
        height = int(height * scale)
        width = int(width * scale)

    # Scale up if below minimum
    if current_pixels < min_pixels:
        scale = math.sqrt(min_pixels / current_pixels)
        height = int(height * scale)
        width = int(width * scale)

    # Round to nearest multiple of factor
    height = round(height / factor) * factor
    width = round(width / factor) * factor

    # Ensure at least one patch in each dimension
    height = max(height, factor)
    width = max(width, factor)

    return height, width
```

This smart resize ensures the patch count stays within reasonable bounds. A 4K video (3,840 × 2,160) would produce an unmanageable number of patches at native resolution; smart resize scales it down while preserving the aspect ratio. The constraints ensure pixel counts stay between ~12K (minimum) and ~450K (maximum), with dimensions rounded to multiples of the patch size.

After resizing, pixel values are normalized using ImageNet statistics (the standard for ViTs):

```
# Standard normalization for ViT models
mean = [0.48145466, 0.4578275, 0.40821073]
std = [0.26862954, 0.26130258, 0.27577711]
```

```
# Normalize: (pixel - mean) / std
normalized_frames = (frames - mean) / std
```

## The Complete Processing Pipeline

Figure 6-9 traces the complete path from video file to generated response.

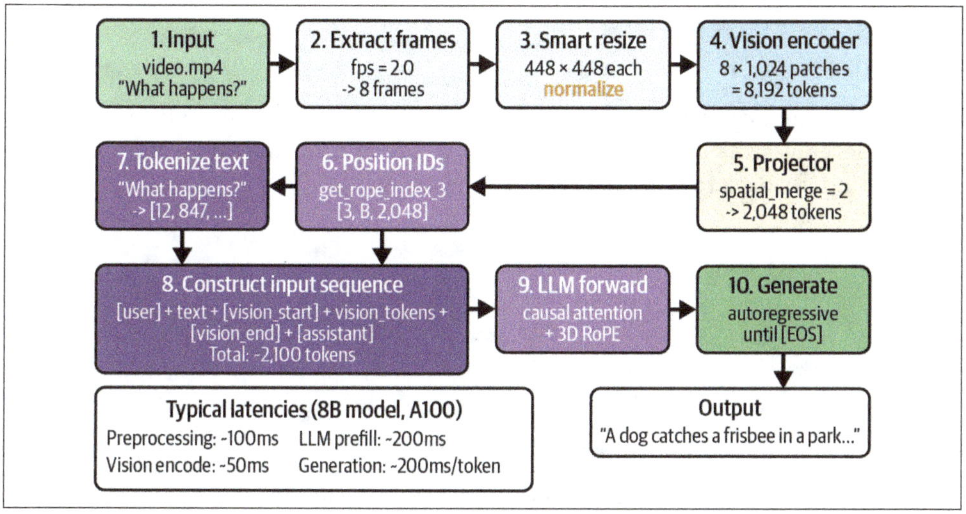


*Figure 6-9. Complete pipeline from video file to generated response*

Each stage transforms the data toward the final goal of text generation. The preprocessing stages (1–3) convert the video file to normalized tensors. The encoding stages (4–6) transform pixels into the token representations and position IDs the LLM expects. The generation stages (7–10) combine these with the text query and produce the response.

## Video Understanding Task Types

The pipeline I've described supports a variety of video-understanding tasks. Each task type places different demands on the model and benefits from different aspects of the architecture.

The 3D positional encoding works like a library catalog optimized for different searches: temporal grounding queries the time dimension; spatial localization uses height and width; and captioning requires all three dimensions together.

*Video Q&A* is the most general task: answer arbitrary questions about video content. The model must understand both the visual content and the question semantics, then generate a coherent response:

```
# Example: Video QA
messages = [{
```

```
        "role": "user",
        "content": [
            {"type": "video", "video": "cooking.mp4"},
            {
                "type": "text",
                "text": "What ingredients does the chef add to the pan?",
            }
        ]
}]
# Model response: "The chef adds olive oil, diced onions, and minced garlic."
```

*Temporal grounding* identifies when specific events occur in the video. This task directly leverages the 3D positional encoding—the model must map from temporal position indices back to human-readable timestamps:

```
# Example: Temporal grounding
messages = [{
    "role": "user",
    "content": [
        {"type": "video", "video": "sports_highlight.mp4"},
        {"type": "text", "text": "When does the player score the goal?"}
    ]
}]
# Model response: "The player scores the goal at 00:47-00:49."
```

*Video captioning* generates a natural language description of the video content, requiring understanding of temporal progression and coherent narrative structure:

```
# Example: Video captioning
messages = [{
    "role": "user",
    "content": [
        {"type": "video", "video": "nature.mp4"},
        {"type": "text", "text": "Describe what happens in this video."}
    ]
}]
# Model response: "A group of elephants approaches a watering hole at sunset.
#                  The adults drink while a
#                  young calf plays in the shallow water.
#                  After several minutes, they walk away into the savanna."
```

## Inference Code Example

This section looks at a complete inference example that ties together all the pipeline components. We'll break this into logical parts for clarity.

### Part 1: Model loading

First, load the model and processor with appropriate precision settings:

```
import torch
from transformers import AutoModelForImageTextToText, AutoProcessor
```

```python
from qwen_vl_utils import process_vision_info

# Load model and processor
MODEL_ID = "Qwen/Qwen3-VL-8B-Instruct"
model = AutoModelForImageTextToText.from_pretrained(
    MODEL_ID,
    torch_dtype=torch.bfloat16,
    device_map="auto"
)
processor = AutoProcessor.from_pretrained(MODEL_ID)
```

### Part 2: Message construction

Construct the input message with video and text query:

```python
# Construct message with video
messages = [
    {
        "role": "user",
        "content": [
            {
                "type": "video",
                "video": "path/to/video.mp4",
                "fps": 2.0,             # Extract 2 frames per second
                "max_frames": 32        # Limit total frames
            },
            {
                "type": "text",
                "text": (
                    "Describe what happens in this video, including "
                    "timestamps."
                )
            }
        ]
    }
]
```

### Part 3: Processing and generation

Apply templates, process inputs, and generate:

```python
# Apply chat template and process vision inputs
text = processor.apply_chat_template(
    messages,
    tokenize=False,
    add_generation_prompt=True,
)
image_inputs, video_inputs = process_vision_info(messages, image_patch_size=16)
inputs = processor(text=[text], images=image_inputs, videos=video_inputs,
                   padding=True, return_tensors="pt").to(model.device)

# Generate and decode response
with torch.no_grad():
```

```
    outputs = model.generate(
        **inputs,
        max_new_tokens=512,
        do_sample=True,
        temperature=0.7,
    )
response = processor.decode(
    outputs[0][inputs.input_ids.shape[1]:],
    skip_special_tokens=True,
)
print(response)
```

This code handles the entire pipeline: the `process_vision_info` function extracts and preprocesses frames, the processor handles tokenization and tensor construction, and the model performs encoding and generation.

## Handling Long Videos

Videos can be arbitrarily long, but model context windows are finite. Even with Qwen3-VL's 256K token context, a 10-minute video at 2 FPS would produce millions of vision tokens—far exceeding any practical limit. Several strategies address this:

*Frame subsampling*
: This is the simplest approach: reduce the effective FPS for longer videos. A 10-minute video might be sampled at 0.5 FPS instead of 2 FPS, producing 300 frames instead of 1,200:

```
# Adaptive FPS based on video length
def adaptive_fps(duration, max_frames=128):
    """Calculate FPS to stay within max_frames."""
    if duration * 2.0 <= max_frames:
        return 2.0  # Standard rate
    return max_frames / duration  # Reduced rate
```

*Keyframe selection*
: Instead of uniform sampling, select frames based on visual content changes. This preserves more information from dynamic scenes while reducing redundant frames from static segments.

*Hierarchical summarization*
: For very long videos, process in segments: summarize each segment, then query over the summaries. This two-stage approach scales to arbitrary lengths but may lose fine-grained details.

*Sliding window*
: Process the video in overlapping windows, aggregating responses across windows. This works well for tasks that don't require global context (e.g., finding specific events).

Before processing a video, estimate the token budget: `tokens = num_frames × (frame_height / patch_size / merge_size) × (frame_width / patch_size / merge_size)`. For 8 frames at 448 × 448 with `patch_size=14` and `merge_size=2`, this gives 8 × 16 × 16 = 2,048 vision tokens. Add text tokens and ensure the total fits within the model's context window.

With the pipeline understood from end to end, you have all the tools needed for video understanding. Our `VideoQA` and `VideoQAWithGrounding` classes—built progressively throughout this chapter—provide a complete system for answering questions about video content. But what happens when pretrained models don't perform well on your specific domain? Medical procedures, manufacturing inspections, or domain-specific activities may require adaptation. In the "Adapting to Your Domain: Dataset Preparation" section, we'll apply the fine-tuning techniques from Chapter 5 to adapt our video understanding system.

## Adapting to Your Domain: Dataset Preparation

When pretrained models do not perform well on your domain, fine-tuning adapts them. LoRA, which we explored in Chapter 5 for video generation, provides efficient adaptation for VLMs as well, typically training less than 1% of the model's parameters.

The training data follows Qwen's conversation format. Each sample pairs a video with a prompt that includes a <video> placeholder:

```
{
  "video": "data/videos/sample_001.mp4",
  "conversations": [
    {
      "from": "human",
      "value": "<video>\nDescribe what is happening in this video."
    },
    {
      "from": "gpt",
      "value": "A person walks along a path in a park surrounded by trees."
    }
  ]
}
```

The <video> tag marks where video tokens are inserted. During preprocessing, the processor loads the video, encodes it into visual tokens, and replaces the <video> placeholder before passing the input to the model. For multiturn conversations, include the video tag only in the first human message. This format uses `from: "human"` and `from: "gpt"`, not `role: "user"` and `role: "assistant"`.

## Training with LoRA

The training script applies LoRA to the language model's attention layers—the same approach we used for video generation in Chapter 5:

```
import torch
from transformers import AutoModelForImageTextToText, AutoProcessor
from peft import LoraConfig, get_peft_model, TaskType

# Load base model
model_name = "Qwen/Qwen3-VL-8B-Instruct"
model = AutoModelForImageTextToText.from_pretrained(
    model_name, torch_dtype=torch.bfloat16, device_map="auto"
)
processor = AutoProcessor.from_pretrained(model_name)

# Configure LoRA: target attention layers
lora_config = LoraConfig(
    task_type=TaskType.CAUSAL_LM,
    r=64,
    lora_alpha=128,
    lora_dropout=0.05,
    target_modules=["q_proj", "k_proj", "v_proj", "o_proj"],
    bias="none"
)

model = get_peft_model(model, lora_config)
model.print_trainable_parameters()  # ~0.5% trainable
```

With the model configured, we load the dataset and run training:

```
from transformers import TrainingArguments, Trainer
from datasets import load_dataset

# Load dataset
dataset = load_dataset("json", data_files="training_data.json")

training_args = TrainingArguments(
    output_dir="./output",
    num_train_epochs=3,
    per_device_train_batch_size=1,
    gradient_accumulation_steps=8,
    learning_rate=2e-5,
    warmup_ratio=0.1,
    bf16=True,
    save_strategy="epoch",
)

trainer = Trainer(
    model=model,
    args=training_args,
    train_dataset=dataset["train"]
)
```

```
trainer.train()
model.save_pretrained("./output/lora_weights")
```

Figure 6-10 summarizes fine-tuning component selection.

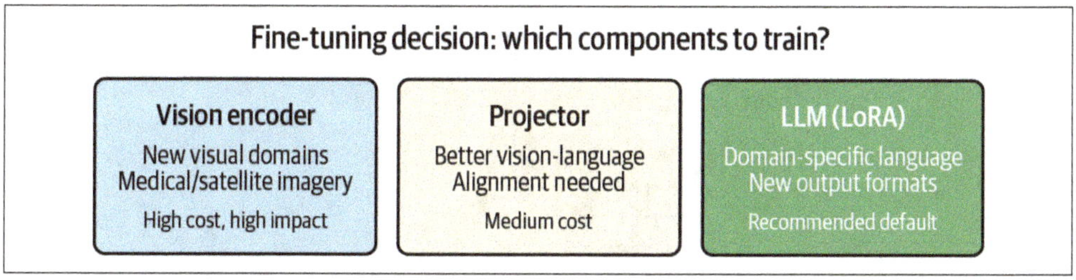


*Figure 6-10. Component selection for fine-tuning*

### Using fine-tuned models

After training, load the LoRA weights and optionally merge them for faster inference:

```
from transformers import AutoModelForImageTextToText
from peft import PeftModel

MODEL_ID = "Qwen/Qwen3-VL-8B-Instruct"
base_model = AutoModelForImageTextToText.from_pretrained(
    MODEL_ID, torch_dtype=torch.bfloat16, device_map="auto"
)
model = PeftModel.from_pretrained(base_model, "./output/lora_weights")
model = model.merge_and_unload()  # Merge for faster inference
```

### Evaluation

Evaluating video understanding requires task-specific metrics. Here's a simple evaluation framework that compares model predictions against expected answers:

```
from dataclasses import dataclass
from typing import List, Dict

@dataclass
class EvalResult:
    accuracy: float
    total: int
    correct: int
    details: List[Dict]

def evaluate_video_qa(
    model: VideoQA,
    test_data: List[Dict],
    fuzzy_match=True,
) -> EvalResult:
    correct = 0
    details = []
```

```
    for item in test_data:
        prediction = model.ask(item["video"], item["question"])
        expected = item["answer"]
        is_correct = (
            expected.lower() in prediction.lower()
            if fuzzy_match
            else prediction.strip().lower() == expected.strip().lower()
        )
        if is_correct:
            correct += 1
        details.append({
            "expected": expected,
            "predicted": prediction,
            "correct": is_correct,
        })

    return EvalResult(
        correct / len(test_data) if test_data else 0,
        len(test_data),
        correct,
        details,
    )
```

Run the evaluation:

```
import json
with open("test_data.json") as f:
    test_data = json.load(f)

qa = VideoQAWithGrounding()
results = evaluate_video_qa(qa, test_data["qa"])
print(
    f"Video QA Accuracy: {results.accuracy:.1%} "
    f"({results.correct}/{results.total})"
)
```

# Summary

In this chapter, we've journeyed from the paradigm shift between video generation and understanding to a complete, working video Q&A system.

Here are the key concepts to remember:

*VLMs transform video understanding into language modeling*
: Instead of predicting pixels, they predict text tokens conditioned on visual input.

*The three-component architecture (vision encoder, projector, LLM)*
: This enables modular training and efficient transfer learning from pretrained components.

*3D positional encoding is critical for video*
: Separate indices for temporal, height, and width dimensions enable precise spatiotemporal reasoning.

*The same fine-tuning principles from Chapter 5 apply*
: LoRA provides parameter-efficient adaptation, and the choice of which components to tune depends on how much your domain differs from the pretraining data.

*Production systems require careful attention to preprocessing*
: Frame sampling rate, smart resizing, and token budget management all affect both quality and performance.

With video generation (Chapters 3 through 5) and video understanding (Chapter 6) now in your toolkit, you have the foundations for building complete video AI systems. The models can work in concert: generate video from text, analyze the results, refine your prompts based on analysis, and iterate. This generation-understanding loop represents the current frontier of video AI, and you now have the knowledge to explore it.

Yet video is only half the story. Real-world video comes with audio dialogue, music, and ambient sounds, which provide crucial context for understanding. A model that can see a person speaking but can't hear their words is fundamentally limited. In Chapter 7, you'll explore audio-visual synchronization with cross-modal fusion, learning how to align and integrate audio and visual streams into unified multimodal representations. We'll implement attention mechanisms that bridge these modalities, enabling models that truly understand video as humans experience it: sight and sound together.

CHAPTER 7

# Audiovisual Synchronization with Cross-Modal Fusion

*Learning objective:* In this chapter, you'll learn how to generate synchronized audio and video simultaneously using cross-modal fusion architectures. By the end of this chapter, you will build a working audio-video generation system using the LTX-2 framework, understand the unified DiT architecture with bidirectional audio-video attention, master the audio VAE pipeline from mel-spectrograms to neural vocoders, and implement two-stage flow matching inference, ensuring that what you see and hear align perfectly in time and meaning.

In the preceding chapters, we've generated silent videos and built systems that understand visual content. But authentic video experiences are inherently multimodal: a crackling fire, footsteps on gravel, the rhythm of speech. The video generation systems from Chapters 3 through 5 produce the modern equivalent of silent films: beautiful to watch but missing half the story. Early cinema audiences accepted orchestras playing alongside projected images, but modern viewers expect perfect synchronization. Sound is the difference between watching an experience and being immersed in one.

This chapter explores how to generate synchronized audio and video simultaneously through the LTX-2 framework's unified transformer architecture. We'll trace the complete path from text prompt to synchronized output, examining each architectural decision that makes joint generation possible.

## The Missing Modality: Audio

The video generation systems from Chapters 3 through 5 produce visually impressive but fundamentally silent content. This silence creates an uncanny valley effect: the barking dog makes no sound, or the speaking person's lips move without voice.

Watch any AI-generated video with realistic human faces, and the lack of audio becomes immediately jarring. We've grown so accustomed to synchronized audiovisual experiences that silence feels like a technical failure.

## Why Post Hoc Audio Fails

One might wonder: why not generate video first, then add audio afterward? The answer lies in the precision required for human perception. True audio-video synchronization requires alignment at multiple scales:

*Frame-level sync*
: A door slam must occur at the exact frame the door closes.

*Phoneme-level sync*
: Lip movements must match speech sounds within 40–80 ms.

*Semantic sync*
: The type of sound must match the visual action.

*Ambient consistency*
: Background audio must remain coherent across the video.

Humans detect lip-sync errors as small as 45 ms, roughly two video frames at 24 FPS. This extraordinary sensitivity evolved for face-to-face communication, and it makes post hoc audio addition fundamentally limited. Even if we could perfectly analyze the generated video, adding audio afterward would require solving a difficult inverse problem: inferring precise timing from ambiguous visual cues.

The solution lies in joint generation (see Figure 7-1): producing audio and video simultaneously with architectural connections enforcing synchronization. Rather than treat audio as an afterthought, we prioritize it in the generation process.

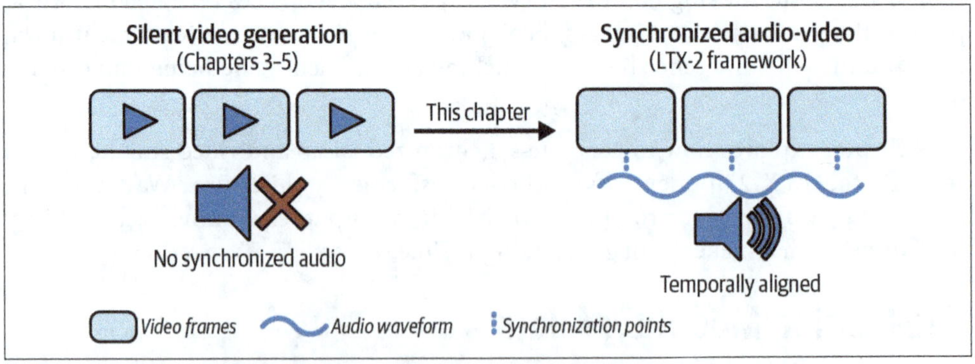


*Figure 7-1. Silent video generation (left) produces visual content without audio and synchronized audio-video generation (right) creates both modalities with temporal alignment enforced through cross-modal attention*

# Audio Representation: From Waveforms to Mel-Spectrograms

Before we can model audio jointly with video, we need to understand its representation. Video is 4D (channels, frames, height, width), while raw audio is 1D (amplitude samples at 16–44 kHz). A 5-second clip contains roughly 120 video frames but 80,000 audio samples at 16 kHz—over 650 samples per frame. Direct modeling of raw audio alongside video would create severe computational bottlenecks and make learning alignment nearly impossible.

The solution is *mel-spectrograms*: a 2D representation capturing frequency content over time. Think of a mel-spectrogram as sheet music for machines: it shows which frequencies (like musical notes) are present at each moment, making patterns visible that would be hidden in raw waveforms. The *mel scale* mimics human auditory perception (which is logarithmic in frequency), reducing dimensionality while preserving perceptually relevant information. Table 7-1 summarizes.

*Table 7-1. Video and audio dimensional comparison for joint modeling in LTX-2*

| Aspect | Video | Audio (raw) | Audio (mel-spectrogram) |
|---|---|---|---|
| Dimensionality | 4D (C × F × H × W) | 1D (samples) | 2D (frequency × time) |
| 5-second size | 128 × F/8 × H/32 × W/32 latent | 80,000 samples | 128 × T mel bins |
| Temporal resolution | ~8 latent frames/sec | 16–44.1 kHz | ~63 FPS (hop-based) |
| Compression (VAE) | 32x spatial, 8x temporal | N/A | ~4x temporal |
| Latent channels | 128 | N/A | 128 |

The compression ratios reveal why video and audio require different treatment. Video's high spatial redundancy (most frames look a lot like the one before) allows for aggressive compression (32x in each spatial dimension). Audio's information density is lower per sample but spans a much longer sequence. The mel-spectrogram VAE compresses temporally while preserving the frequency detail critical for synchronization and perceptual quality.

Raw audio waveforms contain phase information that is perceptually irrelevant but computationally expensive to model. Mel-spectrograms discard phase while retaining perceptually important magnitude information. This makes them ideal for generative modeling—the discarded phase can be reconstructed during synthesis using neural vocoders like HiFi-GAN. The human auditory system is largely insensitive to phase, so this is an excellent trade-off.

## Introducing LTX-2

LTX-2 represents a breakthrough in joint audio-video generation through its unified diffusion transformer (DiT) architecture. Rather than treat audio as an afterthought or using separate neural networks for each modality, LTX-2 processes both through a single 48-layer transformer, where each layer carries two parallel processing paths—a larger video stream and a smaller audio stream—joined by bidirectional cross-modal attention. The current production version is LTX-2.3, a 22-billion-parameter checkpoint released in 2026.

The key insight is architectural: by allowing audio tokens to attend to video tokens (and vice versa) throughout the denoising process, the model learns to generate synchronized content without explicit alignment supervision. The synchronization emerges from the cross-modal attention patterns learned during training on paired audio-video data. It's like having an orchestra where strings and winds rehearse together from day one rather than recording each section separately and hoping they align.

LTX-2's capabilities span multiple generation modes (details outlined in Table 7-2):

*Text-to-audio-video (T2AV)*
: Generate both video and matching audio from text descriptions.

*Image-to-audio-video (I2AV)*
: Animate a static image with motion and corresponding sound.

*Video-to-video (IC-LoRA)*
: Transform videos with in-context control adapters.

*Keyframe interpolation*
: Generate video between specified keyframes with synchronized audio.

The video-to-video mode is worth a closer look. Lightricks publishes four IC-LoRA adapters as separate 19B checkpoints on Hugging Face: `Lightricks/LTX-2-19b-IC-LoRA-Canny-Control` for edge-conditioned generation, `-Depth-Control` and `-Pose-Control` for depth and skeletal-pose conditioning, and `-Detailer` for refining existing footage. Each loads into the same LTXModel pipeline as the base 19B; the `IC-LoRA` weights modify the cross-attention paths so the model conditions on a reference video's structural signal in addition to text.

> These IC-LoRA adapters belong to the conditioning-adapter family. ControlNet (Zhang et al., 2023 (*https://oreil.ly/alAa4*)) introduced the pattern these IC-LoRAs follow: small auxiliary networks that inject a reference signal, depth map, pose skeleton, and edge map into a frozen base model so generation can be conditioned on the reference. The pattern proved productive enough that every modern video model has its successor under a different name. Wan registers a node family in `comfy_extras/nodes_wan.py` that exposes VACE conditioning `vace_frames`, `vace_mask`, and `vace_strength` alongside `WanFunControlToVideo`, `WanPhantomSubjectToVideo` for subject-reference, and `WanAnimateToVideo`. CogVideoX has `CogVideoX-Fun` and the community `TheDenk/cogvideox-controlnet`. Open-Sora 2.0 bakes conditioning into the architecture itself via its `cond_type` parameter (arxiv:2503.09642). HunyuanVideo currently provides image-to-video conditioning only.

*Table 7-2. LTX-2 model architecture and output specifications at the time of writing*

| Specification | Value | Notes |
|---|---|---|
| Production version | LTX-2.3 | Hugging Face: Lightricks/LTX-2.3 |
| Full checkpoint parameters | 22B | ltx-2.3-22b-dev.safetensors (transformer + VAEs + vocoder + upsampler + projections) |
| Transformer parameters (asymmetric) | 19B = 14B video + 5B audio | Asymmetric dual-stream design |
| Transformer layers | 48 | `BasicAVTransformerBlock` |
| Video stream inner dim | 4,096 | 32 attention heads × 128 `d_head` |
| Audio stream inner dim | 2,048 | 32 attention heads × 64 `d_head` |
| Cross-modal attention | Bidirectional | Video ↔ audio at every layer; uses audio-dim heads in both directions |
| Text encoder | Gemma 3 (12B) | `gemma-3-12b-it-qat-q4_0-unquantized`; separate caption projections per stream |
| Video latent channels | 128 in / 128 out | 3D VAE: 32x spatial + 8x temporal compression |
| Audio latent channels | 128 in / 128 out | Mel-spectrogram VAE |
| Audio sample rate | 16 kHz encoder → 24 kHz vocoder out | Mel hop 160 → 100 frames/sec |
| Inference pipelines | 9 variants | See "Hands-On Implementation" on page 223 |
| Frame-count constraint | frames % 8 == 1 | Valid: 1, 9, 17, 25, ..., 121 |

Unlike twin-backbone approaches that process modalities separately before fusing, LTX-2 uses an asymmetric dual-stream architecture inside a single transformer. Each of the 48 `BasicAVTransformerBlock` layers contains a video processing path operating at 4,096 inner dim (14B parameters total across the stack) and an audio processing path operating at 2,048 inner dim (5B parameters), connected by native bidirectional cross-modal attention. The asymmetry is intentional: the video stream needs more capacity for its higher-dimensional pixel manifold, while the audio stream operates on more compact mel-spectrogram latents. The Gemma 3 text encoder feeds two separate projection heads, one matching the 4,096-dim video stream, the other matching the 2,048-dim audio stream, so each modality receives prompt conditioning shaped to its own dimensionality. Despite the size difference, the streams exchange information at every layer through cross-modal attention: video tokens attend to audio tokens, while audio tokens simultaneously attend to video. This continuous exchange allows the model to coordinate timing decisions throughout the network, not just at designated fusion points.

Figure 7-2 shows the full LTX-2 generation pipeline at a glance.

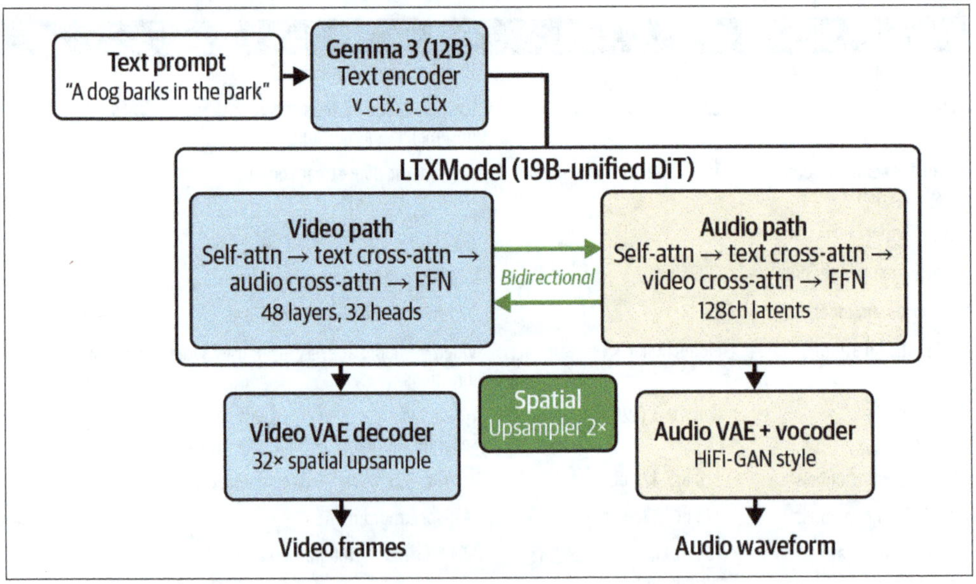


*Figure 7-2. LTX-2 pipeline overview. Text prompts are encoded by Gemma 3, then processed by the unified LTXModel with bidirectional cross-attention between video and audio paths. A spatial upsampler enhances resolution before VAE decoders reconstruct video frames and audio waveforms.*

> A key architectural difference between earlier systems and LTX-2 is the use of a unified backbone rather than twin backbones. Earlier approaches like Ovi used twin backbones—two separate transformer stacks that exchanged information through injected cross-attention projections. LTX-2 uses a unified architecture where video and audio paths are processed within the same transformer blocks, enabling deeper integration and more natural synchronization. Each of the 48 layers contains both video and audio processing with native bidirectional attention.

With this foundational understanding of why joint generation matters, how audio is represented, and the high-level architecture of LTX-2, we're ready to examine the transformer architecture in detail. The "Unified DiT Architecture" section dissects the `BasicAVTransformerBlock` that makes cross-modal synchronization possible.

# Unified DiT Architecture

Having established why joint generation matters and introduced LTX-2's high-level design, we now examine the transformer architecture that makes cross-modal synchronization possible. The core innovation lies in the unified DiT: a single architecture that processes video and audio through parallel paths within each transformer block, connected by bidirectional cross-modal attention.

Think of it like a single orchestra where string and wind sections play simultaneously, each listening to the other in real time. Unlike approaches that record strings first and overdub winds, the unified structure enables natural coordination without explicit choreography. Both sections influence each other's performance from the first note to the last.

## The LTXModel Design

The LTXModel is built as a deep stack of transformer blocks. Each block handles both video and audio, and both are updated together at every step of denoising. This is what allows the model to maintain tight alignment between what is seen and what is heard.

Rather than separate the modalities and stitch them together later, the model keeps them coupled from the beginning. You can see this directly in how the model is constructed:

```
# From ltx_core/model/transformer/model.py - LTXModel initialization
class LTXModel(nn.Module):
    def __init__(self, config: LTXModelConfig):
        super().__init__()

        # Unified transformer blocks for both modalities
        self.transformer_blocks = nn.ModuleList([
            BasicAVTransformerBlock(
                dim=config.inner_dim,                              # 4096
                num_attention_heads=config.num_attention_heads,    # 32
                attention_head_dim=config.attention_head_dim,      # 128
                cross_attention_dim=config.cross_attention_dim,    # 4096
                audio_cross_attention_dim=config.audio_cross_attention_dim,
            )
            for _ in range(config.num_layers)  # 48 layers
        ])

        # Input processing
        self.patchify_proj = nn.Linear(
            config.in_channels * patch_prod,
            config.inner_dim,
        )
        self.caption_projection = nn.Linear(
            config.cross_attention_dim,
            config.inner_dim
        )
        self.adaln_single = AdaLayerNormSingle(config.inner_dim)

        # Output processing with AdaLN scale-shift
        self.scale_shift_table = nn.Parameter(
            torch.randn(6, config.inner_dim) / config.inner_dim**0.5
        )
        self.norm_out = nn.LayerNorm(config.inner_dim, elementwise_affine=False)
        self.proj_out = nn.Linear(
            config.inner_dim,
            config.out_channels * patch_prod
        )
```

The critical design decision is the unified block structure. Each `BasicAVTransformerBlock` contains both video and audio processing paths with built-in cross-modal attention. Instead of passing information between separate networks at a few points, the two modalities interact at every layer. This continuous exchange is what allows synchronization to emerge naturally during generation. Figure 7-3 shows how a single block is structured and how this pattern repeats across all 48 layers.

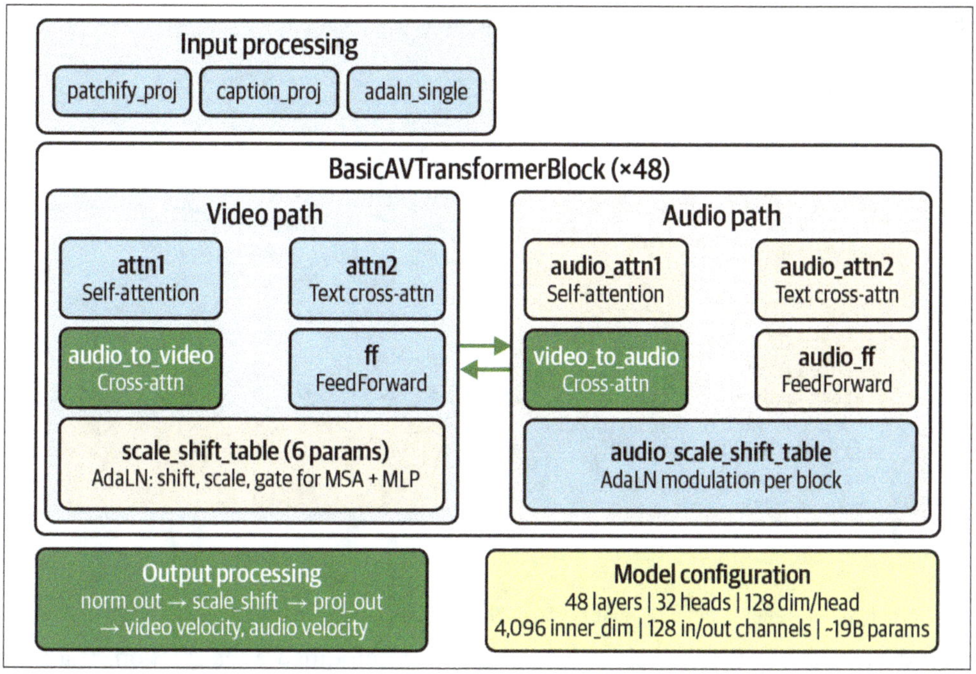


*Figure 7-3. The LTXModel's unified architecture. Video and audio are processed through parallel paths within each of 48 BasicAVTransformerBlocks with native bidirectional cross-attention (green). Each path has self-attention, text cross-attention, cross-modal attention, and feedforward layers with AdaLN modulation.*

## The Modality Dataclass

LTX-2 represents each modality using a simple structure called the `Modality` dataclass. It groups together everything the model needs, including latents, timesteps, positions, and text context, into a single object that moves through the transformer.

Here's how it's defined:

```
# From ltx_core/model/transformer/modality.py
@dataclass(frozen=True)
class Modality:
    enabled: bool               # Whether this modality is active
    latent: Tensor              # [B, seq_len, channels]
    timesteps: Tensor           # [B, seq_len] per-token timesteps
    positions: Tensor           # [B, dims, seq_len, 2] position bounds
    context: Tensor             # Text embeddings for this modality
    context_mask: Tensor | None
```

And here is how it is used during a forward pass:

```
# Usage in forward pass
video = Modality(
    enabled=True,
    latent=video_latents,           # [B, seq_len, 128]
    timesteps=video_timesteps,      # Per-token timesteps
    positions=video_positions,      # [B, 3, seq_len, 2] for F,H,W
    context=video_text_embeds,
    context_mask=None,
)

audio = Modality(
    enabled=True,
    latent=audio_latents,           # [B, seq_len, 128]
    timesteps=audio_timesteps,
    positions=audio_positions,      # [B, 1, seq_len, 2] for time
    context=audio_text_embeds,
    context_mask=None,
)

# Forward returns predictions for both
video_pred, audio_pred = model(video=video, audio=audio, perturbations=None)
```

The dataclass is frozen, which means it cannot be modified after creation. If a field needs to change, a new instance is created using `dataclasses.replace()`. This avoids accidental state changes during the forward pass and makes the flow of data easier to reason about.

## Bidirectional Cross-Modal Attention

The core of synchronization happens inside each transformer block through bidirectional cross-modal attention. This is where audio and video actively influence each other during generation. You can think of it like two performers on stage, each adjusting in real time based on what the other is doing. One listens and responds while at the same time being listened to and influencing the other.

Instead of adding a separate fusion step, cross-modal attention is built directly into the block. Each `BasicAVTransformerBlock` contains both video and audio paths, along with attention layers that allow each modality to attend to the other. Here's how the block is structured:

```
# From ltx_core/model/transformer/transformer.py - BasicAVTransformerBlock
class BasicAVTransformerBlock(nn.Module):
    def __init__(self, dim, num_attention_heads, attention_head_dim, ...):
        # Video path components
        self.attn1 = Attention(...)                  # Video self-attention
        self.attn2 = Attention(...)                  # Video cross-attention (text)
        self.audio_to_video_attn = Attention(...) # Audio → Video cross-attn
        self.ff = FeedForward(...)
```

```
        self.scale_shift_table = nn.Parameter(...)  # AdaLN for video

        # Audio path components
        self.audio_attn1 = Attention(...)          # Audio self-attention
        self.audio_attn2 = Attention(...)          # Audio cross-attention (text)
        self.video_to_audio_attn = Attention(...) # Video → Audio cross-attn
        self.audio_ff = FeedForward(...)
        self.audio_scale_shift_table = nn.Parameter(...)  # AdaLN for audio
```

The forward pass processes both paths with careful ordering to enable bidirectional information flow. Each step builds on the previous one:

*Self-attention*
: Video and audio tokens attend to their own modality (can run in parallel).

*Text cross-attention*
: Both modalities incorporate the text prompt embeddings.

*Cross-modal attention*
: Audio attends to video, while video attends to audio.

*Feedforward*
: Final transformation is established for each modality.

A simplified version of the forward pass looks like this:

```
# Simplified forward logic
def forward(self, video_hidden, audio_hidden, video_context, audio_context, ...):
    # 1. Video self-attention with AdaLN modulation
    video = video + self.attn1(self.norm1(video) * (1 + scale) + shift) * gate

    # 2. Audio self-attention (can run in parallel)
    audio = audio + self.audio_attn1(self.audio_norm1(audio) * ...)

    # 3. Text cross-attention for both
    video = video + self.attn2(video, context=video_context)
    audio = audio + self.audio_attn2(audio, context=audio_context)

    # 4. Bidirectional cross-modal attention
    # Audio attends to video (audio queries, video keys/values)
    audio = audio + self.video_to_audio_attn(audio, context=video)

    # Video attends to audio (video queries, audio keys/values)
    video = video + self.audio_to_video_attn(video, context=audio)

    # 5. Feedforward networks
    video = video + self.ff(self.norm_ff(video) * ...)
    audio = audio + self.audio_ff(self.audio_norm_ff(audio) * ...)

    return video, audio
```

The bidirectional attention uses the updated states from step 3 (after text cross-attention), allowing each modality to see the text-conditioned representation of the other. This is crucial for synchronization: audio tokens can attend to video tokens that have already incorporated the text prompt's description of the visual scene.

## AdaLN: Adaptive Layer Normalization

LTX-2 uses adaptive layer normalization (AdaLN) to condition the model on the diffusion timestep. Instead of treating every step the same, the model adjusts how each layer behaves depending on how much noise remains.

You can think of it like adjusting intensity over time. Early in the process the model focuses on coarse structure, and later it shifts toward fine detail. Each block learns a small set of parameters that control this behavior for both video and audio:

```
# AdaLN applies shift, scale, and gate to attention and FFN outputs
scale_shift_table = nn.Parameter(torch.randn(6, dim))

# During forward:
# [shift_msa, scale_msa, gate_msa, shift_mlp, scale_mlp, gate_mlp]
shift_msa, scale_msa, gate_msa, shift_mlp, scale_mlp, gate_mlp = (
    self.scale_shift_table[None] + timestep_embedding
).chunk(6, dim=-1)

# Applied to attention output
x = x + gate_msa * self.attn(self.norm(x) * (1 + scale_msa) + shift_msa)

# Applied to FFN output
x = x + gate_mlp * self.ff(self.norm_ff(x) * (1 + scale_mlp) + shift_mlp)
```

The key idea is that each layer can adjust how strongly it contributes at different points in the denoising process. Early steps may emphasize structure, while later steps refine details. The gate terms are especially important. They allow the model to scale the contribution of each layer, effectively changing how deep or active the network is as generation progresses.

> Video and audio share parts of the transformer such as normalization but use separate attention and feedforward components. This keeps the model efficient while still allowing each modality to specialize.

With the transformer architecture in place, the next step is to look at how audio itself is represented and processed.

# Audio Pipeline Deep Dive

If video latents are like compressed images, audio latents are a compact representation of sound over time. To generate synchronized audio, the model needs to move between raw waveforms and the structured representations the transformer can process. This section walks through that path from waveform to mel-spectrogram, into latent space, and back to audible output. Figure 7-4 shows the full audio pipeline and how it connects into the LTXModel.

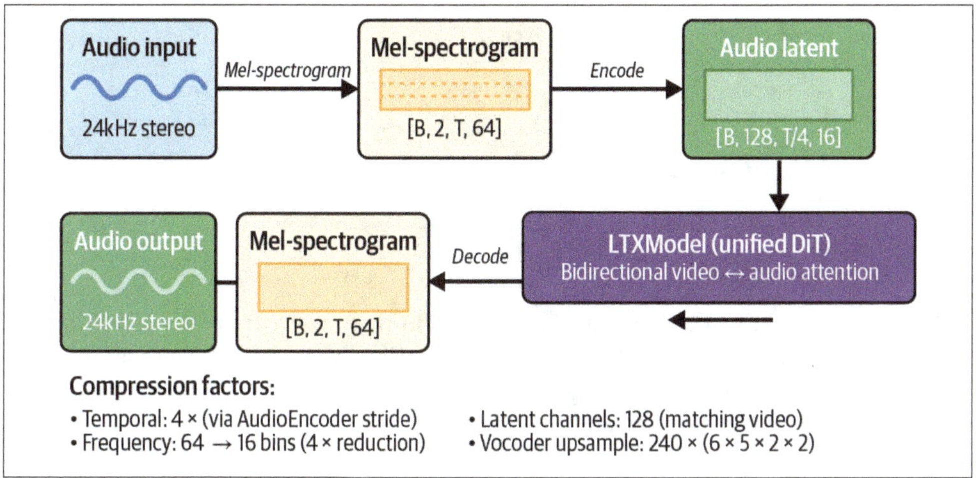


*Figure 7-4. In the LTX-2 audio pipeline, waveforms are converted to mel-spectrograms, encoded to 128-channel latents with 4x temporal compression, denoised by the LTXModel with video cross-attention, decoded back to spectrograms, and finally synthesized to 24 kHz audio by the vocoder.*

## Mel-Spectrogram Representation

Before audio can enter the transformer, it must be converted into a structured representation. LTX-2 uses mel-spectrograms, which organize sound over time and frequency in a format the model can learn from. This reduces the complexity of raw audio while preserving the information needed for synchronization and perceptual quality. Here's how that transformation is implemented:

```
# From ltx_core/model/audio_vae/ops.py - AudioProcessor
class AudioProcessor(nn.Module):
    def __init__(
        self,
        sample_rate: int,
        mel_bins: int,
        mel_hop_length: int,
        n_fft: int,
    ):
```

```
        self.mel_transform = torchaudio.transforms.MelSpectrogram(
            sample_rate=sample_rate,          # 16000 Hz
            n_fft=n_fft,                      # 1024
            win_length=n_fft,                 # 1024
            hop_length=mel_hop_length,        # 160 samples
            f_min=0.0,
            f_max=sample_rate / 2.0,          # 8000 Hz Nyquist
            n_mels=mel_bins,                  # 64 mel bins
            mel_scale="slaney",
        )

    def waveform_to_mel(self, waveform, waveform_sample_rate):
        # Resample if needed, then compute log-mel spectrogram
        waveform = self.resample_waveform(
            waveform,
            waveform_sample_rate,
            self.sample_rate,
        )
        mel = self.mel_transform(waveform)
        mel = torch.log(torch.clamp(mel, min=1e-5))
        return mel.permute(0, 1, 3, 2)  # [B, C, time, freq]
```

Table 7-3 summarizes the key parameters used in this transformation. The choice of 64 mel bins balances frequency detail with efficiency, while the 160-sample hop length produces about 100 frames per second. This resolution is sufficient for capturing speech timing and aligning audio with video.

*Table 7-3. LTX-2 audio processing parameters*

| Parameter | Value | Purpose |
|---|---|---|
| Sample rate | 16,000 Hz | Internal processing rate (speech-optimized) |
| Mel bins | 64 | Frequency resolution (versus 80–128 typical) |
| Hop length | 160 samples | 10 ms frame shift at 16 kHz |
| FFT size | 1,024 | 64 ms window for frequency analysis |
| Output rate | 24,000 Hz | Final waveform sample rate |
| Stereo support | Yes (128 channels) | 2 channels × 64 mel bins = 128 |

## Audio VAE Encoder

The `AudioEncoder` compresses mel-spectrograms into a latent representation that the transformer can process. It uses a hierarchical convolutional architecture that progressively reduces temporal resolution while increasing feature depth. Causal convolutions are used throughout, which means each output depends only on past inputs. This allows the model to operate in streaming settings without relying on future audio. Here's how the LTX encoder is structured:

```python
# From ltx_core/model/audio_vae/audio_vae.py
LATENT_DOWNSAMPLE_FACTOR = 4

class AudioEncoder(torch.nn.Module):
    def __init__(self, *,
        ch: int,                              # Base channels
        # Channel multipliers per stage
        ch_mult: Tuple[int, ...] = (1, 2, 4, 8),
        num_res_blocks: int,                  # ResBlocks per stage
        attn_resolutions: Set[int],           # Resolutions with attention
        z_channels: int,                      # 128 latent channels
        sample_rate: int = 16000,
        mel_hop_length: int = 160,
        mel_bins: int = 64,
        causality_axis: CausalityAxis = CausalityAxis.WIDTH,  # Causal in time
        ...
    ):
        # Per-channel statistics for normalization
        self.per_channel_statistics = PerChannelStatistics(latent_channels=ch)

        # Patchifier for latent preparation
        self.patchifier = AudioPatchifier(
            patch_size=1,
            audio_latent_downsample_factor=LATENT_DOWNSAMPLE_FACTOR,
            sample_rate=sample_rate,
            hop_length=mel_hop_length,
            is_causal=True,
        )

        # Downsampling path: 4 stages with increasing channels
        self.conv_in = make_conv2d(in_channels, ch, kernel_size=3, ...)
        self.down, block_in = build_downsampling_path(
            ch=ch, ch_mult=ch_mult, ...
        )

        # Middle block with attention
        self.mid = build_mid_block(channels=block_in, ...)

        # Output projection (double_z for mean+variance)
        self.conv_out = make_conv2d(block_in, 2 * z_channels, ...)
```

The design centers on a few key ideas:

- Channel multipliers expand feature capacity at each stage, allowing the model to capture more abstract patterns.
- Temporal downsampling reduces sequence length while preserving timing needed for synchronization.

- Causal convolutions ensure that the encoder does not rely on future information.
- The output layer produces both mean and variance, though only the mean is used for the final latent.

Together, these components create a compact representation of audio that remains aligned with the temporal structure needed for joint audio-video generation.

## Per-Channel Statistics Normalization

A key innovation in LTX-2's audio pipeline is the use of per-channel statistics for latent normalization. Think of it like calibrating a mixing board—each channel needs its own gain setting based on what typically flows through it. Rather than use fixed scaling factors, the encoder normalizes each latent channel based on dataset-wide statistics:

```
# From ltx_core/model/audio_vae/ops.py
class PerChannelStatistics(nn.Module):
    """Per-channel statistics computed over the training dataset."""

    def __init__(self, latent_channels: int = 128):
        super().__init__()
        # These buffers are loaded from the checkpoint
        self.register_buffer("std-of-means", torch.empty(latent_channels))
        self.register_buffer("mean-of-means", torch.empty(latent_channels))

    def normalize(self, x: Tensor) -> Tensor:
        # Standardize: (x - μ) / σ
        return (
            (x - self.get_buffer("mean-of-means"))
            / self.get_buffer("std-of-means")
        )

    def un_normalize(self, x: Tensor) -> Tensor:
        # Inverse: x * σ + μ
        return (
            x * self.get_buffer("std-of-means")
            + self.get_buffer("mean-of-means")
        )
```

This normalization ensures audio latents have zero mean and unit variance per channel, which provides three critical benefits:

- Stabilizes the diffusion process by ensuring consistent noise scales across all channels
- Enables effective cross-modal attention with video latents (which use similar normalization)
- Prevents channel-specific biases from dominating the denoising process

## Audio VAE Decoder

The AudioDecoder mirrors the encoder structure, reconstructing mel-spectrograms from latents. Like an artist converting a rough sketch back to a detailed painting, the decoder progressively adds resolution and detail through its upsampling stages:

```python
# From ltx_core/model/audio_vae/audio_vae.py
class AudioDecoder(torch.nn.Module):
    def __init__(self, *,
        ch: int,
        out_ch: int,                          # Output channels (2 for stereo)
        ch_mult: Tuple[int, ...] = (1, 2, 4, 8),
        z_channels: int,                      # 128 input latent channels
        mel_bins: int = 64,
        ...
    ):
        # Denormalization using per-channel stats
        self.per_channel_statistics = PerChannelStatistics(latent_channels=ch)

        # Input projection from latent channels
        self.conv_in = make_conv2d(z_channels, ch * ch_mult[-1], ...)

        # Middle block and upsampling path
        self.mid = build_mid_block(...)
        self.up, final_channels = build_upsampling_path(...)

        # Output projection to mel channels
        self.conv_out = make_conv2d(final_channels, out_ch, ...)

    def forward(self, sample: Tensor) -> Tensor:
        # 1. Denormalize latents
        sample, target_shape = self._denormalize_latents(sample)

        # 2. Project to high-dimensional features
        h = self.conv_in(sample)

        # 3. Middle block processing
        h = run_mid_block(self.mid, h)

        # 4. Upsampling path (4 stages, reverse of encoder)
        h = self._run_upsampling_path(h)

        # 5. Final normalization and output
        h = self._finalize_output(h)

        return self._adjust_output_shape(h, target_shape)
```

The decoder handles variable-length audio through careful shape management, cropping, or padding outputs to match the target temporal length.

## HiFi-GAN Style Vocoder

The final stage converts mel-spectrograms to waveforms using a vocoder based on the HiFi-GAN architecture. If the audio decoder is like converting a sketch to a painting, the vocoder is like bringing that painting to life. This process transforms the static frequency representation into vibrant, audible sound waves. This is a learned synthesis model that produces high-quality audio from mel features:

```
# From ltx_core/model/audio_vae/vocoder.py
class Vocoder(torch.nn.Module):
    def __init__(self,
        resblock_kernel_sizes: List[int] = [3, 7, 11],
        upsample_rates: List[int] = [6, 5, 2, 2, 2],      # Total: 240×
        upsample_kernel_sizes: List[int] = [16, 15, 8, 4, 4],
        upsample_initial_channel: int = 1024,
        stereo: bool = True,
        output_sample_rate: int = 24000,
    ):
        # Input: 128 channels for stereo (2 × 64 mel bins)
        in_channels = 128 if stereo else 64
        self.conv_pre = nn.Conv1d(
            in_channels, upsample_initial_channel, 7, padding=3
        )

        # 5 upsampling stages with transposed convolutions
        self.ups = nn.ModuleList()
        for i, (stride, kernel_size) in enumerate(zip(
            upsample_rates,
            upsample_kernel_sizes,
        )):
            self.ups.append(nn.ConvTranspose1d(
                upsample_initial_channel // (2**i),
                upsample_initial_channel // (2**(i+1)),
                kernel_size, stride,
                padding=(kernel_size - stride) // 2,
            ))

        # Multi-receptive field fusion ResBlocks
        self.resblocks = nn.ModuleList()  # 3 kernels × 5 stages = 15 blocks

        # Output: 2 channels for stereo waveform
        self.conv_post = nn.Conv1d(
            final_channels, 2 if stereo else 1, 7, padding=3
        )

        # Total upsampling: 6 × 5 × 2 × 2 × 2 = 240
        self.upsample_factor = math.prod(stride for stride in upsample_rates)
```

The vocoder's multireceptive field (MRF) architecture is crucial for audio quality. By applying three parallel `ResBlocks` with different kernel sizes (3, 7, 11) and averaging their outputs, the model captures patterns at multiple temporal scales simultaneously:

```
    # Multi-receptive field fusion in forward pass
    def forward(self, x: Tensor) -> Tensor:
        # Rearrange stereo mel: [B, 2, T, 64] → [B, 128, T]
        x = einops.rearrange(x, "b s c t -> b (s c) t")

        x = self.conv_pre(x)  # [B, 1024, T]

        for i in range(self.num_upsamples):  # 5 stages
            x = F.leaky_relu(x, LRELU_SLOPE)
            x = self.ups[i](x)  # Transposed conv upsample

            # Apply 3 ResBlocks with different receptive fields
            # kernels: [3, 7, 11] with dilations [1, 3, 5]
            block_outputs = torch.stack([
                self.resblocks[idx](x) for idx in range(start, end)
            ], dim=0)

            # Average outputs for multi-scale fusion
            x = block_outputs.mean(dim=0)

        x = self.conv_post(F.leaky_relu(x))
        return torch.tanh(x)  # [B, 2, T×240]
```

Why 240x upsampling? The vocoder upsamples 240x because mel-spectrograms have approximately 100 frames per second (16 kHz/160 hop), whereas the output waveform needs 24,000 samples per second. Thus: 24,000 / 100 = 240. The factorization 6 × 5 × 2 × 2 × 2 distributes this across 5 stages with decreasing complexity (larger upsamples when channels are high, smaller when they're low).

## AudioPatchifier

Before audio latents enter the transformer, the `AudioPatchifier` converts them to the sequence format expected by attention layers and computes timing metadata. This is analogous to how a video editor marks timecodes, providing precise temporal anchors that enable synchronization:

```
# From ltx_core/components/patchifiers.py
class AudioPatchifier(Patchifier):
    def __init__(self,
        patch_size: int,                        # 1 (no frequency patching)
        sample_rate: int = 16000,
        hop_length: int = 160,
        audio_latent_downsample_factor: int = 4,
        is_causal: bool = True,
    ):
        self.hop_length = hop_length
        self.sample_rate = sample_rate
        self.audio_latent_downsample_factor = audio_latent_downsample_factor
```

```
def patchify(self, audio_latents: Tensor) -> Tensor:
    # [B, C, T, F] → [B, T, C×F] - flatten freq into features
    return einops.rearrange(audio_latents, "b c t f -> b t (c f)")

def unpatchify(self, audio_latents: Tensor, output_shape) -> Tensor:
    # [B, T, C×F] → [B, C, T, F] - restore structure
    return einops.rearrange(
        audio_latents, "b t (c f) -> b c t f",
        c=output_shape.channels, f=output_shape.mel_bins
    )

def _get_audio_latent_time_in_sec(self, start_latent, end_latent, ...):
    # Convert latent indices to real-time seconds
    audio_latent_frame = torch.arange(start_latent, end_latent)
    audio_mel_frame =
        audio_latent_frame * self.audio_latent_downsample_factor

    if self.is_causal:
        # Offset for causal alignment
        audio_mel_frame = (
            audio_mel_frame
            + 1 - self.audio_latent_downsample_factor
        ).clip(min=0)

    # Convert mel frames to seconds
    return audio_mel_frame * self.hop_length / self.sample_rate
```

The `AudioPatchifier` provides timing information that enables the model to align audio events with video frames at subframe precision. Each audio latent frame represents approximately 40 ms of audio (4 mel frames × 10 ms hop = 40 ms), which maps to roughly 1 video latent frame at 25 FPS.

> Unlike video, which uses 2D spatial patching, audio uses `patch_size=1` with no frequency patching. This preserves the full frequency resolution within each latent frame, treating frequency bins as channels rather than spatial dimensions. The temporal axis is handled by the 4x downsampling in the encoder.

With the audio pipeline explained, we can now examine how these components integrate into LTX-2's production inference system. The "Two-Stage Inference Pipeline" section explores the two-stage pipeline that balances generation quality with computational efficiency.

## Two-Stage Inference Pipeline

If generating a video is like painting, LTX-2's two-stage approach starts with a lower-resolution pass to establish structure, then refines it at full resolution. This allows the model to balance quality and efficiency without requiring a full high-resolution diffusion process. The pipeline is split into two phases: an initial generation stage with guidance, followed by a short refinement stage that adds detail. Figure 7-5 shows how these two stages fit together from prompt to final output.

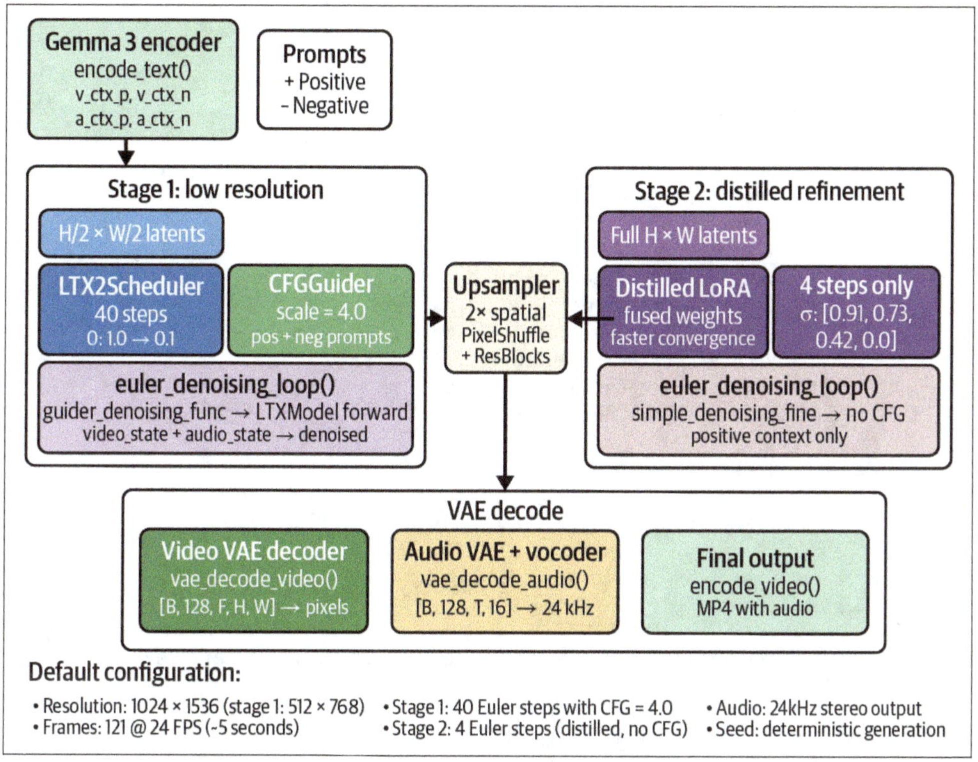


*Figure 7-5. LTX-2 two-stage inference pipeline. Stage 1 generates video and audio at half resolution using 40 Euler steps with CFG guidance. The spatial upsampler doubles resolution, then Stage 2 refines with a distilled LoRA using only 4 steps without CFG. Final outputs are decoded through Video VAE and Audio VAE + Vocoder.*

## Pipeline Initialization: ModelLedger

The `ModelLedger` class serves as the central coordinator for lazy model loading and LoRA management. Think of it as a production stage manager knowing where every prop and actor are but only bringing them on stage when their cue arrives. Rather than load all 19B parameters upfront, it creates builders that instantiate models on demand:

```
# From ltx_pipelines/utils/model_ledger.py
class ModelLedger:
    """Central coordinator for loading and building LTX-2 models."""
```

```
    def __init__(self,
        dtype: torch.dtype,                        # torch.bfloat16
        device: torch.device,                      # cuda
        checkpoint_path: str,                      # Path to .safetensors
        gemma_root_path: str,                      # Path to Gemma weights
        spatial_upsampler_path: str,               # 2x upsampler weights
        loras: list[LoraPathStrengthAndSDOps],     # Optional LoRAs
        fp8transformer: bool = False,              # FP8 quantization
    ):
        # Create builders for each component
        self.transformer_builder = Builder(
            model_path=checkpoint_path,
            model_class_configurator=LTXModelConfigurator,
            loras=tuple(loras),
        )
        self.vae_decoder_builder = Builder(...)
        self.vae_encoder_builder = Builder(...)
        self.audio_decoder_builder = Builder(...)
        self.vocoder_builder = Builder(...)
        self.text_encoder_builder = Builder(...)
        self.upsampler_builder = Builder(...)

    def with_loras(self, loras) -> "ModelLedger":
        # Create a new ledger with additional LoRAs (for stage 2 distilled)
        return ModelLedger(..., loras=(*self.loras, *loras))

    # Factory methods - build model on demand
    def transformer(self) -> X0Model:
        return (
            X0Model(self.transformer_builder.build(...)).to(self.device).eval()
        )

    def video_decoder(self) -> VideoDecoder: ...
    def video_encoder(self) -> VideoEncoder: ...
    def audio_decoder(self) -> AudioDecoder: ...
    def vocoder(self) -> Vocoder: ...
    def text_encoder(self) -> AVGemmaTextEncoderModel: ...
    def spatial_upsampler(self) -> LatentUpsampler: ...
```

The two-stage pipeline creates two ledgers sharing the same base weights but with different LoRA configurations:

```
# Stage 1: Base model (optional LoRAs)
self.stage_1_model_ledger = ModelLedger(
    checkpoint_path=checkpoint_path,
    loras=loras,
    ...
)

# Stage 2: Add distilled LoRA on top
self.stage_2_model_ledger = self.stage_1_model_ledger.with_loras(
    loras=distilled_lora,
)
```

Why lazy loading? With a 19B parameter model, loading everything into VRAM simultaneously would exceed most GPU capacities. `ModelLedger` enables loading components only when needed and freeing them after use. The pipeline explicitly deletes references and calls `cleanup_memory()` between stages to reclaim VRAM.

## Stage 1: CFG-Guided Generation

The first stage generates video and audio at half the target resolution using classifier-free guidance. This is where the model establishes the overall structure of the scene, including motion, layout, and coarse audio alignment. At this stage, the model is not focused on fine detail. Instead, it builds a consistent representation that both modalities can refine later.

Here's how the pipeline initializes and runs Stage 1:

```
# From ltx_pipelines/ti2vid_two_stages.py
class TI2VidTwoStagesPipeline:

    @torch.inference_mode()
    def __call__(
        self,
        prompt,
        negative_prompt,
        seed,
        height,
        width,
        num_frames,
        ...,
    ):
        # Initialize random state and components
        generator = torch.Generator(device=self.device).manual_seed(seed)
        noiser = GaussianNoiser(generator=generator)
        stepper = EulerDiffusionStep()
        cfg_guider = CFGGuider(cfg_guidance_scale)  # default: 4.0

        # Encode both positive and negative prompts
        text_encoder = self.stage_1_model_ledger.text_encoder()
        context_p, context_n = encode_text(
            text_encoder, [prompt, negative_prompt]
            )
        v_context_p, a_context_p = context_p  # Video/audio positive
        v_context_n, a_context_n = context_n  # Video/audio negative

        # Free text encoder memory
        del text_encoder
        cleanup_memory()

        # Stage 1 at half resolution
```

```
stage_1_output_shape = VideoPixelShape(
    batch=1,
    frames=num_frames,
    width=width // 2,    # Half width
    height=height // 2,  # Half height
    fps=frame_rate,
)

# Generate sigma schedule
sigmas = LTX2Scheduler().execute(steps=num_inference_steps)  # 40 steps

# Run denoising loop with CFG
video_state, audio_state = denoise_audio_video(
    output_shape=stage_1_output_shape,
    noiser=noiser,
    sigmas=sigmas,
    denoising_loop_fn=first_stage_denoising_loop,  # Uses CFG
    ...
)
```

### Classifier-free guidance (CFG)

CFG steers generation by computing the difference between conditioned and unconditioned predictions. Imagine asking two artists to paint the same scene—one following your detailed description, one working without any guidance. CFG amplifies what makes the guided version different:

```
# From ltx_core/components/guiders.py
@dataclass(frozen=True)
class CFGGuider(GuiderProtocol):
    """Classifier-free guidance guider."""
    scale: float  # Default: 4.0

    def delta(self, cond: Tensor, uncond: Tensor) -> Tensor:
        # Amplify difference between positive and negative
        return (self.scale - 1) * (cond - uncond)

    def enabled(self) -> bool:
        return self.scale != 1.0
```

During each step:

```
# Usage in guider_denoising_func:
def guider_denoising_step(video_state, audio_state, sigmas, step_index):
    # Forward pass with positive prompt
    pos_video, pos_audio = transformer(video=pos_modality, audio=pos_modality)

    if guider.enabled():
        # Forward pass with negative prompt
        neg_video, neg_audio = transformer(
            video=neg_modality,
            audio=neg_modality,
```

```
        )

        # Apply CFG: output = pos + scale*(pos - neg)
        denoised_video = pos_video + guider.delta(pos_video, neg_video)
        denoised_audio = pos_audio + guider.delta(pos_audio, neg_audio)

    return denoised_video, denoised_audio
```

### The Euler denoising loop

Once initialized, the model iteratively removes noise using a fixed schedule of sigma values. Each step updates both video and audio latents together:

```
# From ltx_pipelines/utils/helpers.py
def euler_denoising_loop(
    sigmas: torch.Tensor,
    video_state: LatentState,
    audio_state: LatentState,
    stepper: DiffusionStepProtocol,
    denoise_fn: DenoisingFunc,
) -> tuple[LatentState, LatentState]:
    """Joint audio-video denoising over a diffusion schedule."""

    for step_idx, _ in enumerate(tqdm(sigmas[:-1])):
        # Get denoised predictions from model
        denoised_video, denoised_audio = denoise_fn(
            video_state, audio_state, sigmas, step_idx
        )

        # Apply conditioning mask (blend with clean latent where applicable)
        denoised_video = post_process_latent(
            denoised_video, video_state.denoise_mask, video_state.clean_latent
        )
        denoised_audio = post_process_latent(
            denoised_audio, audio_state.denoise_mask, audio_state.clean_latent
        )

        # Euler step: x_{t-1} = x_t + v * dt
        video_state = replace(video_state,
            latent = stepper.step(
                video_state.latent,
                denoised_video,
                sigmas,
                step_idx,
            )
        )
        audio_state = replace(audio_state,
            latent=stepper.step(
                audio_state.latent,
                denoised_audio, sigmas,
                step_idx
            )
```

```
        )

    return video_state, audio_state
```

Both modalities are updated together at every step, which preserves alignment as noise is removed.

## Spatial Upsampling

Between Stage 1 and Stage 2, the video latents are upsampled from half resolution to full resolution. This is done using a learned upsampler rather than simple interpolation. The upsampler is trained to add plausible detail while preserving the structure generated in Stage 1. Here's how it's implemented:

```
# From ltx_core/model/upsampler/model.py
class LatentUpsampler(torch.nn.Module):
    """2x spatial upsampling for video latents."""

    def __init__(self,
        in_channels: int = 128,
        mid_channels: int = 512,
        num_blocks_per_stage: int = 4,
        spatial_scale: float = 2.0,
    ):
        # Initial projection
        self.initial_conv = nn.Conv3d(in_channels, mid_channels, 3, padding=1)
        self.initial_norm = nn.GroupNorm(32, mid_channels)
        self.initial_activation = nn.SiLU()

        # Pre-upsample ResBlocks
        self.res_blocks = nn.ModuleList([
            ResBlock(mid_channels) for _ in range(num_blocks_per_stage)
        ])

        # 2x spatial upsampling via PixelShuffle
        self.upsampler = nn.Sequential(
            nn.Conv2d(mid_channels, 4 * mid_channels, 3, padding=1),
            PixelShuffleND(2),  # Rearranges channels into 2x spatial
        )

        # Post-upsample ResBlocks
        self.post_upsample_res_blocks = nn.ModuleList([...])

        # Final projection back to latent channels
        self.final_conv = nn.Conv3d(mid_channels, in_channels, 3, padding=1)
```

In the pipeline, the latent is briefly converted out of normalized space, upsampled, and then normalized again:

```
# Usage in pipeline:
def upsample_video(latent, video_encoder, upsampler):
    # Denormalize before upsampling
```

```
    latent = video_encoder.per_channel_statistics.un_normalize(latent)
    # Apply learned 2x upsampling
    latent = upsampler(latent)
    # Re-normalize for stage 2
    return video_encoder.per_channel_statistics.normalize(latent)
```

This step prepares the latent for high-resolution refinement without losing the structure established in Stage 1.

## Stage 2: Distilled Refinement

Stage 2 takes the upsampled latents and refines them at full resolution. Unlike Stage 1, this phase is short and focused on adding detail rather than building structure. There are a few key differences:

- Only 4 steps instead of 40
- No classifier-free guidance
- Uses a distilled LoRA for faster convergence
- Operates at full resolution

Here's how Stage 2 is executed:

```
# Stage 2 in TI2VidTwoStagesPipeline.__call__

# 2x upsample the Stage 1 video latent
upscaled_video_latent = upsample_video(
    latent=video_state.latent,
    video_encoder=video_encoder,
    upsampler=self.stage_2_model_ledger.spatial_upsampler(),
)

# Load transformer with distilled LoRA fused
transformer = self.stage_2_model_ledger.transformer()

# Only 4 distilled sigma values
distilled_sigmas = torch.Tensor(STAGE_2_DISTILLED_SIGMA_VALUES).to(device)
# [0.909375, 0.725, 0.421875, 0.0] - 4 steps instead of 40!

# Simple denoising (no CFG - just positive prompt)
def second_stage_denoising_loop(...):
    return euler_denoising_loop(
        sigmas=sigmas,
        denoise_fn=simple_denoising_func(
            video_context=v_context_p,  # Only positive
            audio_context=a_context_p,
            transformer=transformer,
        ),
        ...
    )
```

```
# Run Stage 2 with upsampled latents as starting point
video_state, audio_state = denoise_audio_video(
    output_shape=stage_2_output_shape,  # Full H×W
    sigmas=distilled_sigmas,
    initial_video_latent=upscaled_video_latent,
    initial_audio_latent=audio_state.latent,
    noise_scale=distilled_sigmas[0],  # Start at 0.909375
    ...
)
```

Stage 2 does not rebuild the scene. It sharpens it. Because the structure is already in place, the model can focus entirely on improving detail and coherence across both modalities. Table 7-4 summarizes the differences between the two stages.

*Table 7-4. Stage 1 versus Stage 2 comparison*

| Aspect | Stage 1 | Stage 2 |
|---|---|---|
| Resolution | H/2 × W/2 | H × W (full) |
| Steps | 40 (default) | 4 (distilled) |
| Guidance | CFG (scale = 4.0) | None |
| Sigma range | 1.0 → 0.1 → 0.0 | 0.91 → 0.0 |
| Model | Base + optional LoRA | Base + distilled LoRA |
| Initial latent | Random noise | Upsampled Stage 1 |
| Purpose | Structure generation | Detail refinement |

## Final Decoding

After Stage 2, the refined latents are converted back into video frames and audio waveforms. The two outputs are then combined into a final video file:

```
# Decode video: [B, 128, F, H/32, W/32] → [B, 3, F, H, W]
decoded_video = vae_decode_video(
    video_state.latent,
    self.stage_2_model_ledger.video_decoder(),
    tiling_config,  # For memory-efficient tiled decoding
    generator,
)

# Decode audio: [B, 128, T, 16] → [B, 2, samples]
decoded_audio = vae_decode_audio(
    audio_state.latent,
    self.stage_2_model_ledger.audio_decoder(),
    self.stage_2_model_ledger.vocoder(),
)

# Combine into final video file
encode_video(
    video=decoded_video,
```

```
        fps=frame_rate,
        audio=decoded_audio,
        audio_sample_rate=24000,
        output_path=output_path,
    )
```

At this point, the pipeline transitions from latent space back into a format that can be viewed and heard.

> Tiled decoding allows longer videos to be processed in smaller chunks, reducing memory usage during reconstruction.

With the inference pipeline complete, we can now move into hands-on implementation.

# Hands-On Implementation

With the architecture and pipeline in place, we can now walk through how to run and extend LTX-2 in practice. This section covers environment setup, model loading, inference, and fine-tuning.

## Environment Setup

LTX-2 uses uv for dependency management, providing fast, reproducible installations:

```
# Clone the repository
git clone https://github.com/Lightricks/LTX-2
cd LTX-2

# Install dependencies with uv (recommended)
uv sync --frozen

# Activate the virtual environment
source .venv/bin/activate

# Alternative: pip installation for specific packages
pip install -e packages/ltx-pipelines
pip install -e packages/ltx-trainer  # For fine-tuning
```

## Hardware Requirements

LTX-2's 19B parameters require substantial compute resources. Table 7-5 provides configuration recommendations for different use cases.

*Table 7-5. Hardware requirements by use case*

| Use case | GPU VRAM | Configuration | Resolution |
|---|---|---|---|
| Inference (FP8) | 24 GB | `--enable-fp8` | 512 × 768, 49 frames |
| Inference (BF16) | 48 GB+ | Default | 1024 × 1,536, 121 frames |
| LoRA training | 32 GB | `ltx2_av_lora_low_vram.yaml` | 960 × 544, 49 frames |
| LoRA training | 80 GB | `ltx2_av_lora.yaml` | 960 × 544, 49 frames |
| Full fine-tuning | 4–8x 80 GB | FSDP distributed | Variable |

## Required Model Downloads

LTX-2 requires four model components. You'll need to download these before running inference:

```
# 1. Main checkpoint (19B parameters)
# Download from: https://huggingface.co/Lightricks/LTX-2
ltx-2-19b-dev.safetensors      # ~38GB
# Or FP8 quantized version:
ltx-2-19b-dev-fp8.safetensors # ~19GB

# 2. Spatial upsampler (for two-stage pipeline)
ltx2_spatial_upscaler.safetensors

# 3. Distilled LoRA (for Stage 2 refinement)
ltx2_distilled_lora.safetensors

# 4. Gemma 3 text encoder (12B)
# Download from:
# https://huggingface.co/google/gemma-3-12b-it-qat-q4_0-unquantized/
```

## Text-to-Video Generation

The recommended pipeline for production use is `TI2VidTwoStagesPipeline`:

```
from ltx_core.loader import (
    LTXV_LORA_COMFY_RENAMING_MAP,
    LoraPathStrengthAndSDOps,
)
from ltx_pipelines.ti2vid_two_stages import TI2VidTwoStagesPipeline

# Configure distilled LoRA for Stage 2
distilled_lora = [
    LoraPathStrengthAndSDOps(
        path="/path/to/ltx2_distilled_lora.safetensors",
```

```
            strength=0.6,
            sd_ops=LTXV_LORA_COMFY_RENAMING_MAP,
        ),
]

# Initialize the two-stage pipeline
pipeline = TI2VidTwoStagesPipeline(
    checkpoint_path="/path/to/ltx-2-19b-dev.safetensors",
    distilled_lora=distilled_lora,
    spatial_upsampler_path="/path/to/ltx2_spatial_upscaler.safetensors",
    gemma_root="/path/to/gemma-3-12b",
    loras=[],  # Optional: additional custom LoRAs
    fp8transformer=True,  # Enable FP8 for lower VRAM
)

# Generate video with audio
pipeline(
    prompt = (
        "A serene mountain lake at sunrise, with mist rising "
        "from the water and birds singing"
    ),
    output_path="output.mp4",
    seed=42,
    height=1024,          # Final output height (Stage 1 uses 512)
    width=1536,           # Final output width (Stage 1 uses 768)
    num_frames=121,       # Must satisfy frames % 8 == 1
    frame_rate=25.0,
    num_inference_steps=40,  # Stage 1 steps (Stage 2 uses 4)
    cfg_guidance_scale=4.0,
)
```

There is a frame constraint: LTX-2 requires the number of frames to satisfy `frames % 8 == 1`. Valid values include: 1, 9, 17, 25, 33, 41, 49, 57, 65, 73, 81, 89, 97, 121.

## Command-Line Interface

All pipelines can be run directly from the command line:

```
# Two-stage text-to-video (recommended for production)
python -m ltx_pipelines.ti2vid_two_stages \
    --checkpoint-path /path/to/ltx-2-19b-dev.safetensors \
    --distilled-lora /path/to/ltx2_distilled_lora.safetensors 0.6 \
    --spatial-upsampler-path /path/to/ltx2_spatial_upscaler.safetensors \
    --gemma-root /path/to/gemma-3-12b \
    --prompt "A beautiful sunset over the ocean" \
    --output-path output.mp4 \
    --height 1024 --width 1536 \
    --num-frames 121
```

```
# Enable FP8 for lower memory usage
PYTORCH_CUDA_ALLOC_CONF=expandable_segments:True \
python -m ltx_pipelines.ti2vid_two_stages --enable-fp8 ...

# Fast distilled pipeline (8 steps total)
python -m ltx_pipelines.distilled ...

# View all options
python -m ltx_pipelines.ti2vid_two_stages --help
```

## Image-to-Video Generation

Animate still images by conditioning on keyframes:

```
# Image conditioning: specify (image_path, frame_index, strength)
pipeline(
    prompt="A cat slowly turning its head and blinking",
    output_path="animated_cat.mp4",
    seed=42,
    height=1024,
    width=1536,
    num_frames=49,
    frame_rate=25.0,
    # Condition on input image at frame 0 with full strength
    images=[("cat_photo.jpg", 0, 1.0)],
)

# Multiple keyframes for interpolation
from ltx_pipelines.keyframe_interpolation import KeyframeInterpolationPipeline

keyframe_pipeline = KeyframeInterpolationPipeline(...)
keyframe_pipeline(
    prompt="Smooth transition between scenes",
    images=[
        ("frame_start.jpg", 0, 1.0),
        ("frame_end.jpg", 120, 1.0),
    ],
    ...
)
```

## Speech Synthesis

LTX-2 supports synchronized speech generation using special tags in the prompt:

```
# Speech tags: <S>...<E> marks spoken content
prompt = """
A news anchor sitting at a desk, speaking clearly to the camera.
<S>Good evening. Today we bring you breaking news from around the world.
Scientists have made a remarkable discovery that could change everything
we know about renewable energy.<E>
"""
```

```
pipeline(
    prompt=prompt,
    output_path="news_anchor.mp4",
    num_frames=121,
    frame_rate=25.0,
    ...
)

# The generated audio will contain synchronized speech
# matching the visual lip movements
```

## Fine-Tuning with LoRA

The `ltx-trainer` package enables efficient fine-tuning on custom datasets. The process involves three main steps: dataset preparation, configuration, and training.

### Dataset preparation

The following example shows the typical dataset preparation workflow used before LoRA fine-tuning with the `ltx_trainer`:

```
# Step 1: Organize videos with captions
# Create JSON with video paths and captions
[
    {"video": "video1.mp4", "caption": "A dog playing in the park"},
    {"video": "video2.mp4", "caption": "Ocean waves at sunset"}
]

# Step 2: (Optional) Auto-caption videos
uv run python scripts/caption_videos.py videos_dir/ --output dataset.json

# Step 3: Precompute latents and embeddings
uv run python scripts/process_dataset.py dataset.json \
    --resolution-buckets "960x544x49" \
    --model-path /path/to/ltx-2-19b-dev.safetensors \
    --text-encoder-path /path/to/gemma-3-12b
```

### Training configuration

The following YAML configuration provides a typical starting point for LoRA fine-tuning with `ltx-trainer`:

```
# configs/my_training.yaml
model:
  model_path: "/path/to/ltx-2-19b-dev.safetensors"
  text_encoder_path: "/path/to/gemma-3-12b"
  training_mode: "lora"

training_strategy:
  name: "text_to_video"
  first_frame_conditioning_p: 0.1
  with_audio: true  # Enable audio training
```

```
  audio_latents_dir: "audio_latents"

lora:
  rank: 64
  target_modules:
    - "to_k"   # Matches video, audio, and cross-modal attention
    - "to_q"
    - "to_v"
    - "to_out.0"

data:
  preprocessed_data_root: "/path/to/preprocessed/data"

optimization:
  learning_rate: 1e-4
  train_batch_size: 1
  gradient_accumulation_steps: 4
  max_train_steps: 1000

output_dir: "outputs/my_lora"
```

#### Launch training

Once the dataset has been prepared and the training configuration is complete, you can launch fine-tuning using either a single GPU or a multi-GPU setup:

```
# Single GPU
uv run python scripts/train.py configs/my_training.yaml

# Multi-GPU with Accelerate
uv run accelerate launch scripts/train.py configs/my_training.yaml
```

## Using Trained LoRAs for Inference

After training completes, the resulting LoRA can be loaded during inference and applied to new prompts:

```
# Load pipeline with custom LoRA
custom_loras = [
    LoraPathStrengthAndSDOps(
        path="/path/to/my_trained_lora.safetensors",
        strength=0.8,
        sd_ops=LTXV_LORA_COMFY_RENAMING_MAP,
    ),
]

pipeline = TI2VidTwoStagesPipeline(
    checkpoint_path=checkpoint_path,
    distilled_lora=distilled_lora,
    spatial_upsampler_path=upsampler_path,
    gemma_root=gemma_root,
    loras=custom_loras,  # Your trained LoRA
```

```
)

# Generate with your style/concept
pipeline(
    prompt="Your custom style applied to a new scene",
    ...
)
```

Table 7-6 summarizes the available training modes and highlights the trade-offs between memory requirements, output size, and intended use cases.

*Table 7-6. Training mode selection guide*

| Training mode | Use case | Memory | Output size |
|---|---|---|---|
| LoRA | Style, character, or effect adaptation | 32–80 GB | ~200 MB |
| Audio-video LoRA | Synchronized audio-video styles | 32–80 GB | ~200 MB |
| IC-LoRA | Video-to-video transformations | 40–80 GB | ~200 MB |
| Full fine-tuning | Major capability changes | 4–8x 80 GB | ~38 GB |

For production evaluation, a best practice would be to combine automated metrics with human evaluation. Automated metrics capture technical quality (FID, CLIP score, audiovisual sync), but human raters better assess subjective aspects like realism, artistic quality, and semantic coherence.

## Architectural Evolution: From Research to Production

LTX-2 reflects a shift from research prototypes to production-ready systems. Compared to earlier approaches, it consolidates multiple design decisions into a single, scalable architecture. Table 7-7 summarizes that progression.

*Table 7-7. Evolution from Ovi to LTX-2*

| Aspect | Ovi (Research) | LTX-2 (Production) |
|---|---|---|
| Architecture | Twin backbone (2x WanModel) | Unified DiT (48 layers) |
| Parameters | ~5B | ~19B |
| Text encoder | T5 | Gemma 3 (12B) |
| Cross-modal | Injected projections | Native bidirectional attention |
| Latent channels | 48 (video), 20 (audio) | 128 (both) |
| Pipeline | Single-stage | Two-stage with upsampler |
| Scheduler | UniPC/DPM++ | LTX2Scheduler (Euler) |
| Training | Research scripts | Full LoRA |

The shift from twin backbones to a unified transformer, the 4x increase in parameters, and the move to native bidirectional attention all reflect lessons learned from scaling audio-video generation to production quality. Figure 7-6 provides a visual summary of the complete LTX-2 pipeline:

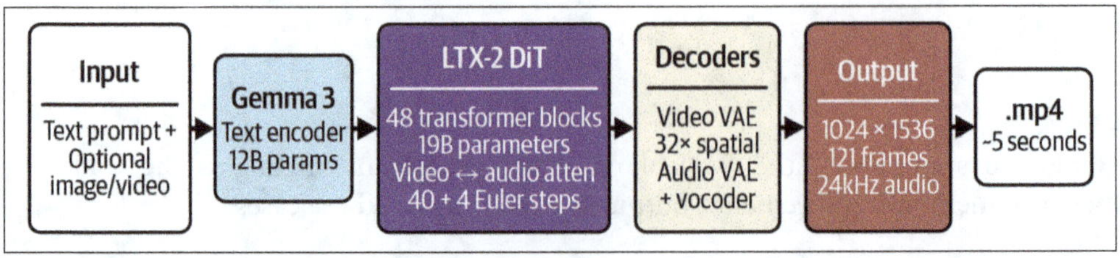


*Figure 7-6. Complete LTX-2 pipeline: from text prompt through Gemma encoding, unified DiT denoising, and VAE decoding to synchronized audio-video output*

# Summary

This chapter introduced the core ideas behind synchronized audio-video generation and how they are implemented in LTX-2:

- A unified transformer processes audio and video together, allowing alignment to emerge during generation.
- Cross-modal attention at every layer enables continuous interaction between modalities.
- Audio is compressed into a structured latent space that preserves timing and perceptual detail.
- A two-stage pipeline separates structure generation from detail refinement.
- Practical deployment relies on patterns like lazy loading, LoRA composition, and efficient decoding.

Taken together, these pieces form a complete system for generating synchronized audio and video from a single prompt. With video generation, video understanding, and now audio-video synthesis in place, you have the core components of a multimodal pipeline. These capabilities can be combined into a loop of generation, evaluation, and refinement.

The next step is turning these building blocks into real workflows. In Chapter 8, we move from model architecture to system design using ComfyUI, where these ideas become reusable, production-ready pipelines.

CHAPTER 8

# From Models to Systems

*Learning Objective:* In this chapter, you will learn what changes when a generative AI model becomes a product. By the end of this chapter, you will recognize the eight architectural patterns that distinguish production AI applications from research scripts, see how each is solved differently across LTX Desktop, ComfyUI, and InvokeAI, and have implemented the same custom extension on all three.

Throughout this book we've moved through video AI from the inside out: foundations and a first generated video (Chapter 1); the data behind generation (Chapter 2); the model itself across pipelines, training, and fine-tuning (Chapters 3 through 5); understanding video with vision-language models (Chapter 6); and synchronizing audio with cross-modal attention (Chapter 7). By the end of Chapter 7, you could load LTX-2's 22-billion-parameter checkpoint from Hugging Face, drive it from Python, and reason about why each architectural decision was made.

But a model is not a product. Research code lives in notebooks and scripts; production code lives in systems. Think of the difference as the gap between a working engine on a workbench and a car you can drive home from the dealership. The engine matters, but everything around it is what turns it into something an actual person can use. The eight architectural patterns of this chapter are concrete answers to the work created in going from model to product.

## The Gap Between a Model and a Product

When a model is just a model, the user is the engineer who downloads it. When a model becomes a product, the user is anyone who installs the app. That single shift creates an enormous amount of work that has nothing to do with diffusion timesteps or transformer blocks. Installing the model brings license acceptance recorded as durable state, GPU and platform capability detection, an API-mode fallback for users without sufficient hardware, and model downloads with per-file progress and atomic recovery. Driving it brings a UI that lets people use the model without touching Python and real-time progress streamed back from a different process. Maintaining it brings updates that ship without breaking installs, telemetry that reports what works without leaking user content, and security taken seriously even when the whole system runs on a single laptop.

None of this is machine learning (ML). All of it is the difference between a model and a product.

## What "Production AI System" Means in 2026

The phrase *production AI system* gets used loosely, so let's be concrete. Across the three reference architectures I examine in this chapter, five qualities consistently distinguish production codebases from ad hoc scripts:

*Modularity*
: Components can be swapped, upgraded, and reused independently. A new VAE doesn't require rewriting the entire pipeline.

*Composability*
: Simple building blocks combine into complex pipelines. The same denoising primitive serves text-to-video, image-to-video, audio-to-video, and retake.

*Observability*
: Logs, metrics, progress events, and health probes let you understand and debug behavior even when the system runs on a user's machine half a continent away.

*Extensibility*
: New capabilities arrive through documented extension points without modifying core code.

*Reliability*
: The system handles errors gracefully, validates inputs, and degrades predictably when something it depended on becomes unavailable.

These five aren't the patterns of this chapter; they're the qualities that the patterns produce.

## Three Reference Architectures

Three open source projects dominate contemporary video-AI workflow tooling:

- LTX Desktop is the production surface Lightricks ships for LTX-2: a three-layer Electron + React + Python application with strong typing, clear process boundaries, and a vendor-controlled extension model.

- ComfyUI is the most widely used community tool: a Python plug-in mesh with loose contracts where the long tail of capabilities comes from third-party nodes—breadth over rigor.
- InvokeAI is a service-oriented monolith with typed invocations, a session queue, and an explicit services layer.

Diffusion-MagiUI, SwarmUI, and several proprietary tools occupy adjacent space, but these three cover the design space well enough that any contemporary project will recognize itself somewhere on the map.

# LTX Desktop: Eight Patterns

The eight patterns in this section are the spine of the chapter, each one a concrete answer to a piece of the work that turns a model into a product. Figure 8-1 maps the codebase those patterns describe: a sandboxed React renderer, an Electron main process for OS integration, and a FastAPI Python backend for ML execution. The renderer talks to Electron over a typed inter-process communication (IPC) bridge for OS concerns, and to Python directly over HTTP and WebSocket for ML work.

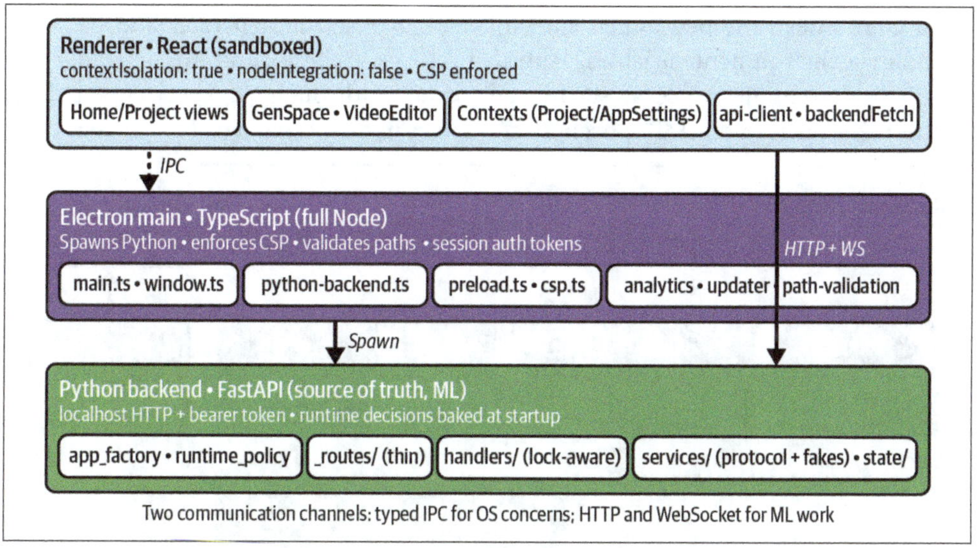


*Figure 8-1. LTX Desktop's three-layer architecture and the channels between processes*

## Pattern 1: The Two-Process Architecture

Why does his matter? A generative AI desktop app needs to do two very different jobs: paint pixels on screen with a modern UI framework and run inference on a multibillion-parameter model. Picking one process to do both means picking which job to make harder. Run everything in Python, and you give up modern UI frameworks and native desktop integration; run everything in TypeScript, and you give up the entire Python ML ecosystem. Two processes (the renderer for the UI, Python for the work) let each tool do what it is best at, with an orchestration layer between them that owns operating-system integration. The complexity cost is real (lifecycle management, IPC, error propagation across the boundary), but it is bounded; the productivity gain is open-ended.

#### Electron owns lifecycle, Python owns work

The division lives in `electron/python-backend.ts`. Spawning, monitoring, and shutdown of the Python backend all happen there; the renderer never touches the Python process directly. It asks Electron, and Electron asks Python. The reverse direction is similarly clean: the Python backend exposes a localhost HTTP API and does not know or care that Electron is the parent. You could drive it from a CLI tool or CI pipeline without changing a line of Python.

#### Spawning the backend

The startup sequence is worth tracing because it surfaces several other patterns we will see later. Figure 8-2 walks app launch to the first frame. Two details matter for what comes next: the per-launch auth tokens that Electron generates and passes to Python via environment variables (Pattern 4 returns to these), and the capability policy Python computes once at startup and exposes through `/api/runtime-policy` (Pattern 2 returns to that). The orchestration lives in `electron/python-backend.ts`.

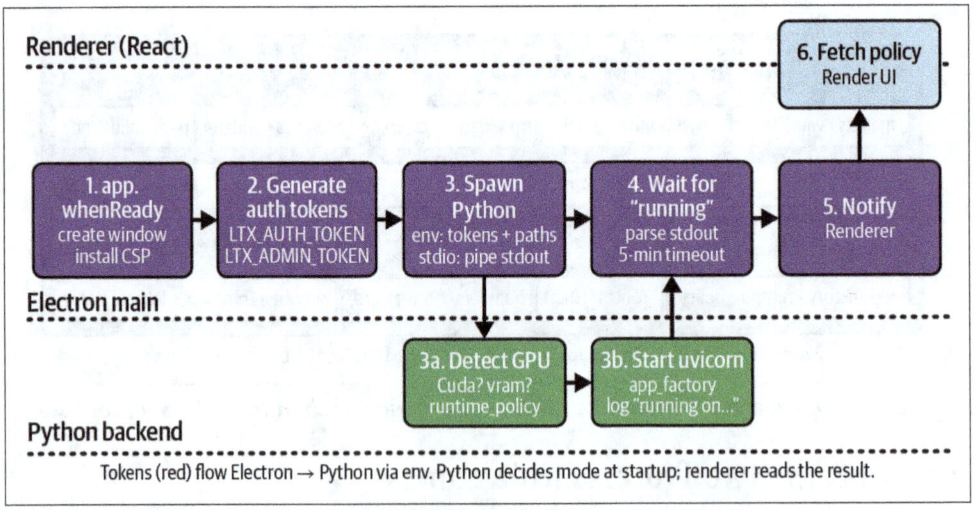


*Figure 8-2. The Electron-spawns-Python startup sequence, from app launch (step 1) to first UI frame (step 6)*

### Health monitoring and restart

Electron polls `/health` and listens for unexpected process exits. If Python dies, Electron publishes `{status: 'restarting'}` and attempts a fresh spawn, with a 10-second debounce to prevent restart storms when the failure is deterministic. If restart still fails, Electron publishes `{status: 'dead', exitCode}` and stops trying; the renderer subscribes and shows a clear error rather than an unresponsive UI. This is the difference between an app that survives a transient GPU driver glitch and one that requires a force-quit.

### Backend adoption: Surviving stale processes

Every developer of a Python-spawning desktop app eventually hits this: a previous run crashed without cleaning up, the Python process is still bound to the port, and the new run cannot start. Naive code prints "`EADDRINUSE`" and gives up. LTX Desktop instead probes the port. If a backend is alive (identifiable by `/health`), it adopts the existing process, attempts a graceful takeover via `POST /api/system/shutdown`, and waits up to eight seconds before spawning fresh. The user sees a brief delay; they do not see an installer-level error.

The two-process architecture pattern applies to any desktop application that needs to combine a modern UI framework with a heavy compute backend. The specific tools differ (you might use Tauri instead of Electron, or Rust instead of Python), but the lifecycle responsibilities are the same: one side owns the OS surface, the other side owns the work, and the boundary between them is explicit, typed, and observable.

> The most common mistake I see in practice is letting Python concerns leak into the renderer (for example, having the renderer directly spawn or signal the Python process). This entangles two layers that should be independent and makes either layer hard to replace. The discipline that separates a well-architected two-process app from a tangled one is this: the renderer talks to Python only over HTTP or WebSocket, never over OS primitives.

## Pattern 2: Backend as Source of Truth

A production AI application has to answer the same capability questions over and over: Can this user run the model locally? Is the GPU sufficient? Are the required model files present? Should this request route to the local model or the hosted API? Think of these like the rules of the road. If every car decides for itself which side to drive on, you get crashes, not traffic. The backend-as-source-of-truth pattern picks one layer to be the authority: capability decisions are made in one place, baked at startup, and exposed to the rest of the system as a read-only fact. Every other layer asks; nobody decides on its own.

### Capability detection at startup

LTX Desktop concentrates capability detection in `backend/runtime_config/runtime_policy.py`:

```
# From backend/runtime_config/runtime_policy.py (LTX Desktop @ 81f7f45)
def decide_force_api_generations(
    system: str,
    cuda_available: bool,
    vram_gb: int | None,
) -> bool:
    if system == "Darwin":              # Always API-only on macOS
        return True
    if system in ("Windows", "Linux"):
        if not cuda_available:
            return True
        if vram_gb is None:
            return True
        return vram_gb < 15             # <15GB VRAM forces API mode
    return True                          # Fail closed for unknown platforms
```

Figure 8-3 traces this same logic as a decision tree, showing how the local-versus-API choice flows from the startup capability check.

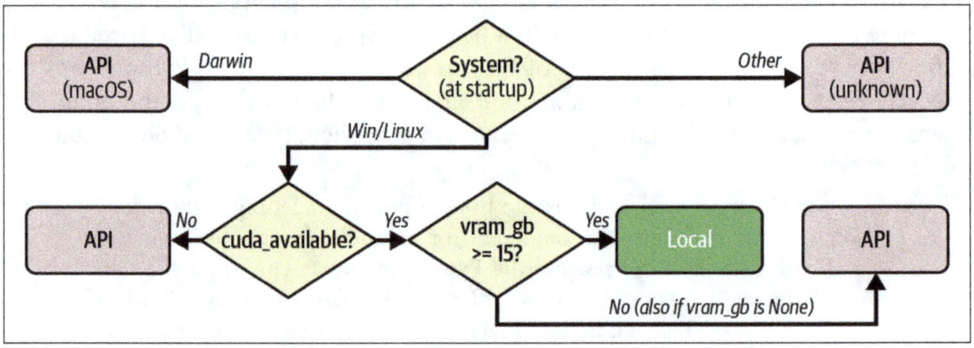


*Figure 8-3. The local-versus-API decision tree, computed once at Python startup*

The 15 GB threshold is deliberate: below that, generations would risk an out-of-memory (OOM) error midrun, and a partial failure 60 seconds into a 90-second job is worse than telling the user up front.

### The local-versus-API decision

Notice the complexity this small function eliminates. Without backend as source of truth, "local or API?" gets answered by the React generation form, the Python request handler, and the model loader that decides which checkpoint to fetch. Three answers, three sources of bugs. With this pattern, one answer: computed once, stored once, read by everything. Features compose: if `force_api_generations` is true, `REQUIRED_MODEL_TYPES` is empty, no downloads are triggered, no download UI is shown, and no GPU settings appear. You do not have to remember to disable each one individually.

### Exposing the decision via /api/runtime-policy

The Python-side decision reaches the frontend through one endpoint:

```
# From backend/_routes/runtime_policy.py (LTX Desktop @ 81f7f45)
GET /api/runtime-policy → { "force_api_generations": bool }
```

The frontend reads this once at startup, stores it in `AppSettingsContext`, and renders the right UI. The frontend never decides; it asks. Tighten the VRAM threshold to 16 GB in a future release, and no frontend change is required. The next startup returns a different value, the UI adjusts, and that is the end of it.

The lesson goes beyond capability detection and beyond AI desktop apps. Anywhere your system has a runtime answer that depends on the environment (web app feature flags, multiregion routing by geography, a CLI choosing between local and remote backends), pick one layer to be the canonical source and have every other layer ask. The pattern's name in distributed-systems literature is "configuration as a service"; the name I prefer is "make the decision once, then publish it." Cost: one round-trip on startup. Benefit: an entire class of subtle inconsistency bugs goes away.

> Two pitfalls show up consistently. First, it is tempting to recompute the decision per request to handle "what if the GPU appeared mid-session?" This is rarely worth the complexity. GPUs do not actually appear midsession, and the rare cases where capability does change (a model finished downloading) are better handled by a different pattern: capability changes trigger a runtime-policy republish event. Second, do not let the published policy drift from reality. If the Python backend caches a stale answer because nothing prompted it to recompute, the frontend will believe a lie. The cleanest discipline is "policy is computed at startup; the only way to change it is to restart the backend."

## Pattern 3: The Typed IPC Bridge

Every Electron app accumulates IPC surface area: the renderer needs the main process to open files, show dialogs, manage windows, save settings, and control updates. Without discipline, those channels grow into a sprawl of string identifiers, untyped payloads, and silent disagreements about what each side expects.

The result is the most frustrating class of Electron bug: a renderer call that works in one version, breaks in the next, and produces no compile-time error because no compiler ever saw both sides at once. The typed IPC bridge pattern fixes the drift architecturally by making the IPC contract a single shared object that both sides derive their behavior from. Think of it like a treaty signed by two governments: neither side can pretend it says something different from what the other side has signed.

### contextBridge and the sandboxed renderer

LTX Desktop's renderer is sandboxed in the strict sense: `contextIsolation: true, nodeIntegration: false`. The renderer process has zero direct access to node APIs, the file system, or any Electron internals. The only way the renderer can ask the main process to do anything is through `window.electronAPI`, an object exposed via Electron's `contextBridge` in the preload script:

```
// From electron/preload.ts (LTX Desktop @ 81f7f45)
import { contextBridge } from 'electron';
import { electronAPISchemas } from '../shared/electron-api-schema';

const electronAPI = buildClientFromSchemas(electronAPISchemas);
contextBridge.exposeInMainWorld('electronAPI', electronAPI);
```

That last line is the entire surface: every capability the renderer has is in that object, and adding or removing one involves a single edit there.

### One Zod schema, two sides

The piece that makes this scale is `shared/electron-api-schema.ts`. It uses a runtime-validation library called Zod to declare every IPC method's input and output as a typed schema:

```
// From shared/electron-api-schema.ts (LTX Desktop @ 81f7f45)
export const electronAPISchemas = {
  acceptLicense: {
    input:  z.void(),
    output: z.object({ accepted: z.boolean() }),
  },
  fetchLicenseText: {
    input:  z.void(),
    output: z.object({ text: z.string() }),
  },
  approvePath: {
    input:  z.object({ path: z.string() }),
    output: z.object({ approved: z.boolean() }),
  },
  // ... all other IPC methods
} as const;
```

Both sides of the bridge derive from this object. The Electron handler-registration code uses it to know what each handler should accept and return; the renderer's TypeScript types are derived from it via TypeScript's type inference. The implementation in `electron/ipc/typed-handle.ts` is small but load-bearing:

```
// From electron/ipc/typed-handle.ts (LTX Desktop @ 81f7f45)
export function handle<K extends keyof Schemas>(
  key: K,
  handler: (input: z.infer<Schemas[K]['input']>)
           => Promise<z.infer<Schemas[K]['output']>>
) {
  ipcMain.handle(key, async (_event, raw) => {
    const input = Schemas[key].input.parse(raw);     // validate at boundary
    const output = await handler(input);
    return Schemas[key].output.parse(output);        // validate response shape
  });
}
```

The handler's input and output are both fully typed from the schema. The Zod parse on input throws on malformed payloads, catching bad renderer code or, hypothetically, malicious renderer code. The output parse catches handler bugs that produce unexpected response shapes. Both call site and handler check against the same source.

### Adding a new IPC method

The workflow is one file edit: add the method's input/output schema to `electronAPISchemas`, register the handler with typed `handle()`—TypeScript refuses to compile if the signature disagrees—and call `window.electronAPI.<methodName>(...)` from the renderer with full autocomplete. No second file, no protobuf to regenerate, no string identifier to type twice and misspell once.

The single-schema-as-source-of-truth pattern applies anywhere two sides of a wire need to agree on a contract: client/server JSON APIs, Wasm boundaries, RPC schemas. The specific tools differ (Zod is one good choice for TypeScript, TypeScript's own type system is another, JSON Schema with code generation is a third), but the principle is the same: define the contract once, derive both sides from it, and never let either side disagree silently.

> Two pitfalls show up consistently. First, do not let the contract become "anything goes" by typing every payload as `z.any()` to skip validation. The discipline only works if the schema is restrictive enough to catch real bugs. Second, when removing a method from the schema, remove the renderer's call to it in the same commit. TypeScript will catch this for you if both sides type-check together; ensure your CI does. Schema-side cleanups that leave dangling renderer calls produce runtime errors that the type system was meant to prevent.

## Pattern 4: Localhost as a Security Boundary

"It is just localhost" is the most common security shortcut taken by developers building desktop AI apps, and it's the kind of shortcut that ages badly. It's the same shortcut as a hotel that doesn't lock internal doors because "we trust the guests." The assumption holds, until it doesn't. The reasoning sounds airtight: "The only thing that can talk to my Python backend is my own renderer process, both running on the same machine." Until you remember that any other process on that machine can also talk to the backend, browser tabs from other applications can sometimes reach localhost ports through subtle vulnerabilities, and the next version of the app might want to expose the backend to a remote orchestrator. Treating localhost as a security boundary from day one costs almost nothing; treating it as trusted and discovering otherwise costs much more.

### Per-session auth tokens

LTX Desktop generates two random 32-byte tokens at every Electron start and passes them to the Python subprocess via environment variables:

```
// From electron/python-backend.ts (LTX Desktop @ 81f7f45)
import { randomBytes } from 'crypto';

const LTX_AUTH_TOKEN  = randomBytes(32).toString('base64url');
const LTX_ADMIN_TOKEN = randomBytes(32).toString('base64url');
// Both tokens are passed to the Python subprocess via env vars (see Pattern 1).
```

The Python backend reads these tokens at startup and gates every request: HTTP calls carry one in `Authorization: Bearer`; WebSocket connections carry one in a query parameter. A request without a valid token is rejected with 401 before any handler sees it. The two-token split is intentional: `LTX_AUTH_TOKEN` authorizes ordinary inference and configuration; `LTX_ADMIN_TOKEN` authorizes a small set of administrative endpoints (graceful shutdown, health introspection, path approval). An exfiltrated user-facing token can drive generations but cannot shut the backend down or grant filesystem access.

### Constant-time token comparison

The middleware uses constant-time comparison rather than ==:

```
# From backend/app_factory.py (LTX Desktop @ 81f7f45)
import hmac

def verify_token(provided: str, expected: str) -> bool:
    return hmac.compare_digest(provided.encode(), expected.encode())
```

A naive == short-circuits on the first differing byte, leaking how much of the token an attacker has guessed correctly. The constant-time variant takes the same time regardless. This is overkill for localhost in practice, but also for one line of code, with the discipline transferring cleanly if the backend is ever reachable beyond localhost.

### Content security policy in production

The renderer's content security policy is enforced by Electron itself, not declared in HTML, so the renderer cannot relax it:

```
// From electron/csp.ts (LTX Desktop @ 81f7f45) – production
session.defaultSession.webRequest.onHeadersReceived((details, callback) => {
  callback({
    responseHeaders: {
      ...details.responseHeaders,
      'Content-Security-Policy': [
        "default-src 'self'; "
        + "script-src 'self'; "          // no inline scripts
        + "style-src 'self' 'unsafe-inline'; "
        + "object-src 'none'; "
        + "connect-src 'self' http://127.0.0.1:* ws://127.0.0.1:*"
      ],
    },
  });
});
```

Dev mode relaxes CSP for Vite's hot-module reload (`script-src 'self' 'unsafe-inline'`); production is strict. The renderer can load scripts only from its own bundle, can connect only to localhost, and cannot embed plug-ins or arbitrary objects. Even a cross-site scripting (XSS) injection would be sharply limited.

### Path validation across platforms

The renderer can ask Electron to read or expose certain filesystem paths: generated outputs, custom model directories, and project folders. Every such request flows through `electron/path-validation.ts`, which enforces a white list:

```
// From electron/path-validation.ts (LTX Desktop @ 81f7f45)
const isWindows = process.platform === 'win32'

function normalize(p: string): string {
  return isWindows ? path.resolve(p).toLowerCase() : path.resolve(p)
}

export function validatePath(inputPath: string, allowedRoots: string[]): string {
  const cleaned = inputPath.startsWith('file://')
    ? stripFileUrl(inputPath)
    : inputPath
  const resolved = path.resolve(cleaned)
  const norm = normalize(resolved)
```

```
    for (const root of allowedRoots.map(normalize)) {
      if (norm === root || norm.startsWith(root + path.sep)) return resolved
    }
    // ... per-call approvePath() additions checked similarly
    throw new Error(`Path not allowed: ${inputPath}`)
  }
```

The implementation is case-sensitive on Linux or Mac and case-insensitive on Windows, which catches the surprising number of path-traversal attacks that exploit case-folding mismatches. Relative paths are resolved before checking. `file://` URLs are stripped. The white list is small and explicit; the per-call `approvePath()` escape hatch is auditable.

The pattern applies to any local service: an SQL Server install, a developer-tooling daemon, a desktop AI app, a local-first sync engine. The moves are the same: authenticate every request even from local callers, constant-time compare credentials, scope them to a session, run least-privilege, and validate user-controllable inputs at every trust boundary. The cost of the discipline is small; the cost of skipping it and later discovering you needed it is much larger.

> Two pitfalls account for most security regressions I see in apps trying to adopt this pattern. The first pitfall is persisting tokens to disk for "convenience": at which point they are no longer session-scoped and the threat model changes. The second pitfall is relaxing the CSP in production because "we ship safe scripts": the renderer's promises about its own behavior are exactly what an attacker would compromise. CSP enforced from the main process is strictly stronger than CSP declared by the renderer.

## Pattern 5: Model Lifecycle: Download, License, Storage

Generative AI models are large: LTX-2.3's 22 GB checkpoint is around 44 GB in bfloat16 (bf16) form, plus a 7 GB upsampler, plus a 25 GB Gemma 3 text encoder. Bundling them into the installer is impractical, so the files have to be downloaded after install. None of this is exotic, but the moments it goes wrong are the moments users abandon the app. Think of model lifecycle as the airport jetway: the user has just bought a ticket (installed the app); they need a clear walkway from terminal to seat, with someone telling them exactly where they are in the boarding process. License acceptance, GPU-aware download decisions, per-file progress, recovery from interrupted transfers, platform-canonical storage: each one is a step on that jetway. A well-designed lifecycle gives the user a clear story of what is happening and recovers from interruptions without losing all prior progress.

### Storage roots across platforms

LTX Desktop stores its application data in platform-canonical locations:

*Windows*
: *%LOCALAPPDATA%\LTXDesktop*

*macOS*
: *~/Library/Application Support/LTXDesktop/*

*Linux*
: *$XDG_DATA_HOME/LTXDesktop/ (default ~/.local/share/LTXDesktop/)*

Models live under *<app_data>/models/*, with an optional user-specified override in app settings. The platform-appropriate root means application data integrates correctly with operating-system tools: Time Machine on macOS backs it up by default, Linux respects the XDG Base Directory specification, and Windows shows it as application data when the user uninstalls. The override lets advanced users store models on a separate drive without symlink games.

### The first-run flow

The sequence between "user finishes installing the app" and "user can generate their first video" is the most fragile part of any AI desktop application. LTX Desktop scripts it explicitly. Figure 8-4 traces what happens.

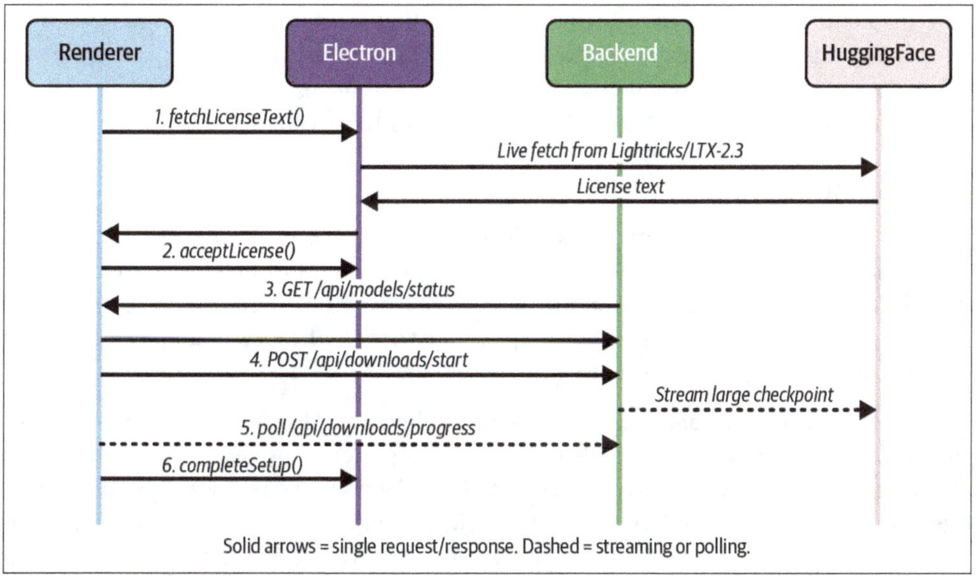


*Figure 8-4. First-run sequence across renderer, Electron, Python backend, and HuggingFace*

Two details in this flow generalize beyond first-run. First, the license text is fetched live rather than bundled: a vendor update reaches subsequent first-run flows without an app update, and acceptance is recorded against the install, not the license version. Second, the long-operation pattern (kick off, return ID, poll for status) is the default for any API call that takes more than a few seconds: it shows progress, supports cancel, and survives renderer reloads.

### Streaming download progress

Progress reporting is intentionally per file. If the user starts downloading the 44 GB checkpoint, the 7 GB upsampler, and the 25 GB Gemma encoder simultaneously, they need three independent progress bars, not one aggregate that creeps forward for hours. The `DownloadingSession` state captures this:

```
# From backend/state/app_state_types.py (LTX Desktop @ 81f7f45)
@dataclass
class DownloadingSession:
    session_id: UUID
    requested_files: tuple[ModelFileType, ...]
    completed_files: frozenset[ModelFileType]
    current_file: ModelFileType | None
    bytes_downloaded: int
    bytes_total: int
    download_speed_bps: float
    started_at: datetime
```

The frontend can render each file as either pending (in `requested_files` but not in `completed_files` and not current), in progress (`current_file`), or done (in `completed_files`). The exhaustive shape of the state means the UI never has to guess what to display. Every download is in exactly one of three categories at any moment.

### License acceptance as state

License acceptance is part of the application state machine, not a side effect of a "Click here to continue" dialog. A user who declines does not produce an error; they remain on the license screen, durably, across crashes and forced quits. This sounds obvious; it is also routinely missed in apps that wire the license dialog as a one-shot modal and the acceptance flag into a click handler.

Platform-canonical storage, license-as-state, background download with per-file progress, async job model with poll-for-status: the pattern applies to any application fetching large external resources after install. Updaters work this way; package managers work this way; cloud sync clients work this way. The cost of getting it right is one well-bounded subsystem; the cost of getting it wrong is the percentage of new users who churn before they see the product work.

There are two implementation mistakes we see often. The first is using temp directories for in-progress downloads and "moving" the file on completion. On a different filesystem, the move becomes a copy that doubles disk usage briefly. On Windows locked files can fail the move entirely. Download to a sibling *.partial* file alongside the final path and rename atomically. The second is treating license acceptance as a global preference rather than per-application version and model. If the license text materially changes, users may need to reaccept, and your state should be rich enough to detect that.

## Pattern 6: State as Discriminated Unions

Production AI applications spend a lot of time in transient states: a generation is running and we know the partial latent shape but not the final output; a model is loading and we know the file path but not the loaded module; a download is partly complete and we know which files are done and which are in flight. Representing these states with one big nullable-field struct (where `output` is `None` until done, `error` is `None` unless errored, `current_step` is `None` unless running) accumulates correctness debt rapidly. It is like trying to describe a soccer match using a single scoreboard that has columns for "goals scored," "penalty taken," "yellow card given," and "match concluded," and trusting every observer to fill in only the cells that apply at any given moment. Discriminated unions solve the problem by making illegal states unrepresentable: every transition produces a new value of a different shape, pattern matching is exhaustive, and the compiler enforces what code used to merely hope was true.

### Why nullable-field structs hurt

Consider the alternative LTX Desktop did not choose. A monolithic generation state class might look like this:

```
# anti-pattern: what LTX Desktop deliberately avoids
@dataclass
class GenerationState:
    job_id: UUID
    status: Literal["pending", "running", "complete", "error", "cancelled"]
    progress: float | None
    current_step: int | None
    output_path: str | None
    error_message: str | None
    cancelled_at: datetime | None
    completed_at: datetime | None
```

Every consumer of this struct now needs to remember which fields are valid in which status. Every check is a runtime check; a typo in the status value is silent until production. A function that handles "completed" generations will, at some point, get one with `output_path=None` because some other code path failed to set it. The bug looks like a UI glitch; the cause is the type system having no way to require the invariant.

### Tagged unions in Python

LTX Desktop's actual representation *is* a discriminated union over five concrete types:

```
# From backend/state/app_state_types.py (LTX Desktop @ 81f7f45)
@dataclass(frozen=True)
class GenerationPending:
    job_id: UUID
    submitted_at: datetime

@dataclass(frozen=True)
class GenerationRunning:
    job_id: UUID
    started_at: datetime
    progress: float                    # always present, 0.0 - 1.0
    current_step: int                  # always present
    estimated_completion: datetime | None

# GenerationComplete, GenerationError, GenerationCancelled defined similarly,
# each with the fields meaningful only to its phase (see Figure 8-5).

GenerationState = (
    GenerationPending
    | GenerationRunning
    | GenerationComplete
    | GenerationError
    | GenerationCancelled
)
```

Figure 8-5 shows how the generation state moves from pending to running and then into one of three terminal states: complete, error, or canceled.

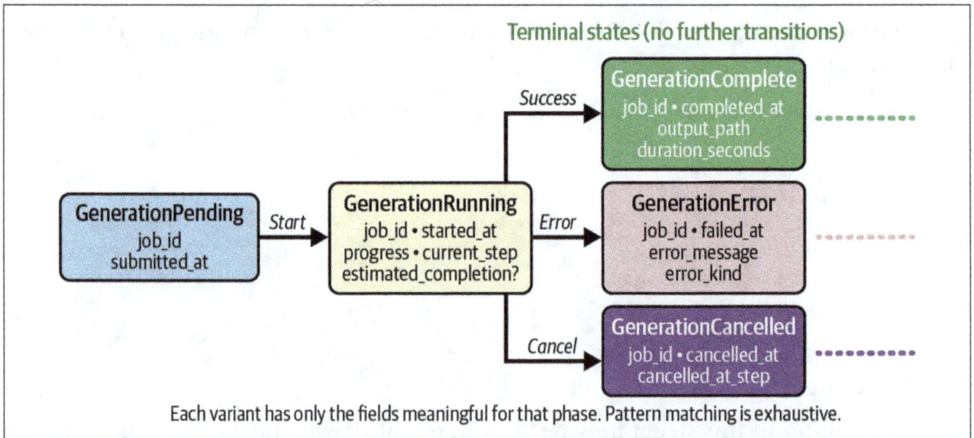


*Figure 8-5. The five variants of GenerationState. Pyright catches missing cases when a sixth variant is added.*

Each variant has the fields meaningful to its phase, nothing more. `GenerationRunning` has no `output_path` to forget; `GenerationComplete` has no `error_message` to confuse the UI. A function that takes a `GenerationComplete` cannot be passed a `GenerationRunning` by accident. The type system will not allow it.

### Exhaustive pattern matching in handlers

Handlers consume the discriminated union with structural pattern matching:

```
# from a handler operating on GenerationState
match state:
    case GenerationPending(job_id=jid):
        return {"status": "queued", "job": str(jid)}
    case GenerationRunning(progress=p, current_step=step):
        return {"status": "running", "progress": p, "step": step}
    case GenerationComplete(output_path=path, duration_seconds=dur):
        return {"status": "done", "output": path, "elapsed_s": dur}
    case GenerationError(error_message=msg, error_kind=kind):
        return {"status": "error", "kind": kind, "message": msg}
    case GenerationCancelled(cancelled_at_step=step):
        return {"status": "cancelled", "at_step": step}
```

A static analyzer (`pyright` in LTX Desktop's case) flags missing cases. Add a sixth state variant, and every handler that matches on `GenerationState` is flagged at type-check time. The compiler does the bookkeeping the human used to do. The same pattern is repeated for downloads, text encoder state, and several other state machines that benefit from explicit shapes per phase.

Discriminated unions are the right representation for any state machine where each phase has different relevant data. The pattern translates across languages: TypeScript discriminated unions, Rust `enums`, Haskell sum types, Scala `case` classes, Swift `enums` with associated values, and C++ `std::variant` all enable the same discipline. Python's pattern matching (3.10+) and `dataclasses` make the pattern readable; `pyright` or `mypy` in strict mode make it enforceable.

> Two pitfalls show up consistently. The first is "almost discriminated unions," where the variants share a base class with a status field but the variant-specific fields still live on the base, optionally. You get the worst of both worlds. The discipline only works if each variant is its own concrete shape. The second pitfall is defining variants and then never matching on them: accessing via `isinstance()` everywhere, which the compiler cannot verify is exhaustive. Pattern matching is the payoff; without it, the variants are merely organized data.

## Pattern 7: Service Protocols and Fakes (No Mocks)

Testing AI orchestration code without a GPU is essential (nobody runs a 19B parameter model in CI), but the standard answer of "use a mock library" produces tests that are brittle, fail on every refactor, and document the implementation rather than the behavior. Mocks are like crash-test dummies that record exactly which seatbelt you fastened in which order; they verify procedure, not safety. The service-Protocol-plus-fake pattern asks a different question: each side effect (GPU execution, network call, filesystem read, model download) hides behind a `typing.Protocol` interface, production code uses real implementations, and tests use handwritten fakes. The tests describe what the system should do, not how it should do it; refactoring the implementation doesn't break the tests as long as the Protocol contract holds.

### Side effects behind protocols

LTX Desktop concentrates its service interfaces in *backend/services/interfaces.py*. Each side effect that the rest of the application depends on appears as a Protocol:

```
# From backend/services/interfaces.py (LTX Desktop @ 81f7f45)
from typing import Protocol

class FastVideoPipeline(Protocol):
    def __call__(
        self,
        prompt: str,
        image: PIL.Image.Image | None,
        size: VideoSize,
        duration_seconds: float,
        on_progress: Callable[[float, int], None],
    ) -> Path: ...

class ModelDownloader(Protocol):
    def download(
        self,
        file_type: ModelFileType,
        target_path: Path,
        on_progress: Callable[[int, int, float], None],
    ) -> None: ...

class GpuInfo(Protocol):
    @property
    def cuda_available(self) -> bool: ...
    @property
    def vram_gb(self) -> int | None: ...
```

The protocols define what the rest of the code can ask for. They do not say where the work happens; they say what the contract is. Anything that satisfies the Protocol can be plugged in at the seam.

### Real and fake implementations

Production code provides concrete implementations:

```
# From backend/services/ltx_fast_video_pipeline.py (LTX Desktop @ 81f7f45)
class LTXFastVideoPipeline:
    def __init__(
        self,
        checkpoint_path: Path,
        gemma_root: Path,
        device: torch.device,
    ):
        self.transformer = load_transformer(checkpoint_path, device)
        ...  # full real loading

    def __call__(
        self, prompt, image, size, duration_seconds, on_progress) -> Path:
        ...  # real inference: 40 Euler steps with CFG, etc.
```

Tests provide fake implementations of the same Protocol:

```
# From backend/tests/fakes.py (LTX Desktop @ 81f7f45)
class FakeFastVideoPipeline:
    """Test double: returns a tiny canned video file after a short delay."""

    def __init__(self, fixture_video_path: Path = FIXTURE_TINY_MP4):
        self.fixture = fixture_video_path
        self.calls: list[FakeCall] = []  # tests can assert on this

    def __call__(
        self, prompt, image, size, duration_seconds, on_progress) -> Path:
        self.calls.append(FakeCall(
            prompt=prompt,
            size=size,
            duration=duration_seconds,
        ))
        for step in range(0, 100, 10):
            on_progress(step / 100.0, step)
            time.sleep(0.01)
        on_progress(1.0, 100)
        return self.fixture
```

The fake is handwritten, is type-checked against the same Protocol, and has its own behavior worth thinking about: records calls for later inspection, produces realistic progress callbacks, returns a real (tiny) MP4 file so downstream code that decodes the video can run end to end. It is more code than a mock, but it is honest code that reflects how the real implementation behaves.

### Composing the ServiceBundle

The pattern's payoff comes at composition time. The application has a single `ServiceBundle` that holds every side-effect Protocol:

```
# From backend/services/bundle.py (LTX Desktop @ 81f7f45)
@dataclass
class ServiceBundle:
    fast_video_pipeline: FastVideoPipeline
    model_downloader: ModelDownloader
    gpu_info: GpuInfo
    text_encoder: TextEncoder
    ...  # ~12 services total
```

Production startup builds the bundle with real implementations, and tests build it with fakes for whichever services the test cares about and real implementations of the rest:

```
# Production
bundle = ServiceBundle(
    fast_video_pipeline = LTXFastVideoPipeline(
        checkpoint_path,
        gemma_root,
        device,
    ),
    model_downloader=HuggingFaceModelDownloader(api_token),
    gpu_info=GpuInfoImpl(),
    ...
)

# Test of generation orchestration
bundle = ServiceBundle(
    fast_video_pipeline=FakeFastVideoPipeline(),
    model_downloader=FakeModelDownloader(),
    gpu_info=FakeGpuInfo(cuda_available=True, vram_gb=24),
    ...
)
```

Handlers receive the bundle by dependency injection. They know nothing about the difference between real and fake. Tests set up the bundle, call the handler, and assert on the fake's recorded calls and the handler's response. No patches, no monkey-patching, no stubbing import paths.

Service-Protocol-plus-fake is the structurally correct answer to "how do I test code that has side effects?" in any language with structural subtyping or interfaces: TypeScript, Java, Go, Rust, C++, and OCaml all afford the same discipline. The pattern is sometimes called "ports and adapters" or "hexagonal architecture." The principle is consistent: define what you need, let production wire in real and tests wire in fakes, and never use a mock library to fake what should have been a Protocol.

Two pitfalls are worth naming. The first is getting the fake's complexity wrong: too smart, and your tests are testing the fake instead of the system; too dumb, and downstream code under test can't run. The balance is "fake enough to satisfy the Protocol contract, plus expose what tests need to assert on." The second pitfall is the temptation to use both protocols and mocks. Pick one. A codebase that uses protocols + fakes for some services and mocks for others becomes a confusing patchwork. Choose the discipline at the codebase level.

## Pattern 8: Lock-Aware Handlers

Generative AI applications are concurrent whether you planned for it or not. A user clicks "generate" while a previous job is still running; downloads complete in a background thread while the model loader holds GPU memory; the renderer polls for progress while the handler that sets that progress is mid-update. Without explicit concurrency discipline, state corruption is a matter of when, not if. Think of state mutation as the single doorway into a kitchen: only one cook goes through at a time, but the cook should also leave fast so the next one can come in. The lock-aware handler pattern enforces both halves architecturally, so every contributor doesn't have to remember the rules.

### The @with_state_lock decorator

LTX Desktop's handlers all inherit from a base class that exposes a state lock and provides a decorator for state-mutating methods:

```
# From backend/handlers/base.py (LTX Desktop @ 81f7f45)
import threading
from functools import wraps

class HandlerBase:
    def __init__(self, state_provider: StateProvider):
        self._state = state_provider
        self._lock = threading.RLock()

def with_state_lock(method):
    """Acquire the handler's RLock for the duration of the method."""
    @wraps(method)
    def wrapper(self, *args, **kwargs):
        with self._lock:
            return method(self, *args, **kwargs)
    return wrapper
```

The decorator makes lock acquisition explicit at the API surface (you can see at a glance which methods touch state) and guarantees release even on exception. Without it, contributors would scatter with `self._lock` blocks throughout the code base, some would forget, and the bugs would be intermittent.

### The "never hold the lock" doctrine

The decorator is half the pattern. The other half is a discipline: never hold the lock during heavy work. *Heavy* means anything beyond microseconds: filesystem I/O, network calls, GPU operations, sleeps. A handler holding the state lock during a 90-second inference call serializes the UI for 90 seconds. State-mutating handler methods therefore do their state work under the lock and return; the actual heavy work happens in a `TaskRunner` thread the handler kicks off:

```
# From backend/handlers/generation_handler.py (LTX Desktop @ 81f7f45)
class GenerationHandler(HandlerBase):

    @with_state_lock
    def start_generation(self, request) -> UUID:
        # Holds the lock briefly for state mutation only.
        if self._state.current_generation is not None:
            raise GenerationAlreadyRunningError()
        job_id = uuid4()
        self._state.current_generation = GenerationPending(job_id=job_id, ...)
        # Lock will release when this method returns.
        self._task_runner.submit(self._run_generation, job_id, request)
        return job_id

    def _run_generation(self, job_id: UUID, request: GenerationRequest) -> None:
        # Runs in a background thread. Does NOT hold the lock.
        # Long-running GPU work happens here.
        result = self._services.fast_video_pipeline(...)
        # Updates state by acquiring the lock briefly when ready.
        with self._lock:
            self._state.current_generation = GenerationComplete(
                job_id=job_id,
                output_path=result,
                ...
            )
```

The handler submits and returns. The runner works without the lock. When it has results, it reacquires the lock briefly to write them. The lock window is short and deterministic.

### Background tasks and the TaskRunner

The `TaskRunner` makes "kick off long work and return" tractable: a thin wrapper around a thread pool that handles thread lifecycle, exception capture, and task identification. The shape is conventional; the discipline is that handlers always submit long work to the runner. Combined with `@with_state_lock`, the result is an architecture where state mutations are atomic, long operations are nonblocking, and contributors only need to remember: "if you mutate state, decorate it; if you do work, submit it."

Lock-aware handlers and the no-heavy-work-while-locked discipline apply to any concurrent stateful system: HTTP servers, GUI applications, game engines, and financial systems. The specific primitives differ across languages (Python's `RLock`, Java's `ReentrantLock`, Rust's `parking_lot::Mutex`, Go's `sync.Mutex`, and Erlang's `GenServer`), but the pattern is the same: make the lock acquisition explicit at the API surface, keep the critical section short, and put long-running work in a worker pool that does not hold the lock.

> Three failure modes are worth naming. The first is holding the lock during a callback to user code: an `on_progress` callback that the user might supply could do anything, including reentrantly calling back into the handler. Use callbacks defensively and never hold the lock across a call into code you do not control. The second failure mode is using a nonreentrant lock in a code path that is naturally recursive: a handler that calls another handler that calls back into the first will deadlock. `RLock` (reentrant) is the safer default. The third failure mode is a "fast path" that bypasses the decorator for "trivial" updates. The trivial updates are exactly where race conditions hide. If the method touches state, decorate it; the cost is one function call.

## The Landscape: Three Architectures, One Problem

The eight patterns describe one architectural philosophy: tight typing, clear process boundaries, and treating every trust boundary as a security concern even when the threat model is benign. LTX Desktop is by no means the only way to build a production AI workflow system. ComfyUI and InvokeAI solve the same fundamental problem (let users compose generative AI pipelines on their own machines) with substantively different choices. Reading those choices side by side is how you learn to recognize the ones LTX Desktop made and to choose intelligently when you build your own system. Each project is the right answer to a different set of priorities.

### ComfyUI: Community Plug-in Mesh

ComfyUI is the most widely used open source workflow tool in the video- and image-generation ecosystem. Its source code lives on the GitHub platform (*https://oreil.ly/8yppA*). The project's reach (tens of thousands of custom nodes) is earned by community size more than by any architectural property of the codebase. The barrier to writing a node is intentionally low. ComfyUI is the answer to the question "what if extension is the most important thing?"

#### Architecture philosophy

Where LTX Desktop separates Electron from Python by process boundary and contract, ComfyUI runs as a single Python process with a web server (`server.py`) and a browser-based React frontend that fetches its capabilities at runtime. Where LTX

Desktop's IPC surface is defined once in a typed schema, ComfyUI's API surface is whatever endpoints `server.py` registers. Where LTX Desktop's services hide behind `typing.Protocol` interfaces, ComfyUI's nodes are plain Python classes. This is deliberate, not careless: the smaller the contract, the more developers can extend the system without learning a framework first.

### The node abstraction

A ComfyUI node is a Python class with four conventional class attributes:

```
# From nodes.py (ComfyUI @ 5e3f15a)
class CLIPTextEncode(ComfyNodeABC):
    @classmethod
    def INPUT_TYPES(s) -> InputTypeDict:
        return {
            "required": {
                "text": (IO.STRING, {"multiline": True, ...}),
                "clip": (IO.CLIP, {"tooltip": "..."})
            }
        }
    RETURN_TYPES = (IO.CONDITIONING,)
    FUNCTION = "encode"
    CATEGORY = "conditioning"

    def encode(self, clip, text):
        tokens = clip.tokenize(text)
        return (clip.encode_from_tokens_scheduled(tokens),)
```

That is the entire contract. `INPUT_TYPES` describes the inputs and their types; `RETURN_TYPES` is a tuple of output type strings; `FUNCTION` names the method to call; and `CATEGORY` groups the node in the UI palette. The class itself can do anything Python can do. ComfyUI does not constrain how the work is implemented, where it imports from, or what side effects it has. A newer typed schema-based API exists in `comfy_api.latest`, but the duck-typed legacy API is what the ecosystem of community nodes is overwhelmingly built on.

### The custom node extension model

To install a community node, a user drops a Python file (or directory) into ComfyUI's `custom_nodes/`. On startup, ComfyUI iterates that directory, `importlib`-loads each module, and merges the module's `NODE_CLASS_MAPPINGS` dict into the global registry:

```
# Simplified from nodes.py:2207 (ComfyUI @ 5e3f15a)
async def load_custom_node(
    module_path,
    ignore=set(),
    module_parent="custom_nodes",
):
    module_spec = importlib.util.spec_from_file_location(name, path)
    module = importlib.util.module_from_spec(module_spec)
```

```
        sys.modules[name] = module
        module_spec.loader.exec_module(module)

        if hasattr(module, "NODE_CLASS_MAPPINGS"):
            for name, node_cls in module.NODE_CLASS_MAPPINGS.items():
                NODE_CLASS_MAPPINGS[name] = node_cls
```

The contract is: set the right module-level attribute. No manifest, no plug-in SDK, no sandbox. The custom node runs inside the same Python process as ComfyUI, with full access to the filesystem, the network, and every loaded module. That is the cost of "lowest possible extension barrier." And for an ecosystem that has produced tens of thousands of community nodes, the cost has been worth paying.

### Strengths

The extension API is small enough to memorize: a developer who has never seen ComfyUI can read a single example node and write their first one. The community has built an enormous library of nodes covering use cases the core team would never have prioritized. And the runtime engine (`execution.py`) is sophisticated where it matters: hierarchical and least-recently-used (LRU) caches for intermediate latents, graph-walk execution that reruns only affected subgraphs on input changes, and lazy-evaluated inputs for branches that may not be needed.

### Trade-offs

There is no story for type safety in the legacy API; `INPUT_TYPES` is a dict, `RETURN_TYPES` is a tuple of strings, and a typo in either fails at runtime. Custom nodes cannot be tested in isolation in any structured way, so most ship without tests, and a bug in one can propagate up the whole graph. And custom nodes run with full process privileges: a malicious or buggy node can do anything the ComfyUI process can. The project is honest about this and provides a `--disable-all-custom-nodes` flag for security-conscious environments.

ComfyUI is the right architecture if your priority is the size and creativity of the community of extensions. It is the wrong one if your priority is type-safe contracts, isolated tests, or sandboxing. The result of the choice is the largest visual AI workflow ecosystem in existence.

## InvokeAI: Service-Oriented Monolith

InvokeAI is a different answer to the same problem. Its source can be found on the GitHub platform (*https://oreil.ly/7ln9Q*). Where ComfyUI optimizes for extension surface area, InvokeAI optimizes for architectural rigor. A one-line characterization, InvokeAI is what a senior backend engineer would build if asked to design a generative AI workflow system for production deployment.

### Architecture philosophy

InvokeAI is a service-oriented monolith. A single Python application contains an explicit services layer (`invokeai/app/services/`), an invocation registry, a session queue, a session processor, an event bus, and a typed graph execution engine. Each service has a clear responsibility; each invocation is a typed Pydantic model; each session through the graph executor is tracked, resumable, and observable. The shape is closer to a Django application than to a desktop app or a plug-in mesh.

### The invocation abstraction

Where ComfyUI's node is a duck-typed class, InvokeAI's invocation is a typed Pydantic model:

```
# From invokeai/app/invocations/baseinvocation.py (InvokeAI @ 3b2d2ef)
@invocation(
    "denoise_latents",
    title="Denoise Latents",
    tags=["latents", "denoise"]
)
class DenoiseLatentsInvocation(BaseInvocation):
    """Denoises noisy latents to decodable latents"""

    positive_conditioning: ConditioningField = InputField(
        description="Positive conditioning tensor",
    )
    noise: LatentsField = InputField(description="Noise tensor")
    steps: int = InputField(
        default=10,
        ge=1,
        description="Number of denoising steps",
    )
    cfg_scale: float = InputField(default=7.5, description="CFG scale")
    # ... more typed inputs

    def invoke(self, context: InvocationContext) -> LatentsOutput:
        # implementation
        return LatentsOutput(latents=...)
```

Every input has a declared type, default, validator, and UI description. The registry is built from class decorators and provides exhaustive metadata to the frontend at startup. The graph executor knows the type of every output before any work happens; type compatibility is checked when edges are added, not at runtime.

### The services layer

The container in *invokeai/app/services/invocation_services.py* composes around 30 cross-cutting services: model management, session queue, configuration, events, image and latent storage, board management, and download queue. Invocations receive an `InvocationContext` that exposes whichever services they need. The pattern resembles dependency injection: invocations declare what they consume; the container wires in the right implementations.

#### Strengths

InvokeAI's choices map almost cleanly onto the eight patterns. The typed invocation contract corresponds to LTX Desktop's typed IPC bridge. The services layer corresponds to LTX Desktop's `ServiceBundle` and `Protocol-fake` pattern. The graph executor's session queue and session processor map to LTX Desktop's `TaskRunner` and discriminated-union state. Architecturally, InvokeAI is LTX Desktop's closest cousin; both prioritize disciplined contracts over extension surface area.

#### Trade-offs

The higher contract bar makes extension significantly harder than ComfyUI: writing an invocation requires learning `BaseInvocation`, the input/output typing system, the `InvocationContext`, and the registration decorators. This is the learning curve ComfyUI deliberately eliminates. The community of third-party invocations is correspondingly smaller, and first-time contributors face more reading before they can be productive.

> InvokeAI is the right architecture if your priority is rigor, type safety, and a long-lived production deployment. It is the wrong one if your priority is the broadest possible community of extensions.

#### Comparison matrix

The three architectures sit at different points on a small set of axes. Each row in Table 8-1 is one of the eight patterns above or a closely related dimension.

*Table 8-1. Architectural comparison across LTX Desktop, ComfyUI, and InvokeAI*

| Concern | LTX Desktop | ComfyUI | InvokeAI |
|---|---|---|---|
| Process model | Two-process: Electron + Python | Single Python process | Single Python process |
| Frontend | React renderer (sandboxed Electron window) | React in a browser | React in a browser |
| Capability decisions | Backend as source of truth, baked at start | Per request, mostly | Service container with policy services |
| Extension contract | Vendor-controlled (no plug-in SDK) | Duck-typed Python class + dict registry | Typed Pydantic invocation + registry |
| Type safety | Pydantic + Zod, strict end to end | Mostly duck-typed; new typed API present | Strict Pydantic everywhere |
| Auth on local API | Per-session bearer tokens, constant-time compare | None by default (trusts browser) | None by default (trusts browser) |

| Concern | LTX Desktop | ComfyUI | InvokeAI |
|---|---|---|---|
| State representation | Discriminated unions | Plain dicts and class attributes | Pydantic models with explicit shapes |
| Side-effect testing | Protocol + handwritten fakes | Limited; community nodes mostly untested | Service interfaces + dependency injection |
| Concurrency discipline | Lock-aware decorators, `TaskRunner` | Async + caches; less explicit | Session queue + session processor |
| Custom-extension privilege boundary | None (no public extension API) | None (custom nodes run in-process) | None (invocations run in-process) |
| Primary trade-off | Architectural rigor, narrower extension | Extension breadth, weaker contracts | Architectural rigor, midsized ecosystem |

Read the matrix: the "best" cell in each row depends on what you are optimizing for. When building for paying customers who expect security and reliability, LTX Desktop's choices look obvious. When building infrastructure for a research community that needs to extend in directions you cannot anticipate, ComfyUI's choices look obvious. Building a long-lived production service that you and your team will maintain for years, InvokeAI's choices look obvious. The mistake is treating any column as universally right (see Figure 8-6).

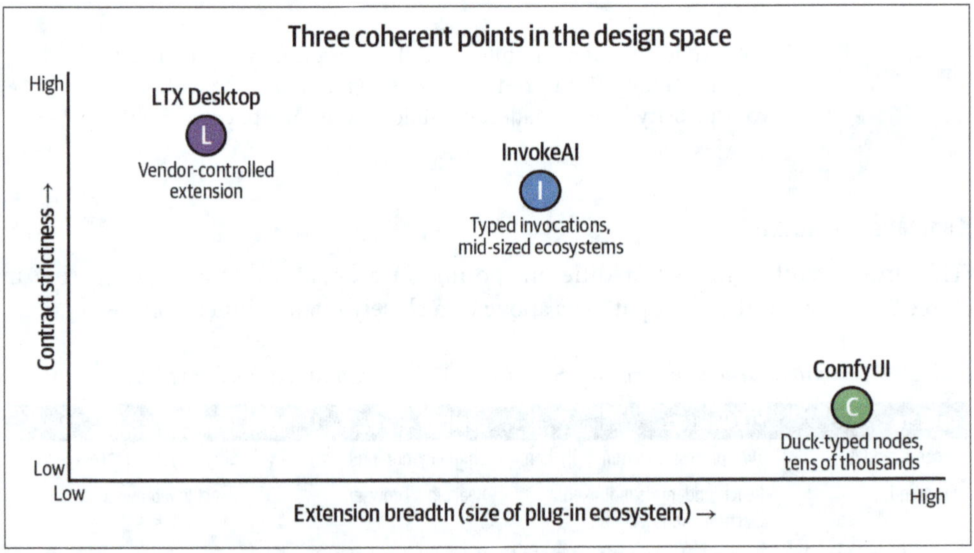


*Figure 8-6. The three reference architectures are plotted by extension breadth (size of plug-in ecosystem) against contract strictness (rigor of the API contract)*

# Capstone: Building a Custom Extension Across Three Platforms

The patterns and contrasts discussed so far do their real teaching when you put them to work. This capstone implements the same custom feature across all three reference architectures. The conceptual goal (exposing LTX-2.3's audio-to-video pipeline as a user-accessible feature) takes a different shape in each platform, and the differences surface what each architecture optimizes for in a way no diagram can match.

The complete code lives in this book's companion repository at *github.com/jenochs/video-ai-book-companion* (chapter-08 folder), pinned to the same commits this chapter cites. The walk-through is detailed enough that you could write your own from scratch; the companion exists so you can verify your understanding by running it.

## The Feature: Add LTX-2 Audio-to-Video as a New Capability

The audio-to-video pipeline from Chapter 7 (`a2vid_two_stage in ltx_pipelines`) takes an audio waveform and a text prompt and produces a video synchronized to the audio. We choose it as the capstone feature for two reasons. First, every reader has the prerequisite knowledge: the capstone is "expose what the model can already do," with no novel ML to learn. Second, audio-to-video stresses each platform's extension API: nontrivial input (an audio file), meaningful parameters (duration, resolution, conditioning strength), nontrivial output (a video file), and long enough runtime that the user needs progress reporting.

The user-visible behavior we target in all three platforms: the user supplies an audio file (*.wav* or *.mp3*) and an optional text prompt then picks a target duration and resolution; the platform invokes `ltx_pipelines.a2vid_two_stage` with the right configuration and reports progress; and the output video lands in the platform's normal output flow. The pipeline call is identical across all three implementations. What differs is the scaffolding around it (see Figure 8-7).

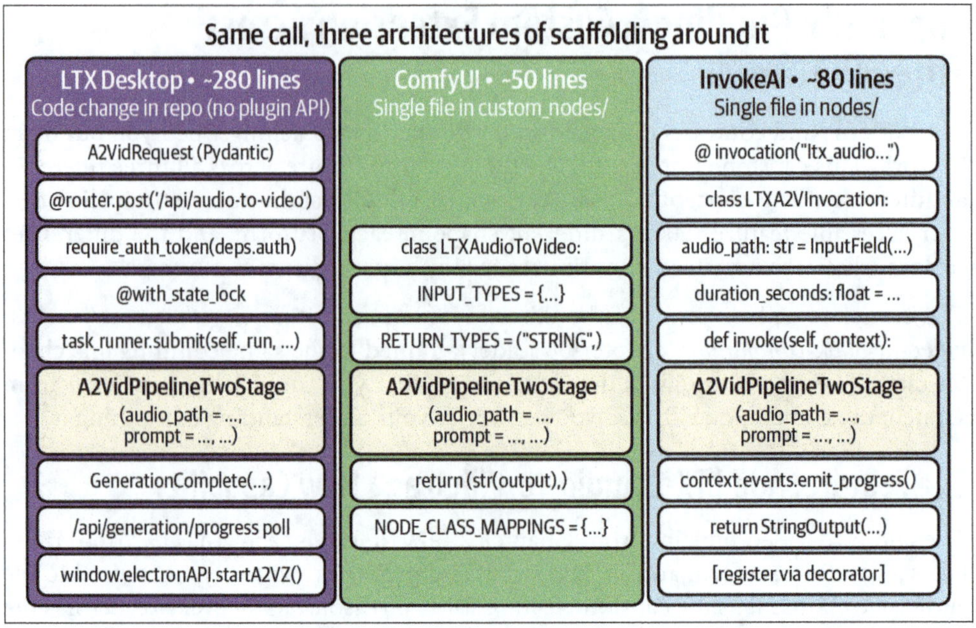


*Figure 8-7. The same A2VidPipelineTwoStage call (yellow) at the center of three implementations. The 280/50/80 line counts at the top are the price each architecture charges for the same feature.*

## Implementation in LTX Desktop

LTX Desktop has no public extension API; its architecture deliberately keeps the IPC contract vendor-controlled. Adding a feature is therefore a code change in the LTX Desktop repository itself, not a plug-in. For the capstone, we work in a fork at the pinned commit `81f7f45`. The change touches all three layers. In the Python backend, a new handler invokes the `a2vid` pipeline:

```
# From backend/handlers/audio_to_video_handler.py (companion @ ch8-capstone)
from ltx_pipelines.a2vid_two_stage import A2VidPipelineTwoStage
from ltx_pipelines.utils.types import OffloadMode
from ltx_core.quantization import QuantizationPolicy

class AudioToVideoHandler(HandlerBase):
    def __init__(self, services: ServiceBundle, state_provider: StateProvider):
        super().__init__(state_provider)
        self._services = services
        self._pipeline: A2VidPipelineTwoStage | None = None

    @with_state_lock
    def start(self, request: A2VidRequest) -> UUID:
        if self._state.current_generation is not None:
            raise GenerationAlreadyRunningError()
```

```python
        job_id = uuid4()
        self._state.current_generation = GenerationPending(
            job_id=job_id,
            submitted_at=datetime.utcnow(),
        )
        self._services.task_runner.submit(self._run, job_id, request)
        return job_id
```

`start()` is decorated with `@with_state_lock`, which acquires the handler's `RLock` for the duration. It checks the invariant (no concurrent generation), mutates state to `GenerationPending`, kicks the heavy work to the `TaskRunner`, and returns immediately with a `job_id`.

The actual generation runs in `_run()`, which begins by lazy-constructing the pipeline and defining a progress callback:

```python
    def _run(self, job_id: UUID, request: A2VidRequest) -> None:
        # Lazy-construct the pipeline to amortize Python imports.
        if self._pipeline is None:
            self._pipeline = A2VidPipelineTwoStage(
                checkpoint_path=self._services.config.checkpoint_path,
                distilled_lora=self._services.config.distilled_lora,
                spatial_upsampler_path=self._services.config.upsampler_path,
                gemma_root=self._services.config.gemma_root,
                loras=[],
                quantization=QuantizationPolicy.fp8_cast(),
                offload_mode=OffloadMode.NONE,
            )

        def on_progress(step: int, total: int) -> None:
            with self._lock:
                self._state.current_generation = GenerationRunning(
                    job_id=job_id,
                    started_at=self._state.current_generation.submitted_at,
                    progress=step / total,
                    current_step=step,
                    estimated_completion=None,
                )
```

The pipeline is constructed lazily so the cost of Python imports is amortized across the first call rather than paid at startup. `on_progress` is a closure that captures `job_id` and acquires the lock briefly to mutate state to `GenerationRunning` as the pipeline reports progress. With those in place, the rest of `_run()` runs the pipeline and emits the terminal state `GenerationComplete` on success, `GenerationError` on failure:

```python
        try:
            output_path = self._pipeline(
                audio_path=request.audio_path,
                prompt=request.prompt,
                duration_seconds=request.duration_s,
                size=request.size,
```

```python
                on_progress=on_progress,
            )
            with self._lock:
                self._state.current_generation = GenerationComplete(
                    job_id=job_id,
                    completed_at=datetime.utcnow(),
                    output_path=output_path,
                    duration_seconds=request.duration_s,
                )
        except Exception as e:
            with self._lock:
                self._state.current_generation = GenerationError(
                    job_id=job_id,
                    failed_at=datetime.utcnow(),
                    error_message=str(e),
                    error_kind=type(e).__name__,
                )
```

The handler embodies several of the eight patterns at once: it inherits `HandlerBase` for the state lock, decorates the state-mutating method with `@with_state_lock`, kicks the heavy work off in the `TaskRunner`, holds the lock only briefly, and emits state transitions as discriminated-union variants. The HTTP route is thin plumbing in the established style:

```python
# From backend/_routes/audio_to_video.py (companion @ ch8-capstone)
@router.post("/api/audio-to-video", response_model=A2VidResponse)
async def start_a2vid(
    request: A2VidRequest,
    deps: BackendDeps = Depends(get_deps),
):
    require_auth_token(deps.auth)
    job_id = deps.handlers.audio_to_video.start(request)
    return A2VidResponse(job_id=str(job_id))
```

The route enforces the auth token, parses the typed Pydantic request, and delegates to the handler. The handler returns immediately with a job ID; the renderer polls */api/generation/progress* for state transitions. The renderer side is a single new HTTP call (the renderer calls the Python backend directly for ML; IPC is reserved for OS concerns):

```typescript
// From frontend/api-client.ts (companion @ ch8-capstone)
export async function startAudioToVideo(
    req: A2VidRequest,
): Promise<{job_id: string}> {
  return backendFetch<A2VidResponse>('/api/audio-to-video', {
    method: 'POST',
    body: JSON.stringify(req),
  });
}
```

The OpenAPI types are regenerated; TypeScript will not let the call site compile if the request shape disagrees with Pydantic. From the user's perspective, a new "Audio to Video" tab appears in GenSpace; they upload audio plus a prompt and click Generate; and the output appears in the project gallery.

The full change is around 200 lines of Python and 80 lines of TypeScript across a dozen files. It ships as a code change, not a plug-in. That is the cost (and the discipline) of the no-extension-API choice.

## Implementation in ComfyUI

ComfyUI's extension API is exactly suited for this capstone. The feature becomes a single custom node that any user installs by dropping a file into `custom_nodes/` and restarting. Here's the entire implementation:

```
# custom_nodes/ltx_a2vid_node.py
import torch
from ltx_pipelines.a2vid_two_stage import A2VidPipelineTwoStage
from ltx_pipelines.utils.types import OffloadMode
from ltx_core.quantization import QuantizationPolicy

# Module-level cache so repeated calls reuse the loaded model.
_PIPELINE_CACHE = None

def _get_pipeline(checkpoint_path, distilled_lora, upsampler_path, gemma_root):
    global _PIPELINE_CACHE
    if _PIPELINE_CACHE is None:
        _PIPELINE_CACHE = A2VidPipelineTwoStage(
            checkpoint_path=checkpoint_path,
            distilled_lora=distilled_lora,
            spatial_upsampler_path=upsampler_path,
            gemma_root=gemma_root,
            loras=[],
            quantization=QuantizationPolicy.fp8_cast(),
            offload_mode=OffloadMode.NONE,
        )
    return _PIPELINE_CACHE
```

The module-level cache exists because ComfyUI's node lifecycle has no hook for "construct expensive resources once." Each call to `generate()` needs the pipeline; loading 22 GB checkpoints on every call is unworkable. The cache is a pragmatic work-around for the missing lifecycle event. With that in place, the node itself is a class with the four conventional attributes plus the work method:

```
class LTXAudioToVideo:
    @classmethod
    def INPUT_TYPES(cls):
            "required": {
                "audio_path": ("STRING", {"default": "", "multiline": False}),
                "prompt": ("STRING", {"default": "", "multiline": True}),
```

```
                "duration_seconds": (
                    "FLOAT",
                    {"default": 5.0, "min": 1.0, "max": 30.0, "step": 0.5}
                ),
                "checkpoint_path": (
                    "STRING",
                    {"default": "/path/to/ltx-2.3-22b-dev.safetensors"}
                ),
                "distilled_lora_path": (
                    "STRING",
                    {"default":
                     "/path/to/ltx-2.3-22b-distilled-lora-384-1.1.safetensors"},
                ),
                "upsampler_path": (
                    "STRING",
                    {"default":
                     "/path/to/ltx-2.3-spatial-upscaler-x2-1.1.safetensors"}
                ),
                "gemma_root": ("STRING", {"default": "/path/to/gemma-3-12b"}),
            }

        RETURN_TYPES = ("STRING",)
        RETURN_NAMES = ("output_video_path",)
        FUNCTION = "generate"
        CATEGORY = "LTX/Audio-to-Video"

        def generate(self, audio_path, prompt, duration_seconds,
                     checkpoint_path,
                     distilled_lora_path,
                     upsampler_path,
                     gemma_root,
        ):
            pipeline = _get_pipeline(
                checkpoint_path=checkpoint_path,
                distilled_lora=[(distilled_lora_path, 0.6)],
                upsampler_path=upsampler_path,
                gemma_root=gemma_root,
            )
            output = pipeline(
                audio_path=audio_path,
                prompt=prompt,
                duration_seconds=duration_seconds,
            )
            return (str(output),)

    NODE_CLASS_MAPPINGS = {
        "LTXAudioToVideo": LTXAudioToVideo,
    }

    NODE_DISPLAY_NAME_MAPPINGS = {
        "LTXAudioToVideo": "LTX-2.3 Audio to Video",
    }
```

That is the entire installation. No manifest, no *pyproject.toml*, no plug-in SDK, no registration step. Restart ComfyUI, and the new node appears in the LTX/Audio-to-Video category. Wire it up in the visual editor: a Load Audio node feeds `audio_path`, a String Constant feeds prompt, and the `output_video_path` feeds Save Video.

Read the contrasts honestly. The implementation is ~50 lines of Python in one file. There is no auth: the node runs with full process privileges and honors the filesystem paths verbatim. There is no progress reporting integrated with the node API; we'd have to use ComfyUI's preview hooks or print to stdout, neither of which feeds back to the workflow editor naturally. The pipeline is module-level cached because nothing in the node lifecycle hints at when to construct or destruct expensive resources. These are not flaws; they are the consequence of optimizing for ease of extension. Fifty lines is genuinely fifty lines. The user installs without learning a framework. The node is forkable, modifiable, and shareable as a single file.

## Implementation in InvokeAI

InvokeAI sits between LTX Desktop and ComfyUI on this axis. The feature packages as a custom invocation that registers through the framework's decorator-based extension API. It offers stronger typing than ComfyUI while requiring less application-level integration than LTX Desktop:

```
# nodes/ltx_a2vid_invocation.py
from invokeai.app.invocations.baseinvocation import (
    BaseInvocation,
    InputField,
    InvocationContext,
    invocation,
)
from invokeai.app.invocations.fields import StringField
from invokeai.app.invocations.primitives import StringOutput

from ltx_pipelines.a2vid_two_stage import A2VidPipelineTwoStage
from ltx_pipelines.utils.types import OffloadMode
from ltx_core.quantization import QuantizationPolicy


@invocation(
    "ltx_audio_to_video",
    title="LTX-2.3 Audio to Video",
    tags=["ltx", "audio", "video"],
    category="generation",
)
class LTXAudioToVideoInvocation(BaseInvocation):
    """Generate a video synchronized to an input audio file using LTX-2.3."""

    audio_path: str = InputField(
        description="Path to input audio file (wav/mp3)"
    )
```

```
    prompt: str = InputField(
        description="Text prompt for video content",
        default="",
    )
    duration_seconds: float = InputField(
        default=5.0, ge=1.0, le=30.0,
        description="Output video duration in seconds",
    )
    checkpoint_path: str = InputField(description="Path to LTX-2.3 checkpoint")
    distilled_lora_path: str = InputField(description="Path to distilled LoRA")
    upsampler_path: str = InputField(description="Path to spatial upsampler")
    gemma_root: str = InputField(description="Path to Gemma 3 weights")
```

The `@invocation` decorator registers the class with InvokeAI's invocation registry. Each `InputField` declares a description, default, and—where appropriate—a range constraint (`ge=1.0, le=30.0`); InvokeAI's frontend reads these and renders the right UI controls automatically. The reader gets type-checked inputs without writing UI code. The actual work happens in `invoke()`:

```
def invoke(self, context: InvocationContext) -> StringOutput:
        pipeline = A2VidPipelineTwoStage(
            checkpoint_path=self.checkpoint_path,
            distilled_lora=[(self.distilled_lora_path, 0.6)],
            spatial_upsampler_path=self.upsampler_path,
            gemma_root=self.gemma_root,
            loras=[],
            quantization=QuantizationPolicy.fp8_cast(),
            offload_mode=OffloadMode.NONE,
        )

        def on_progress(step: int, total: int) -> None:
            context.events.emit_invocation_progress(
                queue_item_id=context.queue_item.item_id,
                node_id=self.id,
                progress=step / total,
                step=step,
            )

        output = pipeline(
            audio_path=self.audio_path,
            prompt=self.prompt,
            duration_seconds=self.duration_seconds,
            on_progress=on_progress,
        )
        return StringOutput(value=str(output))
```

The implementation is ~80 lines: longer than ComfyUI because of the typed inputs and explicit progress emission, shorter than LTX Desktop because the framework provides the handler scaffolding (state, queueing, progress events) for free. The user installs by dropping the file in InvokeAI's *nodes/* directory; on next start, the invocation appears in the palette.

The progress emission works the same way. It goes through `context.events.emit_invocation_progress`, which feeds the existing WebSocket channel the rest of the app already consumes, so the new invocation gets observability for free.

## What the Three Implementations Reveal

The same pipeline call appears in all three, surrounded by different scaffolding. The scaffolding tells the architectural story.

LTX Desktop required the most code (~280 lines across a dozen files) and the deepest codebase knowledge. The change ships as a fork or pull request, not an installable plug-in. The discipline produces a result that slots cleanly into the existing app: the feature gets the existing auth and progress channels, the existing UI controls, and every other architectural pattern the rest of the app uses. The cost is the inability of a third party to add it without modifying the application source:

*ComfyUI*
: Required the least code (~50 lines in one file) and the least platform-specific knowledge. Anyone with the LTX-2.3 model files and an installed ComfyUI can drop the file into `custom_nodes/`, restart, and have a working node. The cost is the absence of integrated progress reporting, manual pipeline lifecycle management, and no sandboxing: a buggy or malicious version could do anything its Python process can.

*InvokeAI*
: Required a moderate amount of code (~80 lines in one file) and moderate platform knowledge. Typed inputs become UI automatically; progress events feed the existing WebSocket channel; the invocation slots into the workflow graph. Extension is possible without modifying core; the contract is more demanding than ComfyUI's, but the payoff is integration. The result is closer to LTX Desktop's polish without LTX Desktop's no-extension-API constraint.

Three platforms, one feature, three architectures of code that bring it to life. Choose the architecture that matches what you are optimizing for, and the choice will repay you for the life of the system.

### Architectural principles recap

The eight patterns of this chapter, distilled to one sentence each:

*The two-process architecture*
: Separates application lifecycle (Electron) from compute work (Python), letting each tool do what it is best at and making the boundary between them explicit.

*The backend as source of truth*
: This pattern concentrates capability decisions in one layer, bakes them at startup, and exposes them as data, eliminating the class of bugs that arises when multiple layers decide independently.

*The typed IPC bridge*
: Makes the contract between two sides of a wire one shared object that both sides derive from, eliminating drift architecturally rather than relying on convention.

*Treating localhost as a security boundary*
: Applies authentication, CSP, path validation, and sandboxing even when the threat model is benign, because the cost is small and the discipline transfers cleanly to less-benign futures.

*The model lifecycle pattern*
: Handles license acceptance, downloads, and storage as durable state with platform-canonical roots, per-file progress, and atomic file operations, because the percentage of users who churn before they see the product work is set in this code path.

*State as discriminated unions*
: Makes illegal states unrepresentable, enabling exhaustive pattern matching and replacing runtime correctness arguments with compile-time guarantees.

*Service protocols and fakes*
: Enable testing of side-effect-heavy code without mock libraries, producing tests that describe behavior rather than implementation.

*Lock-aware handlers*
: With the no-heavy-work-while-locked discipline, enforce concurrency safety at the API surface, not in every contributor's head.

### Practical applications

The patterns are not exclusive to generative AI. They show up in code editors, music production tools, design applications, and scientific computing platforms. What is distinctive about generative AI is the combination of long-running compute, large model files, hardware-dependent capabilities, and a compelling but fragile UX that punishes every unhandled failure mode. The patterns are well suited to that combination.

### Design lessons

LTX Desktop's choices are defensible because they are coherent. Strong typing in the IPC bridge pairs naturally with strong typing in the state machine; per-session auth tokens pair naturally with sandboxed renderer plus path validation; service protocols pair naturally with a container that injects them. The patterns reinforce each other; you do not adopt one and reject the others without paying a coherence cost.

ComfyUI and InvokeAI make coherent choices for different priorities: each is the right answer to a different question. The mistake to avoid is mixing patterns from different coherent architectures without thinking about whether they fit together.

## Summary and Conclusion: The Video AI Landscape

Across these chapters you have built understanding from the inside out: the math of diffusion, the mechanics of training, the architecture of the LTX-2 model, and now the patterns that turn a model into a product. A practitioner who only understands models cannot build production systems; a practitioner who only understands systems cannot evaluate the models they integrate. Ground in both, and the pipeline from research to deployment becomes navigable.

The video-AI tooling landscape at the time of writing is in roughly the same state web frameworks were in around 2008: multiple ambitious, fragmented, credible architectures competing for the future. LTX Desktop, ComfyUI, and InvokeAI are three coherent points in that design space. New entrants will appear, and the specific products this chapter cites may look different in 18 months. What will not change as quickly is the underlying problem (how do you take a model and make it a product?) or the patterns that answer it. Code references age; patterns endure.

Core things to take away. If you build production AI applications, treat the eight patterns as a checklist, not a creed: adopt what fits your priorities, reject what doesn't. If you contribute to one of the three reference architectures, the comparison here gives you vocabulary for design discussions. And if you are designing a new system from scratch, write down what you are optimizing for first; the architectural choices follow from the answer.

The model is not the product. The system around the model is. With the eight patterns in your toolkit and the three reference architectures in your mental map, you are equipped to build that system well.

# Index

## B



## C



## D



## E

## F



## G



## H



## I



## K

## L



## M

## N



## O



## P

## Q



## R



## S



## T

## U



## V

## W



## Y



## Z

## About the Author

**Joseph Enochs** is the Chief AI Officer at EVT, where he leads artificial intelligence strategy and specializes in bridging the gap between cutting-edge research and production-ready systems. His work spans generative AI, agentic systems, multimodal learning, trustworthy AI, and governance, translating emerging capabilities into practical solutions.

Throughout his career, Joseph has led initiatives across healthcare, utilities, financial services, manufacturing, media, and the public sector. He believes technology is most valuable when it solves real-world problems. His career has been defined by translating innovation into practical systems that solve real-world problems and earn the trust of the people who rely on them.

Joseph is the creator of the L.E.V.E.L.S. methodology, a framework for helping individuals and enterprises adopt emerging technologies through structured learning, experimentation, and continuous improvement. He is a frequent speaker on enterprise technology strategy, governance, and the future of intelligent systems.

He holds a Bachelor of Science in Information Technology, a Master of Business Administration, and a postgraduate diploma in Applied Machine Learning and Artificial Intelligence from Columbia University.

## Colophon

The animal on the cover of *Video Generation with AI* is the rainbow lorikeet (*Trichoglossus moluccanus*), a species of parrot native to northern and eastern Australia.

Rainbow lorikeets are playful, social birds that are sometimes kept as pets. Like other parrots, they can mimic human speech and can learn to say many words and phrases. In the wild, they often travel in flocks. They are known for their vibrant colors, with deep blue heads and bellies, red or orange breasts, and bright green wings and tails.

Their diet is highly specialized, consisting of mainly nectar and pollen, along with soft, ripe fruits and occasionally insect larvae. To effectively harvest nectar and pollen, their tongues are shaped like a paintbrush, with tiny hairlike structures covering the tip. To find food, they will travel up to 40 miles in a single day.

Relying on tree hollows for nesting, they can live in a variety of environments as long as there are enough trees, ranging from rainforests and eucalyptus woodlands to suburbs and urban parks. In some locations where they have been introduced, such as New Zealand, they are considered invasive.

Rainbow lorikeets have a stable population and are classified as Least Concern by the International Union for Conservation of Nature (IUCN). Many of the animals on O'Reilly covers are endangered; all of them are important to the world.

The image on the cover of *Video Generation with AI* is an original illustration by José Marzan Jr. The series design is by Edie Freedman, Ellie Volckhausen, and Karen Montgomery. The cover fonts are Gilroy Semibold and Guardian Sans. The text font is Adobe Minion Pro; the heading font is Adobe Myriad Condensed; and the code font is Dalton Maag's Ubuntu Mono.

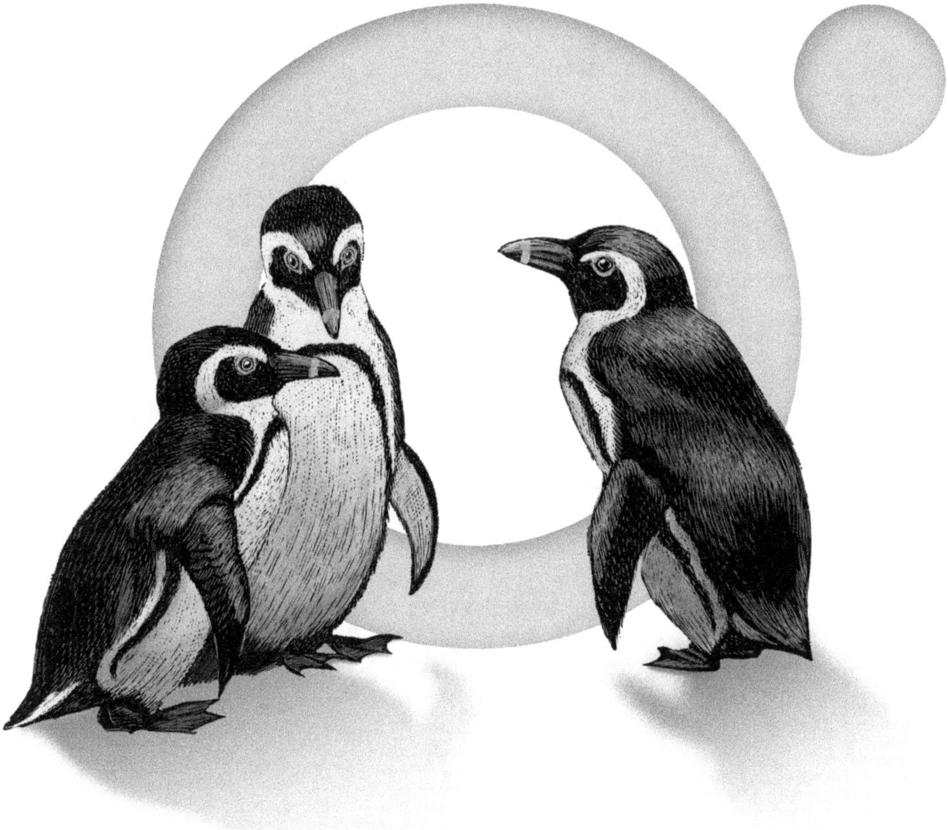

www.ingramcontent.com/pod-product-compliance
Lightning Source LLC
LaVergne TN
LVHW080032210926
848481LV00011B/3170